SOURCES OF THE HISTORY OF ARUNACHAL PRADESH

SOURCES OF THE HISTORY OF ARUNACHAL PRADESH

Editors
Prof. S. Dutta
Dr. B. Tripathy

GYAN

Published by

Gyan Publishing House
5, Ansari Road
Daryaganj, New Delhi-110002
Phone: 011-47034999, 9811692060
E-mail: books@gyanbooks.com

Distribution Network
gyanbooks.com
India, USA, Canada, UK, Australia, France

ISBN: 978-81-212-1008-9 (HB)

Reprint in India, 2024
First Published, 2008

Printed at: Gyan Press, Delhi.

Sources of the History of Arunachal Pradesh
Author: Prof. S. Dutta & Dr. B. Tripathy

Contents

List of Contributors

J.B. Bhattacharjee : *Professor in History, North-Eastern Hill University, Shillong and Former Vice-Chancellor, Assam University, Silchar.*

P.K. Shukla : *Member Secretary, Indian Council of Historical Research, New Delhi.*

N. Joykumar Singh : *Professor in History, Manipur University, Imphal.*

N.T. Rikam : *Sr. Lecturer, Department of History, Dera Natung Govt. College, Itanagar, Arunachal Pradesh.*

Gindu Borang : *Sr. Lecturer, Department of History, J.N. (Govt.) College, Pasighat, Arunachal Pradesh.*

Lakhi Nath Pegu : *Sr. Lecturer, Department of History, North Lakhimpur College, Assam.*

Ashan Riddi : *Sr. Lecturer, Department of History, Rajiv Gandhi University (Formerly Arunachal University), Rono Hills, Itanagar, Arunachal Pradesh.*

Pura Tado : *Reader, Department of Political Science, Rajiv Gandhi University, Rono Hills, Itanagar, Arunachal Pradesh.*

Byomakesh Tripathy : *Reader & Head, Department of History, Rajiv Gandhi University, Rono Hills, Itanagar, Arunachal Pradesh.*

Ramesh Chandra Joshi : *Reader & Head, Department of Geography, Rajiv Gandhi University, Rono Hills, Itanagar, A.P*

J.B. Ganguly : *Former Vice-Chancellor, Tripura University, Agartala.*

J.N. Phukan : *Retired Professor, Department of History, Gauhati University, Guwahati, Assam.*

I.S. Mumtaza : *Sr. Reader, Department of History, Gauhati University, Guwahati, Assam.*

Jahnabi Gogoi : *Professor, Department of History, Dibrugarh University, Dibrugarh, Assam.*

S. Dutta : *Professor, Department of History, Rajiv Gandhi University, Rono Hills, Itanagar, A.P.*

A.K. Thakur : *Reader, Department of History, North-Eastern hill University, Shillong, Meghalaya.*

Dipanker Banerjee : *Sr. Reader, Department of History, Gauhati University, Guwahati, Assam.*

S.D. Goswami : *Professor, Department of History, Dibrugarh University, Dibrugarh, Assam.*

B. Mallick : *Archaeologist, State Archaeology Department, Govt. of West Bengal, Kolkata.*

M.C. Behera : *Reader, Department of Tribal Studies, Rajiv Gandhi University, Rono Hills, Itanagar, A.P.*

1

Keynote Address—Folk Materials as Alternative Indigenous Sources for History of Arunachal Pradesh

J.B. Bhattacharjee

The research in the history of Arunachal Pradesh has shown commendable progress in recent years. However, the researchers are facing the difficulty in locating the source materials, which are very few and far between. On the other hand, it should be said, even at the risk of repetition, that the starting point in the historians' craft is the identification of the sources. Therefore, I consider this seminar on 'Sources of the History of Arunachal Pradesh', sponsored by the ICHR, in the series "Sources of the History of North-East India" and in continuation of the seminar held in Guwahati last year, as extremely important and very timely.

1. The society in Arunachal Pradesh, as in case of most of the other tribal communities in Northeast India, was in pre-literacy stage till 19th century and, therefore, could not create or produce written records of what had happened in various stages of socio-political and cultural evolution. For the pre-colonial period, there are only few pre-historic and archaeological sites, which have been explored or excavated (thanks to the Research Department, Govt. of Arunachal Pradesh). However, the findings of those explorations and excavations are yet to be historically evaluated and appropriately integrated in writing the early history of Arunachal Pradesh. Similarly, we are told of the rich collection of manuscripts in the Tawang Monastery, but, although there are some excellent works on the monastery itself (N. Sarkar's

Tawang Monastry, Shillong, 1981, for example), no historian has perhaps so far thoroughly examined those manuscripts. There are references in Ahom and Assamese *Buranjis* on the nature of relations of the border tribes (or at least, the chiefs) with the frontier officials of the Ahom Government, but the information is so limited in scope and nature, and the references are so confusing and thereby difficult to interpret for specific tribes, that the *Buranjis* are hardly helpful in reconstructing the history beyond the Ahom relations with some of the tribes in the border areas. No wonder, L.N.Chakraborty's *Glimpses of the Early History of Arunachal Pradesh* (Shillong, 1973) may be considered as exploratory, sketchy and by and large limited to the origin, myths and migration stories for the pre-colonial period. It is, therefore, incumbent upon the researchers in the history of Arunachal Pradesh to explore the oral materials as indigenous sources, created and conserved by the people themselves. For the colonial and post-colonial periods, the oral materials are not only alternative to archival sources (which are official versions, and not acceptable without criticism) but also the only materials to bridge the gaps as the administration took long time (almost till the end of the Raj) to cover some of the tribes and areas in this frontier territory in their reports and correspondence. [*It is a known fact that the British rule was established in Northeast India much later than the rest of the country, and in case of Arunachal Pradesh, the colonial contacts could not mature into governance till the Raj was in its last days]*. To reconcile a situation like this, the folklore materials can be the alternatives.

2. Folklore is considered to day as a source of history by its own right and the historians, all over the world, are more and more attracted to this category of 'living past' for an understanding of the 'past' of the humankind. It is generally accepted as a source of history, because "Folklore is the material handed down traditionally either by world of mouth or by custom and practice". (Archer Taylor, "Folklore and the Student of Literature"

in Alan Dundas ed. *The Study of Folklore,* New Work, 1965, p. 34) and includes, besides myths and legends, and songs and ballads, "The folk art, folk craft, folk tools, folk costume, folk belief, folk medicine, folk recipes, folk music, folk dance, folk games, folk gestures, and folk speech as well as those verbal forms of expression which have been called folk literature". (W.R.Bascom, "Folklore", *International Encyclopedia of Social Sciences,* 1972, pp. 496). In fact, "Folklore comprises traditional creations of peoples, primitive or civilized. These are achieved by using sounds and words in metric form and prose and include folk beliefs or superstitions, customs and performances, dances and plays". (Jonas Balys in M.Leach ed. *Standard Dictionary of Folklore, Mythology and legends,* San Francisco" 1984, p. 398). Like history, "Folklore is an echo of the past, but at the same time it is also the vigorous voice of the present". (Y.C.Sokolov, *Russian Folklore,* New Work, 1950, p. 15). However, the historian will not use folklore as a source without examining the acceptability of the information according to the standard methods of verification of sources and eliminating the possible impact of ignorance or motive or compulsion in each narration. The use of folklore is recommended when the standard sources are either scanty or absent, or the folklore is able to provide additional information or to supplement the conventional sources. As Dorson tells us, "Certain scholars welcome the use of folklore and folklife materials to recapture vanished historical periods for which other evidence is scanty". (Richard M. Dorson ed. *Folklore and Folklife: An Introduction,* Chicago, 1972, p. 12).

In case of Northeast India, where other sources are so scanty, folklore can be an alternative evidence for historical reconstruction. Birendranath Datta in his excellent work *Folklore and Historiography* (Chennai, 2002), which emerged out of his H.K.Barpujari Endowment Lecture at the Department of History, Dibrugarh University, has discussed some theoretical implications of folkloristics in the context of medieval and modern history of Northeast India. To quote him: "Cooperation between the folklorists and the historians is not only a possibility but also a necessity, in the interest of fuller and better comprehension of the past as related to the present. In India where the two levels of the classical and the folk have been operating in a close symbiotic relationship since ancient times, such cooperation assumes all the more significance. And more so in North East India which offers such a great wealth of material to work with – in terms of the 'written' and the 'un-written', the 'tangible' and the 'believed', the 'documented' and the 'oral' – the prospects of a meaningful dialogue, not only between folklore and history but also encompassing several other disciplines – such as cultural anthropology, archaeology and linguistics – seem to be very bright indeed". (p. 107).

2. The tradition of preserving the past through tales, lore and practices is still very strong in Arunachal Pradesh. The destructive impact of modernization is still less here, in comparison to the several other urbanized parts of the country. Therefore, serious efforts can be made to capture and record the folklores of Arunachal Pradesh before they die out completely. Happily, many of those have already been collected and published. A beginning was made by E.T.Dalton in his *Descriptive Ethnology of Bengal* (Calcutta, 1872). Verrier Elwin's *Myths of the North-East Frontier of India* (Shillong, 1958) and, his other works, contain a lot of those. The monographs on some of the major tribes by the ethnographers, associated with the Research Department, Govt. of Arunachal Pradesh, have also recorded a large of number of the traditions, myths and legends. There are also some excellent collections by freelance scholars. The historians may consider these as alternative sources to recapture and reconstruct the past of the Arunachalese.

3. Arunachal Pradesh is, however, no longer a *terra incognita* for the historians. We come across a number of important monographs and studies on the history of Arunachal Pradesh. The scholars associated with the Research Department (of erstwhile NEFA Administration) made the beginning under the leadership of the great Anthropologist, Verrier Elwin. The tradition has been continued by the officers of the

Department. D.K.Bora's *History and Archeology of Itanagar* (Government of Arunachal Pradesh, 1996) and his study of the Naksha Parvat give a good account of the works of the Research Department. Some doctoral works have been carried out in the Gauhati University, Dibruagarh University and the North Eastern Hill University in the history and culture and institutions of Arunachal Pradesh, and scholars, not professionally connected with Arunachal Pradesh, have also published a number of books on Arunachal Pradesh. However, the establishment of the Arunachal University with a Department of History definitely gave a fillip to the study of the history of Arunachal Pradesh, and the creation of the Department of Tribal Studies has further reinforced the research activities in the University. The teachers in the University and its affiliated colleges are individually and collectively involved in research; the department is conducting doctoral research, the teachers have undertaken projects, and they are regularly publishing their findings in various journals and proceedings. A survey of the *Proceedings of the North East India history Accociation* will testify this point. A few years back, Professor S. Dutta brought out a collection of papers on Arunachal Pradesh published in NEIHA Proceedings (a good number of which are based on non-conventional folklore materials). Many more collections may come out in future.

I am sure this seminar, sponsored by the ICHR, on the Sources of the History of Arunachal Pradesh will bring to light some new sources, make a survey of our current knowledge of the conventional and non-conventional sources, evaluate the sources and discuss appropriate methodologies for use of the sources.

2

Historical Sources: Categories, Mathods and Techniques for Constructing Modern Indian History – An Overview

P.K. Shukla

This paper makes an attempt to discuss the importance of sources for writing the history of modern India. If due importance is not given to the historical sources which are in abundance for writing the history of modern India, history would become a myth dependent largely on faiths and thus it would give rise to the notion that perception of the past by the self is history. Weaving tales, legends and tradition from the classical texts such as the *Mahabharata* and the *Shahnamas* which are, in fact, biblical legends to accommodate Hindu and Muslim myths of the origin of mankind[1] do not point out towards writing objective and scientific history. It is therefore necessary to re-create the significant features of the past on the basis of imperfect and fragmentary evidence. This imperfect and fragmentary evidence (as it may be) is the historian's sources.[2] The imperfect and fragmentary evidence for the construction of the past can only be relied upon on the basis of the scrutiny of the sources which is not more than a 'critical or scientific' history. It is a type of historical thinking in which the historian made up his mind for himself instead of repeating whatever stories he found in the old books.[3] While defining the definition of history Carr has rightly said that 'history is a kind of research or inquiring'[4]. If source material is reliable all social science disciplines require historical evidence, in so far as they deal with social reality. Any attempt to verify or falsify general theoretical models by reference to evidence depends on historical sources. Most social sciences also use more strictly historical materials for various purposes, most probably to establish trends, or more generally for purposes of comparison over time. How far back in time the materials goes, depends partially on its availability and partly on the nature of the inquiry.[5] Thus Census data are usually available in India after 1872 onwards for interpreting the social structure of our past. But demographic evidence is hardly available which is essential for the purpose of establishing the curve of demographic growth of our country.

The problem of data becomes particularly serious when social scientists are not content to use historical materials which is already available in some form or the other. They require historical material which is not available; for instance, in order to verify or falsify their theoretical propositions. This is likely in the case of social scientists concerned with essentially or ostensibly historical questions, as in the theory of economic growth. Calculation of Gross National Product (GNP) or national income at various types may be necessary for this purpose. But hardly any such data were collected before the twentieth century. Still the data for this GNP are less. In such cases the historical material used by the historian or social scientist is not original. But it is an artifact constructed on the basis of assumptions and guess work. To some extent this is the case of available historical sources in so far as they consist of grouped data *i.e.,* the census tabulations. Thus the method of collecting census data has to be critically examined before applying such data for writing the history of modern India. It may be mentioned here that the historians do take cognizance of the problem of the nature, assessment and manipulation of historical evidence. But the social scientists are "often insufficiently aware of the difficulties of using such evidence and insufficiently critical in using it".[6] A common practice among sociologists has been to use secondary historical accounts as their raw material and then to theorize them. Similarly economists are also tempted to use any statistical series that is available just because it is there and they do not inquire too closely into its reliability. For example, what about the data about the subsistence sector of our economy or about the unrecorded or 'black' sector of the economy. There is hardly any authentic data for further study on this subject.

Documents

After having discussed some of problems or limitations regarding the use and misuse of historical data, it is imperative to touch upon the historical sources and their categories. It is well known that the primary source is the raw materials. It is more meaningful to the expert historian than to the layman. A historical work is considered scholarly and reliable if is based exclusively on primary source. But it requires scientific study of primary sources. These sources have hierarchy and the principle behind this hierarchy is the idea that something which is hand-written, and of which there may be only copy, is somehow more primary than something which is printed. If a historian finds such hand-written documents with great difficulty, he feels that the conclusion based on it is so far more significant than the observation made on the basis of printed document. Since the hand-written document is rare, a historian asserts his professional autonomy. It has been held that a document written in a man's hand was more immediate to historical reality.[7] It is more closer to how it really was than a document that has suffered the less direct method of production on a printed press. But there is one problem. The document written in one man's handwriting may be of genuine record of a transaction which took place, or a record in good faith of something the writer has seen with his own eyes or may be the record of a statement dictated by one man to another, or a collective decision, or may be a complete invention on the part of a writer. Whatever may be the situation such hand-written document will yield answer only to certain question. What a historian is required to do is to compare the content of handwritten document with the printed document so as to assess its reliability. Moreover, the policy of the government is to be seen while examining the authenticity of the document. The printed papers, on the other hand, are more readily open to inspection and to be used by scholars in their disciplines like the economists, lawyers and sociologists.

The secondary source is a testimony of someone who was not present at the time of the occurrence of the event. But the historian makes use of the event it is expected that the historian should make use of the secondary sources – the books and the articles of other historians. The books and the articles written on the strength of primary sources fall in the category of secondary sources but the historian should master all the existing secondary sources. Study of such works would give an idea of the gaps in the historical writings. At least a survey of the secondary sources will enable the historians to write good text books of history.

Bibliography

In the hierarchy of primary sources we have bibliography of any substantial piece of historical scholarship. The manuscript materials include the home public records, the Judicial proceedings, foreign affairs files, miscellaneous bundles of papers, parliamentary papers, proceedings of the debates of central and state legislatures, organizational papers (Trade union Papers, Kisan Sabha Papers), intelligence reports, reports of the native news papers which are also called fortnightly report, Agriculture, Revenue and Commerce papers etc. Now a days much emphasis is placed on the *Thana records, Matha and Masjid Papers,* Missionary papers and family records. This example is illustrative and not exhaustive. Having listed and discussed the manuscript papers there is next level of the primary sources. The contemporary pamphlets and periodicals are available in abundance. Private manuscript collection and archival materials from the various embassies are other important sources. It is called foreign correspondence.

Certain materials do not fit neatly into the categorization as primary or secondary sources; some are primary sources from one point of view, secondary from another. The outstanding instance is the autobiography. Biography is generally listed in the bibliography as a primary source. But it assumes the proportions of a secondary history of the times through which the writer has lived, but it is a primary account of his own experience and thoughts. If it is composed long after the events as described, an autobiography is to be treated with greater circumspection. In somewhat similar case it is contemporary history. It has an eye-witness quality of a primary record. For example, Mahatma Gandhijee's *My Experiment with Truth,* may be taken as primary source.

Literature

One primary type of source material which has given rise to much interesting disputation is the imaginative literature left by an age or generation. A novel or a poem if it is source at all, it is a source for the period in which it was written and not for the period about which it is written. For example, *Bharat Durdasha (Plight of India)* written by Bhartendu Harishchancra in the 19th Century tells us about the condition of India in the later half of the 19th century but not about the 20th century. Dinbandhu Mitra's *Nil Darpan,* Prem Chand's *Mahajani Sabhayata (Bousgeoise Civilization)* and Angyana's *Shekhar Ek Jiwani* can be cited as examples for establishing the historical significance of imaginative literature. Special expertise is required to handle imaginative literature to establish historical events. Not doubt imaginative literature is an insight into the mores and folkways of the period, but while interpreting such literature for determining the status of social class, it is essential that a historian must saturate himself in the art and literature of that age.[8] Art and literature of an age can be a mirror of the age only when these are seen in the context of social and economic structure of the periods concerned.

Oral History

Oral history is not just a new technique but it is a part and parcel of history. It increases the possibility of history of the people and for the people. This does not mean that oral history necessarily serves the people; it can very well be used against them also. Oral history meant for the reconstruction of the past mainly on the basis of oral sources, which include oral tradition, folklore and interview. It can be termed as voice from the past. The written word became an effective tool for the ruler. The 'haves' have had power that was perpetuated by their exclusive monopoly of material and intellectual life. The growing monopoly at the written word strengthened their cause. In a country like India it was a well-established cannon that the subalterns should have no access to education.[9] Thus the written word remained confined to a small minority and the majority of the deprived people were sustained only by their oral traditions, which mirrored and projected their hopes and despair. Oral tradition therefore became an indispensable medium for probing the lives of the unprivileged section. This has been amply proved by the research of Vansina on Black Africa.[10] Even in India, Visier Sanya has written the history of Pre-British Kohima mainly on the basis of Oral tradition. In fact oral history and ethno-history have enabled historians to reconstruct the past of many communities. Thus oral history is both a complementary and supplementary to histro-graphical instrument. But the study of the methodology of oral history shows that the collection of oral materials, be it oral tradition or other oral testimony, is quite challenging.

The discipline of history has, over the past two and half decades, undergone a very substantial expansion of its intellectual horizons. Two trends lie behind such expansion. In the first instance, historians influenced by scholars of the Annales school have reached out to new disciplines in the social sciences in a bid to enrich mode of exploration and areas of enquiry. Secondly, the sources have also grown in quantity. In this connection, the use of "oral sources" as a basis of historical writing occupies a very prominent place. The Nehru Memorial Museum and Library, New Delhi, has recorded the activities of individuals who have contributed to the political, social and economic development of modern India. Such collection has enriched the historiography of modern India and therefore it deserved to be drawn increasingly into historical research.[11]

Techniques

Historian's activity is not different from that of an Inspector General while writing sound historical piece. He is like an ambassador reporting to his own government or a newspaper reporter reporting his copy to chief-reporter or chief medical officer reporting on the health of the population. History is easy if the historian does it to ascertain the facts and report them faithfully. Needless to mention that ascertaining the facts is a complicated business. Once a corpus of data has been ascertained the historian of whatever description inevitably has a problem of selection. Added to this is the problem of chronology and periodisation. Keeping in view all such factor as discussed above the task of historian is not an easy one, especially when he relies upon evidence and interprets it for reconstructing the history of the past.

Of late historians have tried to give a special primacy among primary materials to sources of non-literary type like statistics of gross national output, demographic tables, aerial photographic and industrial archaeology. But the professional historians treat every fragment of evidence with suspicion because it is possible that human errors might creep into the compilation and recording of statistics. The statistics do not in themselves provide answers. It is still the historian who must frame the questions on the basis of other types of evidence at his command.

References

1. Rajat Kant Ray "Inventing History, Discovering the Past: A Sketch of Indian Historiography, 1760s to 1990s" in *Contemporary India*, Vol. I no. 2 (April-June 2002) NMM & Library, New Delhi, p. 3.
2. Arther Marwick, *The Nature of History*, Macmillan, 1970 (first edition) p. 131.
3. Eighteenth Century Philosopher, Voltaire quoted in the Introduction to the book, *What is History*, E.H. Carr (reprint 1972) p. 1.
4. *Ibid.*, p. 4.
5. E.J. Hobsbawon "The Contribution of history to Social Science" in *International Social Science Journal*, vol.XXIII, no.4, 1981, p. 626.
6. Ibid., p. 624.
7. Arther Marwick, *op. cit.,*, p. 133.
8. *Ibid.*, p. 139.
9. L.B.Verma, "What and How of Oral History: Transforming of Past into History" in the *Indian Historical Review* (hereafter IHR) vol.XII, nos. 1-2, Delhi, 2000, p. 158.
10. *Ibid.*, p. 158.
11. Ravinder Kumar, *The Making of a Nation: Essay in Indian History and Politics*, Manohar, New Delhi, 1989, p. 245.

3

Reconstruction of Tribal History from Oral Tradition

N. Joykumar Singh

Prof. A.L. Rowse said, "History is essentially the record of the life of men in the societies in their geographical and their physical environment". He was of the view that their social and cultural environments arise from the interaction of the one with the other society and geographical condition. In the same line B. Sheik Ali also said that history is the record of unique events in the life of mankind. In this respect many writers also advanced different ideas and observation about the concept and nature of the history. But as a whole it can be suggested that history is a fact and it is the unfolding story of human freedom. However the process of historical writings and studies has got its own variation. The historians of the early periods had confined their energy to the activities of kings, queens and some important members of the royal family. They did not have the time to see the role of the common people and other different communities in the process of the development of the society. This trend of historical writing was continued for quite long time. But just after having a new idea of the inter-disciplinary approach in the writing of the history the trend of the study of historical research being to enter into a new dimension. Under the new method of the study of history, the historians of the later period began to take strong initiative to study the role and contribution of the common people of different communities in the process of the historical developments. The study on peasants, women, tribal etc. has dominated the process of the historical study. It is a well aware fact that the historical research is based on some important sources that is called historical evidences. The source can be broadly divided into two parts *i.e.,* archaeological evidence and literacy sources. But now a new trend of study in historian and researchers are making a serious attempt to construct the history particularly of the pre-literate society of Tribal people. This type of study is popularly known as 'Oral history'. It is a new phenomenon in the process of historical research. The main objective of the paper is to make a humble attempt to highlight the importance of the oral tradition as a source in the study of the tribal history.

Indeed, oral history is a primary source material obtained by recording the spoken words of persons deemed to harbour hitherto unavailable information worth preserving. This oral tradition was also known as 'popular antiquities'. But in the year 1846 one W.J.Thomas began to use the term of oral tradition as 'folk lore'. It is recorded that he introduced this term into the English usage in a letter written under the pseudonym of Ambrose Merton which appeared in Athenaeum in August 1846. In this letter he wrote, "A good Saxon compound Folk-lore could be more aptly used to describe what we in England designate a popular Antiquities or popular literature..." His main interest was to publish the notes concerning superstition, customs, ballads, saying and other traditional survivals. The older times still exist in Britain. Then the word coined by W.J.Thomas quickly adopted and absorbed into the language of almost all the European countries. However the oral history as an organized activity started only from 1948 when Professor Allan Nevins launched 'The Oral History Project' to obtain and preserve such a valuable record like traditional beliefs, superstitions, manners customs and observance of ordinary people which have persisted from earlier periods.

Oral tradition has got its own variation in every source. This is the character of oral tradition. In this regard many writers gave different theories and observations. However there is a common assumption that 'Oral tradition' is something uniform, something that can be treated as an undifferentiated and self-evident entity. Whatever the case may be the oral tradition may be listed into three main classes *i.e.,*:

1. Recognized literary forms
2. Informal historical knowledge and
3. Personal recollections

Recognized Literary Form

This category of oral tradition is also known as 'oral literature'. However still it is very hard to define precisely about the real character of oral literature. Some writers are of the view that oral literature is relatively formalized, in the sense not of verbal accuracy but of generes clearly recognized in the society. They are of the view that various types of both prose and poetry which correspond to literature in literate socials are also a part of oral literature. The main theme is eulogy. Ruth Finnegan said "it is a political propaganda, and we cannot expect very different historical information, in the sense of exactly description or narration" (D.K.Dunaway and William K. Bauan Page, 127). But if the importance of the eulogy in the value of the society is to be analyzed it can be suggested that praise poetry can lead to insight into the values and ideal of the society. In the case of Manipur the concept of eulogy started on the beginning of 18th century. From this praise poetry the researchers was able to extract the basic values and the ideas of the society and thus it greatly help in the process of the construction of history of the pre-literate society. Apart from this Manipur also enjoyed the contribution of many folk stories like *'Khuman Kangleirol'* (Genealogy of Khuman), *'Moirang Kangleirol'* (Genealogy of Moirang) in the process of the construction of history. Earlier, these were in the form of oral tradition. But finally it was written in the middle of 18th century under the authoritative of royal recognition. Thus these oral literatures was formalized and accepted by the royal court.

Then 'Lyrics' – songs for wedding, dance, work etc., etc. can throw light on values in a society at a particular time. These personal songs are also an excellent source in the process of the construction of the history of the pre-literate society of tribal people. Some writers were of the view that poetry and lyrics in non literate societies can be illuminating for the historian that it gives a direct relevance for the intellectual history of the time and indirectly useful for other aspects of society. It is also true that there would be a lot of exaggeration, element of propaganda personal whim, desire to please etc. in the oral literature. This is also one of the characteristics of folklore. But these elements can be avoided by the historians.

Informal Historical Knowledge

Ruth Finnegan said, "Informal historical knowledge includes not only general notions of what happen in the past, but also a few element which though not eligible for the term 'oral literature' can take a somewhat formalized shape" (ibid. p.130). According to him the items like place names, praise names or genealogies are included in this category. No doubt the place names and its underlying literary concept have played a great role as a source in the reconstruction of history of any particular society. To name a particular place had always associated with certain idea. For example in Manipur naming of place is always associated with the action of the personality. Therefore when we make an attempt to know the historical background of a particular place it has come out together with the history of the personality. In the same way in the tribal area of the different countries, the same pattern is also existed. Theref ore it certainly gave a valuable contribution in the process of the reconstruction of the tribal history.

Genealogy is also equally important as source of the history. In some cases Genealogies are formally recited in, say, prayers or praises but most often they merely form part of the general knowledge of a society or group. But still it exists as an excellent source as far as it goes. Some writers called it as 'Telescopic Source'. In European countries some groups claimed that they were the descendents of Noah and Adam and other groups also claimed that their pedigrees descent from prophet. In Indian context also we find the genealogy of Lunar dynasty and Solar dynasty. Like this among the tribal people also there is a strong belief that their originators are the direct descendents of gods etc., etc. Thus, the genealogies of chiefs also make an important source of information in the process of the reconstruction of tribal history.

Personal Recollection

The personal recollection is also another important category of oral tradition. In a way this category may be observed as one of the best sources in the process of the reconstruction of history. But there is need to cross check because it always includes personal prejudices, romantic memories, exaggeration etc. But as a whole this kind of source is much nearer the primary facts than similar accounts which have been handed down through several generations.

Indeed, oral sources are in many ways even more open than written ones. A written document is certainly liable to many influences as it is written down, but once written it can be taken as permanent. Oral form, on the other hand, is open to all these influences. Whatever the case may be, the oral sources are one of the best contributing factors in the process of the reconstruction of history.

4

Historical Value of Indigenous Oral Tradition: A Study of Nyshi Tribe

N.T. Rikam

I

Introduction

Oral history as a historical source is not a new phenomenon. It has been utilized systematically as an archival and research tool to study the history of given area. Oral history is not strictly a means of retrieval of information, but rather one involving the generation of knowledge. It is a record of perceptions, rather than a re-creation of historical events. It can be employed as a factual source but with corroboration. The difficulty of crosschecking information does not detract, however, from its value for understanding perceptions and recovering levels of experiences, which are not normally available to historians. It offers almost the only feasible route for the retrieval of perceptions and experiences of whole groups who did not normally leave a written record. In societies where the oral narrative is part of the formal culture, no explanation is needed as to why a certain story is significant. The very time honourd practice and the setting within which the oral tradition takes place lend its strength and meaning.

A common definition of oral history among oral historians focuses on the reminiscence about direct personal experience. According to Willa Baum, oral history "involves the tape recording of an interview with a knowledgeable person, someone who knows whereof he or she speaks from personal participation or observation, about a subject of historical interest".[1] Charles Hudson separates folk history from ethno-history from the points of view of what is studied from and how it is studied.

According to him, folk history "denotes the historical beliefs of other societies and cultures", but the aim of ethno-history is "to reconstruct, using all available materials, 'what really happened' in terms that agree with our sense of creditability and our sense of relevance... In a folk history we attempt to find what people in another society believe 'really happened', as judged by their sense of credibility and relevance'. 'Thus, the methodology of ethno-history is essentially 'etic', while the methodology of folk history is essentially 'emic'".[2] These terms were initially borrowed from Kenneth Pike's linguistic theory but now it often appears in contemporary folklore studies. In academic usages "etic" has come to designate an outsider's point of view and system of classification and "emic" the insider's conception of cultural categories and their order.[3]

Oral history mainly focused on the native view of the past, either in collective tradition or in a personal reminiscence. In order to gather data necessary in describing and interpreting that perception of the past, we use the technique of oral history, among others. On the basis of the above conceptual framework, I have tried to put the indigenous oral tradition as an important source of history.

II

The Nyishis

Almost all tribes of Arunachal Pradesh do not have written tradition and there is hardly any historical evidence to study the history of Arunachal and its people. The only available source through which we can deconstruct the past history of the indigenous people is oral sources, embedded in their custom, belief, practice, tradition, and culture.

In this paper an attempt has been made to examine the indigenous oral tradition with special reference to the Nyishi tribe in a historical perspective. Nyishis are academically less known tribe in the state but numerically they are the most important community as they spread over five different districts namely Upper Subansiri, Lower Subansiri, Kurung Kume, Papum Pare and East Kameng. These districts are named after the major rivers *i.e.,* Subansir, Kurung Keme, Papum Pare and Kameng respectively. A few Nyishis are also inhabited in Sonitpur and Lakhimpur districts of Assam.

Few ethnographers and authors tried to describe the Nyishi in their own ways to totality vis-à-vis the other tribes of the state. They had painted wrong picture of the tribe by studying only a few pockets of the Nyishis and unfortunately the subsequent authors (even the contemporary) have repeatedly used the same notion. Thus, F.Hamilton, described the Nyshis (Daflas) as retaining 'the fierce and warlike spirit of the ancient Assamese; they indulge their appetites in eating unclean food as much as the impure nations of China and Europe, and adhere to their old customs, altogether rejecting the instruction of the sacred order of the Hindus and what is called the purity of its law'.[4] Similarly, in his book, *The Daflas of the Subansiri Region,* B.K. Shukla had distracted the truth relating to the temperamental behavour of the Nyishis. This distortion is explicit in his words: 'Their hills have remained terra incognita for centuries, with a long history of acts of brutal vengeance, raids and ransom, assault and murders. Innocent adventurers and intruders were liable to be ambushed and killed.'[5]

The Nyishis in all practical purposes call themselves *Nyeshang, Nishi* or more appropriately as *Nyishi* since the time immemorial. As per their mythology, the term '*Nyishi'* or '*Nyeshang'* is derived from two words *i.e., Nyi or Nyia* – means man or human race that descended from *Atu Nyia* (first real man on earth) and *Eshang or Ishi* – means high hills or highland. Therefore, a compound words *'Nyishi* denotes the descendants of *Atu Nyia* who dwells in the highland. This is the reason they are called highlanders. They are by nature innocent, simple and straightforward. However, due to the variations of topographical and climatic conditions, their physical stature, dress, phonetic accent of language etc. vary slightly from one region to other. But because of the same racial blood, more or less their temperament, attitude and mentality are almost similar.

In absence of standard historical documentation and lack of archaeological sources, there is no definite idea about the early history of Nyishi which is shrouded in the midst of wilderness.[6] Nevertheless, they have rich culture, magnificent tradition and fascinating religious beliefs and practices, which have been vigorously processed and maintained through ethical codes orally and believed to have been handed down from generation to generation since time immemorial. Myth is an important source for deconstructing the history of the origin and evolution of any community. According to K.V.W. Bolle, a myth 'is an expression of the sacred in words: it reports realities and events from the origin of the world that remains valid for the basis and purpose of all there is consequently, a myth functions as a model for human activity, society, wisdom and knowldege'.[7] A myth, whether its subject is the acts of deities or other extraordinary events, always takes us back to 'beginning of all things'; hence, the cosmology, the birth of the world, is a principle theme.[8] Verrier Elwin writes: "Long ago Tylor suggested that myth was primitive history and ethnology expressed in poetic form. The poet contemplates the same natural world as the man of science, but he expresses his discovery in a different way. And the primitive poet who puts his inspiration in the from of myth shapes it out of 'those endless analogies between man and nature, which are soul of all poetry'. The truth of a myth is thus in a way irrelevant. 'Myth is the history of its authors, not of its subjects; it records the lives, not of superhuman heroes, but of poetic nation."[9]

But in the context of Nyishis in particular and the tribes of Arunachal Pradesh in general the above statement can hardly be applied to. The indigenous myths and for that matter the folk literatures are built with elaborate cultural codes some of which hardly one can interprete with authority. The experts or elderly persons in the community lucidly deal these aspects and the ordinary or common man is devoid of understanding the intricacies of creation and evolution processes. Their folk stories are not at all imaginative because many of it is still quite relevant and popular even today as is reflected in their day to day life like dress, food habit, settlement pattern, celebration of festivals, folk songs, dances, etc.

Their cultural ethos is represented in their *Idh-bingnam, Nuya-sonam Nyeme-Kabnam, Bingjam-jamnam, Weyi Barnam, Gumba Banam* and so on and so forth. In other words it can be termed as folk literature based on indigenous oral tradition. The varied nature of folk culture and folk tale depicts as well as narrates some particular events of human activities ranging from birth to death and even after the death or the netherworld. Oral literatures are being appropriated in the society mainly through three institutions *i.e., Barek Meram, Weyi Meram* and *Niting-Harming.*

III

Barek Meram (Socio-Political Institution or Village Council)

Barek Meram is a mechanism through which the entire socio-political issues are being debated. Generally the elderly people well-versed in past history take part in such deliberations. These people are called *Nyegam or Nyejik* and they can be treated as the guardian of the society. However, they are neither appointed nor formally trained. Like the *Nyobus,* they achieve this position through individual efforts and of course with the blessing of *Sobu Weyi* (benevolent deity), as they believe. There is another related term called *Nyele Meram.* It deals exclusively the issues relating to settlement of disputes and maintaining peace and order in the society. Here, the *Bungriang Bungte* (intermediary) plays an important role especially in major disputes like war or murder of a person. The *Nyegam* performs broadly two types of duties. One is *Nyeda Barek* (Marriage negotiation) and the other is *Arum Barek* (friendship ties). Among the number of *Nyegams, a Haakhe* (representative) is arranged who shall negotiate or talk on behalf of the party or individual concerned. While dealing with any given issue, the *Nyegam* uses to trace the entire events of the past and relates it to the present problems; while doing so they would try to gather as much points as possible so as to substantiate or convince the other group to accept the contention (argument). The deliberations in *Barek Meram* continue till both the parties because satisfied or agree upon and the participants goes on talking hours together. This way they enrich their general knowledge about the past history and these are used for understanding occurrences or problems in the society.

Besides direct talking, *Nyegam* and for that matter *Nyobu* can also go for performing folk songs or chanting hymns call *Idh Bingnam. Edh-bingnam* mainly deals the whole process of origin and evolution of the Universe. *Korium Kolu* is the beginning and from there the creation and evolution process started, which is called *Changte-Dote Ho Nyikum Nyia Blah Barnam.*[10] As par their tradition *Jingbu Pabu Abu* was the creator, who used extra-ordinary spirit – *Chene Rolum Dola* in the process of creations. Through *Idh Bingnam,* we can also deconstruct the evolution of human beings too. As we have seen that the power of *Kamchang Chene Dola* was employed to create all living beings including the human being. In this process *Loma Chene Dola* was invoked to create *Nyikh Tani,* the first man on the earth. With the coming of first man, a chain of descendents like *Nyema Tani, Nyiyang Tani, Nyidar Tanik Nyikum Tani* and at last *Nyia Tani* were born on the earth. The Nyishis believe that it was from *Atu Nyia Tani,* the actual human race started.

IV

Weyi Meram (Religious Institution or Priesthood)

Weyi Meram is an institution, which mainly deals with the religious specialities of the Nyishis. Since it deals the spiritual aspect of the society, *Nyobus* (priests) play a vital and multi-facet role. The core meaning of the term priest in the western usage is – (i) the priest performs a sacrificial ritual, usually at a fixed location, such as, altar.[11] (ii) the priest does as a specialist on behalf of a community or congregation.[12] When "both of these are present", says Baruch A. Levine, "We have priesthood in a strict or narrow sense".[13] In the cross cultural and non-western use of the term 'priest', 'a priest is any religious specialist acting ritually for or on behalf of a cummunity'.[14]

In the tribal society, a priest offers himself as a liaison between the human being and the world of unseen powers. J.N.Chowdhury writes, "They are the shamans par excellence with the knowledge and power of negotiating with the spirit world. Their services are sought after during sickness or other misfortunes, when they prescribe the necessary rites or sacrifices for propitiating the inimical or *orams*".[15] When a person is ill, he is called for diagnosis; he is consulted to save crops from damages and enable the farmer to yield rich harvest; he ensures the protection of livestock and makes them to thrive; he also ensures the safe journey and assures a comfortable life even when a person departs from this world; he forecasts impending disasters and averts them; and above all, he has been the refuge, the solace to the people living in the darkness of evils surrounding them. All the activities of priest come under the domain of *Weyi Meram.* Nyobo performs its duty through different modes and methods such *Weyi Binam, Weyi Kuknam or Pachung Kuknam, Weyi Panam, Oram Paknam* etc.[16] While carefully studying all these, it is equally important like that of *Barek Meram.* Although, the rituals and sacrifices are exclusively performed by the priest but every one can have an access to the dealing of the Priest. The preparation and management for the rituals and sacrifices are generally done on community basis.

The performances of the priest also start from the origin and evolution but put more emphasis on the struggle between human being and the world of unforeseen. In the process of evolution we have seen the coming of *Sachang and Nyedo,* the earth and the heaven but later on another world called *Weyi Nyoku or Nel Nyoku* evolved, as a result the Nyishis believed that the entire universe is divided into three worlds *i.e.,* earth, heaven and netherworld respectively. *Sachang* is a dwelling place for living creatures including man, animal and plant; *Nyedo* is the abode of Gods and Goddesses, and other celestial bodies, while *Weyi/Nel Nyoku* is a place meant for the life after death. There is also an imaginary world called *Talang Nyoku,* which lies in between heaven and earth. The people believe that the person who dies at the ripe age or after prolonged illness, their *Yajyalu* (soul) goes to the netherworld, which lies inside the earth. But those who die of unnatural death like accident, murder, suicide etc. their soul will go to *Talang Nyoku,* which the Nyishis treat it as hell.[17]

V

Niting-Harming (Folk Lore)

In a simple term *Niting-Harming* may be interpreted (understood) as 'storehouse' of non-material culture. It is primarily folk literature in the form of story or tale, song, dance, drama, ballad, lullaby etc. Every folk item deals with or depict a particular event or situation. Some folk item can be performed at different occasions but the content or the interpretation will change depending on the given situation or occasion. For instance, *Buya Sonam* may be performed in different occasion like during *Yullo* ceremony, during festival, during marriage and even during house construction. Unlike the other two *i.e., Nyegam* and *Nyobu*, there is no hard and fast rule to perform folk items. Normally a well-versed person led the songs or dances but it is not compulsory. Most of the items are performed in chorus or group and hence any one can initiate it. One striking characteristic of folk items among the Nyishi is that it has no ending. The song or dance goes on for hours together and many items have competitive notion, which will come to an end only when both parties are either satisfied or fully tired of. These are generally performed with lively or in a festivity mood where eating, drinking and merry making goes together.

VI

It is amply clear that the treasure of oral sources is lying within the community. It is being spread over but the primary problem is how and in what way these sources can be used in writing the history of a community. It is very difficult to systematize or categorize and to correctly interpret some of the oral sources as it has been dealt with by using special terminology, which may be called 'cultural codes'. So here the language plays an important role as one need to understand or interpret in a right perspective. Insiders (Indigenous Scholars) can do much better provided they are free themselves from the weaknesses like romanticization, prejudice, emotions, bias, etc. In any case, the oral traditions prevalent among the Nyishis will definitely throw light on writing the history of the community in particular and the state in general.

References

1. Willa Baum, *Oral History for the Local Historical Society*, Nshville: American Association for State and Local History, 1971, p. 7.
2. Charles Hudson, "Folk History and Ethno-history", *Ethno-history*, in David K. Dunaway and Willa K. Baum (ed), second edition, *Oral History*, New Delhi, p. 189.
3. Ibid. 196.
4. F. Hamilton, An Account of Assam, (ed) by S.K.Bhuyan (1940), p. 74, cited in Verrier Elwin, (ed) *India's North East Frontier in the Nineteenth Century*, Oxford University Press, Delhi, 1959, p. 168.

5. *Ibid.*, p. 1
6. N.T. Rikam, *Socio-Cultural Life of the Nishings;* unpublished M.Phil Thesis, Dept. of Tribal Studies, Arunachal University, Doimukh, 1997, p. 22.
7. Kees W. Bolle, "Myths: An Overview" in Mircea Eliade, General, ed. *The Encyclopedia of Religion, op. cit.*, vol. 10, p. 261.
8. Kees W. Bolle, *ibid.*, p. 262.
9. Verrier Elwin, *Myths of the North East Frontier of India,* Directorate of Research, Govt. of Arunachal Pradesh, Itanagar, 1993 (First Edition, 1958), p. xxii.
10. Views expressed by Mr. Tang Epa Tara, interview conducted on 15th June, 2002 at his Official Chamber at Itanagar.
11. Baruch, Levine, Priesthood, An Overview, in Mircea Eliade, ed. *The Encyclopedia of Religion, op. cit.*, Vol. 11, p. 528.
12. *Ibid.*
13. *Ibid.*
14. *Ibid.* p. 529.
15. J.N. Chowdhury, *Arunachal Panorama,* Directorate of Research, Govt. of Arunachal Pradesh, Shillong, 1973, p. 142.
16. N.T. Rikam, *Faith and Philosophy of the Nyishis,* (Booklet), Offset Printing Press, Itanagar, 1999.
17. As narrated by Mr. Tam Tahi, Rachi, February 22, 2001.

5

Oral Tradition: An Important Source of Adi History

Gindu Borang

The Siang valley, which occupies the central part of Arunachal Pradesh, on North Eastern tip of India, is the home of different sub-tribes of the Adis Padam, Minyong, Panggi, Simong, Karko, Bori, Bokar, Pailibo, Pasi, Milang and Ashing. From the Ahom period till the end of the British rule these tribal groups were collectively known as Abor. It is defined variously by different writers, such as, savage or disobedient, independent, unruly etc.[1] This word was considered polluted or derogatory term and later they called themselves as 'Adi' meaning hill people. Actually the word 'Adi' is a geographical term, which means hill or mountain. Generally the altitude of a geographical area is divided into three belts – *Adi*, which mean upper belt (upper part of the hill), *Rape* middle belt and *Monggu* lower belt or plain areas. These tribal groups occupying the three belts right from MacMohan line in the North to the adjoining plains of the Brahmaputra valley in the south. So the most appropriate meaning of the Adi is people coming from the hill. This is because all the sub-tribes covering the three belts claimed that they came to the present habitat from the northern mountain (Namcha Barwa range).

Like other tribal societies, the Adis have rich oral tradition. The Adi tradition says that the wise Man, believed to be the God of Wisdom distributed scripts to all the great ancestors of all human beings. The script for the Adi was written on animal skin and others were written on stone and bark of the tree. It is said that the hungry ancestor of the Adi burnt the skin and ate it. That is why the Adis do not have scripts but have sharp memories till today. In a traditional society where there is no written record, events concerning the remote past often take the form of myth. It is true to the Adi society. The story of an Adi heroes who took part in the Adi-British war in the early part of the 19th century takes the from of a myth due to the absence of written records but British records remains an authentic historical evident of modern Arunachal.

Oral Tradition is an important source of the history of Arunachal Pradesh in particular and all the pree-literate tribal society in general. The dictionary meaning of 'Oral' means spoken and 'Tradition' means beliefs and customs. Thus, the 'Oral Tradition' means beliefs and customs expressed orally by means of specialized voice forms. These literary works circulated by the words of mouth from one person to another and from one generation to the next are known as oral Literature'. 'Oral literature' 'is nothing but a kind of verbal art or expressive literatures which are sung, spoken and voiced forms of traditional utterance'.[2] Such oral literature reflects the culture of a community and brings its people in solidarity, continuity and consistency.

Oral tradition of the Adis is the important sources of Adi history. But writing of an Adi history without the knowledge of their tradition would be misleading and incomplete because in the absence of written records and archaeological evidence there is no base on which one have to rely upon. The research scholars should therefore, collect and analyze the existing tradition, maintain the time sequence, recognize and point out the historical aspects and give it more meaningful historical sense.

The oral traditions of the Adis are preserved in the form of *Abang* (rhapsodies relating myth of creation, origin of several institutions), *Bari* (myth of origin and evolution of various institutions), *Abe* (introductory speech of *kebang i.e.,* village council), *Kongki Bote* (narration of historical facts and exploits of great ancestors in verse in *Abe* tune), *Penge* (the funeral hymn relating birth, material life of deceased, death and journey of the soul to the next world), *Odong* (geneaology), *Doying* (history/ story), *Dobo* (expression of one's desire in the form of songs), *Lutom* (folk proverbs and sayings) and *Dance-Drama* like *Besung Nayi, Nunu Pipi, Padam Nyanyi, Boying Nero Pasi Kongki*, etc.

Abang

The word *'Abang'* literally means possible way of coming or clue of origin. During the seasonal festivals of the Adis, the leader singer called *Miri Abu* (*Miri Ane* in case of female singer) sings and dances in a typical way. The *Miri Abu* goes on singing for whole night narrating the evolution of universe, creation of earth, origin of gods and goddesses, man and animals, evolution of social institutions etc. The narration of all these concepts of traditional songs itself carries the meaning of *Abang*. The presentation of *Miri Abu* through the medium of traditional songs itself carries the meaning of *Abang*. It means when one knows the meaning he would say it is the possible way of origin and evolution of everything. Various types of *Abang* could be composed in different occasions. However, *Ponung Abang, Delong Abang* and *Abang Bapit* or *Bapit* are notable ones.

Ponung Abang is sung in the *Solung* festival and is divided into three parts – *Ardo Bado Abang* (the main theme of this is origin of methun, pig and sacrifice thereof and is sung in the first night of sacrifice day), *Binyat Abang* (the main theme is how paddy came to the land of *Tani* (human being) through the ears of *Sanyi* (dog) from the land of *Kine Nane*, the goddess of Grain and after, in the third night of solung festival and *Ekop Abang* (the main theme is how *Tani* (human being) struggle against the evil spirits and the art of warfare and protection thereafter) in the sixth night of the solung festival. However, the first part of every *Abang* is almost similar *i.e.,* dwell at length on evolution of universe, origin of the earth, sun, moon and other phenomenon without which all *Abang* is baseless, and the slight variation is due the way of presentation of different *Miris*.

In solung one would see the *Miri Abu* wearing *Gale* (lady's skirt), two or more beads decorated with white festoons made of *Ridin* (creeper of religious value) in his head, two hunches of *Kiring* (bell) hung at his neck, and carrying sword in one hand and scabbard in the other, singing and dancing and jerking his sword. He narrates various stories of interest called *Abang* through the medium of songs and in poetical language repeatedly followed by *Ponung* girls, and the villagers go on listening him for hours together. On such nights, the younger generation who want to become *Miri Abu* spend the whole night.

According to *Abang*, there was nothing in this world except darkness. In the dark world came a super woman called *Kamang Mone. Kamang Mone* while flying in the darkness created the earth. Describing this *Abang* says,

"Keyum Kamang e Mone
Mone Taying e gyapit dakla
Sedi beliem pilen to
Among beloem yatlen to"

Regarding the origin of sun and moon, the *Abang* says that after the creation of *Sedi, Sedi* (the earth) and *Melo* (the sky) lay close together. Out of their union things were born in the darkness. With the birth of *Myane* (Sedi-Dir-Irmang-Myane), a super man, the light first appeared in this world. The eyes of *Myane* were as bright as the sun of today and focus the whole world. Every body began to get the light as day when he awoke and night when he was sleeping. After the death of Myane the darkness once again reigned the world. Every body tried their best to find out a source of light but utterly failed. Finally they decided to send *Kongki Yokmo* (*Sedi-Dir-Irkong-Kongki Yokmo*) a blacksmith of repute to the side of *Myane's* dead body. Kongki Yokmo as expected took out the two eyes of *Myane* and made it into two suns called *Bomong* and *Boo. Bomong* the right eye of *Myane* was brighter than *Boo* and began to rise from the higher altitude. And *Boo* less in power began to rise from the lower altitude. These two suns rise alternatively giving no chances of sleeping, love affairs and all plants began to dry up. All beings became restless. Finding no way out they held a *Kebang* and decided to kill one of the suns. As decided by the *Kebang* Attung Tiklung, a small frog shot *Boo* and injured one of his eyes and hid himself inside the hollow part of bamboo. One eyed *Boo* became weak and pale and, transformed into a less light producing celestial body called *Polo* (moon). Thus, the right eye of *Myane* became the present day sun and the left eye moon.

Delong and Bari

Delong and *Bari* are the male songs and dances of the Adi. In *Lutor* or *Etor* festival, all male member of the village gather in the *Musup* and take part in the *Delong* dances. In *Delong* also the *Miri Abu* leads the performance. Like *Ponung Abang* the

Miri Abu goes on singing for whole night the first part of which is almost same *i.e.,* myth of creation. Besides this, he dwells on the topics like origin of *methun,* how some people have many *methuns* and some others do not and various other things. According to *Delong Abang Methun* is created out of a worm of a ground. That is why the *methun,* by treating it as his maternal uncle, does not eat the leaves of a ground till today.

Bari is a special type of *Abang* sung by Minyong particularly *Dorung* and *Unnying/Aran* festivals. It is a solo, followed by chorus. Among Padams, it is usually sung in *kojing gedoku yume i.e.,* the night when roofing materials called *kojing* are finally brought in the village. The very theme of this occasion is how man first came to the earth, built houses and lived together. The traditional *Bari Abang* (Ering 1972) writes, 'mostly concentrates on the belief, imagination and description of an ideal and richly ornamented bride called *Nyanyi Mete'.*[3] Here seasonal physical nature especially the pleasant season beginning from the last month of winter to before scorching heat, flash flood and epidemic of hot summer is artistically compared to *Nyanyi Mete,* meaning reverent foremother. This pleasant season is described as the most beautiful entertaining, warm and most loved bride of the tribe. Traditionally it is believed that her arrival produces endless waves of joy and contentment, which touches all men, animals, trees and creepers of the physical world. As a result, the earth regains freshness of life after dry winter. *Nyanyi Mete,* though a creation of artistic imagination influences the tribe a lot in their way of life. She is depicted as well-dressed and ideal wife of the tribe. So, all females of the tribe are well-dressed and look beautiful and try their best to live up to the ideal of the most loved and reverent bride *Nyanyi Mete.*

Abe

The term *Abe* literally means corner of a circle or anything within which all the *Kebang* decisions should confine. Therefore older members of the *Kebang* generally narrate this introductory speech of the *Kebang* in the beginning of the session. The *Abe* speakers are not only expert in psychological study of the people but also good historians who can narrate the whole story of Adi community from beginning to the latest time within a few minutes. With rhythmic oratory speech they appeal the fellow members to speak out boldly for the betterment of the tribe *i.e.,* application of uniform laws, give impartial justice acceptable to both the parties, etc. Roy (1960) in his 'Aspects of Padam-Minyong Culture' writes, "Every speech begins with a preamble narrating the ancient history and glory of the Adi race and exhortation on the bench for conformity to the traditional laws for impartial justice".[4] During the deliberations of *Abe,* they recall the recorded history of the crimes and disputes and its nature, importance of *Kebang* and its decision and finally payment of penalty. They also caution the listeners particularly the younger generation of the society not to commit offence in order to avoid the *Kebang* and payment of penalty. This act as an agent of moulding the mind of the people

Kongki Bote

Kongki Bote is a narration of historical facts and exploits of worthy ancestors in verse in Abe tune. As per *Kongki Bote, Adi,* being one of the great warrior of the time conquered vast territory running from Kepang Adi (Namcha Barwa Range) in the north to Lopa Baring and Lotong Adi (probably the hill in the north of Lotao village) in the east, Guwahati Lingkok (Pandu Ghat) in the south and Obonori (present Subansiri bridge area in Assam) in the West. One could know the origin and migration of the tribes from *Kongki Bote.* In *Kongki Bote* they mentioned various places as their earlier settlements. The ancestors of the Adis are said to have come from Tibet through *Kepang La* pass and settled at a place called Korbe-Mayung at the source of river Siang. Then they settled in the lovely valley of Jere to Dalda, Nugong valley, Sirang, Gelling Jemum Poklek, Miging Poklek (the present Miging village of Upper Siang District). From here the Adi had split into several clans and later acquired the characters of separate sub-tribes. Such as *Bomi* now called themselves Padam, *Bonyong* now Minyong, *Bobin* to simong, *Boto Topo* to Galo, etc. Every Adi are now curious to prove the authenticity of their oral tradition *Kongki Bote.* So sending of an archaeological team to the selected places mentioned above will be a welcome step.

Penge

Penge is the typical exclamatory expression of an Adi at the death of near and dear one. It is the traditional farewell song to the departed soul. Though the *Penge* is also an *Abang* consisting of the sacred hymn of the religion and not every Miri is in a position to chant it. So, right person is always chosen for the purpose. The *Penge Ngena Abu i.e.,* who experts in *Penge*, chant for hours together, describing the *Lenko-Angko*, the home of origin and end, material life of deceased, death and journey to the next world. The *Adi Penge*, as per N.N. Osik (1992) 'locates the original home of the Adis to the north, also known as Engo Takar (the land of plenty), which has been identified with Tsangpo valley in China'.[5] The *Adi Penge* also furnishes some clues regarding the original home of the tribes.

Odong (Geneaology)

The genealogy of the Adis particularly the first part, beginning from *Keyum* to *Pedong nane* (mythical mother of all living beings and spirits) is mixed up with the myth of creation. *Pedong Nane's* last and youngest son was *Doni* or *Tani* (the first man). He is regarded as the common ancestor of the tribe. However, they count their genealogies not from *Doni* but from *Pedong Nane*. Genealogical chart of Borang clan of Padam sub-tribe is taken as an example. They are as follows: Pedong – Doni – Nibo – Bomi – Midong – Dolo – Lonung – Nuda – Dayi – Yike – Kepang – Paper – Pertin – Tinling (Borang clan) – Litung – Tubang – Bapir – Pirjong – Jotan – Tanling – Lingko – Kotem – Temlom – Lomjong – Jorang – Radu and Rapel – Peltom. Peltom stands the 27th generations from Pedong Nane. The lengthiest genealogy stands around 32 to 35 generations.

The common acceptance of *Pedong* Nane as their progenitor makes us believe that she led her son (*Doni*) from Tibet to the source of river Siang somewhere around Mac Mohan Line. If we accept this view and calculate the 35 generations into 25 years, the Adi came to Arunachal in 1128 AD, exactly one century earlier than the Ahoms in Assam. In the absence of written records, there are definite possibilities of mixing up *Pedong Nane*, the mother of *Doni* and *Doro* with the mythical mother *Pedong Nane*.

Doying (History/Story)

Doying of the Adis is of various types dealing in different subjects. The *Aku Doying* (old history) of the Adis is full of inter-tribal feuds. The main causes of inter-tribal feuds as recorded in the *Doying* were capturing of *mithun*, kidnapping of women and children as slaves, provocative remark on individual with ill motives, etc.

The famous Padam (Damro) and Minyong (Riga) Mimak (War) fought in the early part of the 19th century was the result of the cold blooded murder of Balu Oupir of Perme clan of Damro by Kepsi Sikep also called Matsi Sikep, a rich man and influential person of Sitang village who visited Damro, a Padam village. Balu Lupir, a rich man of Damro wanted to make friendship with him. In their business transaction, both of them decided to meet at Ampe Dumbang (a resting place between the two villages) with proper Adi customs and it was decided Matsi Sikep should take his *Arem* (costly metal plates) and Balu Oupir should being his *mithun*. Balu Lupir came with all his paraphernalia, his slaves following with the cattle. Matsi Sikep who had ill motives in his heart carried only beads necklace, a sword and a jar of *Apong* (local wine). Both reached the rendezvous at the appointed time. Matsi Sikep offered his *Aong* jar to *Balu* Lupie as a friendship gesture. While Balu Lupie was drinking *Apong* Matsi Sikep took the opportunity and beheaded Balu Lupir with his sword. Matsi Sikep then took away all beads and other properties and decamped from there. When the slaves of Balu Lupir arrived there they found their master killed. They immediately followed the murderer and found the Siang Lam (bridge) still jerking which indicates that the murderer just crossed the bridge. They questioned the people of Parong and Riu village but they expressed their ignorance about him. Then they went to Sitang, the village of the murderer, but the villagers did not give them right answer and indirectly hinted that, that day Riga had killed a pig and was having a feast, that possibly they were the culprits and to celebrate the killing they were enjoying the feast. The slaves, without detailed inquiry of the matter, were convinced that it was Riga village, which was responsible for the murder of their master and they carried this information to their village. The Padams of Damro were greatly enraged at this and prepared for launching an attack on Riga. With their allied forces the Padam attacked Riga and burnt the famous *Ereng Lidung* (big stone having spiritual power). This event shows that murder of one person with an ill motive led to a feud on a large scale and followed by killing of many innocent people.

Another story told us that the original inhabitants of Pasighat area were the Digu-Marang people. They were very rich in traditional beads. The Padams who were highly ambitious and established-warrior of the time attacked the village unaware at night and driven out the original people from Pasighat. All original stories were full of facts and could be used as supporting evidence.

But now, many clans or sub-tribes began to compose new history called *Abuk Doying* to avoid the mistake committed by their ancestors or their inferior position within the community. Hence, *Abuk Doying* seems to be biased and needs thorough investigation.

Dance-Drama

There are different types of dance-drama in the Adis. *Tapu* and *Tapo-Rija* are war dances performed by men. In these dance-dramas, the Adis successively narrate the history of war and their victories. *Besung Nayi* is a symbolic dance depicting the relations of monkey with the human being thus coinciding the history of evolution from Ape Man. *Padam Nyanyi, Pasi Kongki, Nunu Pipi, Boying Nero,* etc. also tell us how *Tani* (human beings) clear the jungle, seedling the seeds in the field, weeding the weeds, harvesting the grain, bring it to the granary and perform other domestic works. Thus, social behariour of ancient society is known from these dance-dramas.

Dobo

Dobo is an expression of one's desire in the form of song. The most popular *Dobo* of the Adis is *Oge Gye* narrating the unending emotional attachment of a young couple Aming Goming of Tirgong village and Mayung Yumin of Korbe village, after many years of separation by unavoidable circumstances. This type of *Dobo* composed in the long past mentions the ancient villages inhabited by the Adis and some time the prevailing conditions of the society. So, the importance of *Dobo* as a source of Adi history cannot be ruled out.

Lutom (Proverbs and Sayings)

The traditional folk proverbs and sayings are the important ornaments of oral tradition. It is attached in all other forms of oral literature and is one of the most important cultural devices for maintaining customary laws, imparting knowledge about cultural semantics and ideal behavioural pattern among the people especially the younger generation of the society. Some important *Lutoms* of the Adis are:

1. *Mimine Ngopi ko, miyone Bungko ko;*
   Dik-dikne Tatik do, Dak-dakne Take ko.

Meaning: A person who thinks deeply before performing any work and does it slowly and steadily get good result; but a person who does not think and work hurriedly will get bad result.

2. *Ama dopit mape ka,*
   Ama Donyie kaye

Meaning: Take your food without losing any rice; otherwise the God of Grain curses you to become poorer and poorer.

3. *Dori situng em dobong mapeka,*
   Pari situng em pabong mapeka.

Meaning: Excessive eating is bad, so excessive revengefulness even under provocation is not advisable.

4. *Susenge Paseng ko,*
   Petyange Jajang ko.

Meaning: A small mistake, which we neglect, grows into a great problem. The synonym of this proverb in English is "A spark neglected burns the house".

Lutom literally means Caution, suggesting the people to maintain self-restrain, moderation and wisdom, which are essential for a human being to lead a normal and peaceful life.

Like the Adis, entire Arunachalee tribes are tremendously rich in their oral traditions, which reflect not only the physical and material aspects of life but also the pattern of social behaviour and thought shared by the members of the society. We should therefore take right measures to preserve the oral tradition, the only literature transmitted orally from one generation to another.

References

1. Mackenzie, A., *The North East Frontier of India* (reprint 1994) Mittal Publications, New Delhi, p. 33.
2. Sen, S., (ed.) *Folklore in North East India* 1985, Omsons Publications, New Delhi, p. 7.
3. Ering, Oshong, *Arunachal News*, Vol. I, No. 10, December, 1972, p. 9.

   The term is opposite to forefather in Adi-tribal society.
4. Roy, S., *Aspects of Padam-Minyong Culture*, (Shillong, 1966), p. 219.
5. Osik N.N., *British Relations with the Adis,* Omsons Publications, New Delhi, 1992, p. 5.

6

Oral Sources of the Mising – A Study of Origin and Migration

Lakhinath Pegu

The main purpose of this paper is to throw some light on the origin and early migration of the Misings – a tribe of Arunachal Pradesh and Assam. But before delving deep into the crux of the problem, it may be noted here that history furnishes a very imperfect insight into the origin and early migration of the Misings. The external sources, literary and material, do not provide a comprehensive account of the pre-history of the Misings. Moreover, they have no written historical documents except some inconsistent and scattered oral traditions in the forms of legends, myths, folk-tales and folk-songs, which cannot, however, provide significant authentic facts of their early history. Thus, the history of the Misings' early period doubtlessly is obscure and hence it is difficult to pin-point a definite time as to when they began their early migration, where they came from, and what exact route they followed in reaching their present habitat.

However, fortunately there are few existing sources which come to our succor in gleaning some relevant information pertaining to the origin and migration of the Misings – *i.e.,* early Vedic Aryan literature, Greek and Roman literature, ethnological researches, linguistic studies and other material cultures of 'North-Assam Branch' tribe group. Besides, it is interesting to note that, the host of legends and traditions they posses, that can be used in absence of the conventional history of the tribe already touched upon, can be helpful in tracing out the origin and early migration of the Misings, if they are scientifically utilized.

Therefore, my attempt in this paper is to trace the origin and migration of the Misings on the basis of two distinct sources: 1. The available historical materials and, 2. The legends and traditions of the tribe which are preserved for generations as true. Hence, the entire paper is divided into three sections. The first section gives a brief account of the tribe, the second attempts to glean information regarding their origin and migration on the basis of available historical materials, and the third on the basis of the legends and traditions of the tribe.

SECTION-I

The Misings, also known as Miris, are a well-known tribal community living along the foot-hill belt of Siang, mostly in the East Siang District of Arunachal Pradesh, adjoining the plains of Assam. However, major part of the community lives in eight districts of Assam viz. Lakhimpur, Dhemaji, Dibrugarh, Tinsukia, Sibsagar, Jorhat, Golaghat and Sonitpur along the courses of the river Brahmaputra and its tributaries. The name 'Miri' was given to them, evidently by the plains people, but they always preferred to be known by their name 'Mising'.

Ethnically, the Misings belong to the Tibeto-Burman language speaking group of the great Mongoloid stock[1] and originally they belong to the same group of tribe comprised of Nyishis (Dafla) Minyongs, Padams, Pasis, Galongs (Adis), Apatanis, Hill Miris, Mishmis, etc. of Arunachal Pradesh. G.A.Grierson[2] groups them into one unit under the common appellation of 'North-Assam Branch' of the Tibeto-burman group of the Indo-Chinese language family on the basis of language spoken by them, although they collectively identify themselves as *Tani or Ami,* meaning 'man'. According to Mising myth, *Tani* (also called *Abo-Tani*) is the father of mankind. It is significant to note in this context that besides the Misings, some other renowned tribes of present day Arunachal Pradesh, such as, the Adis, Nyishis, Apatanis and Hill Miris also trace their descent from a common mythical ancestor known as *Abo-Tani or Abo-Teni.*[3] However, it may be surmised that the tribes who identify themselves as descendents of *Tani* were distantly related. These tribes possess similarities in their language, traditions and culture. But more close resemblance in their language and various cultureal traits can be seen between those of the Misings and the Adis only. As Alexander Mackenzie says:[4]

"The Akas (Hrussos) Daflas (Nishis) are, according to ethnologists, one in race with each other, and with the tribes of Abors (Adis) and Miris (Misings) inhabiting the hills North of Lakhimpur.... Coming no doubt originally from the same habitat, they are still alike in all material respects as to warrant us in calling them the earlier and later migrants of the same tribe, the Abors as the last comers retaining more of their pristine savagery and hardihood, while the Miris have been, to some extent, influenced by free association with the plains and settled habitats of cultivation. The intercourse between Abors and the Miris is still nevertheless constant and intimate".

Likewise, W.W.Hunter [5] also writes: "The Miris of the plains were an offshoot from the Abors". Simiarly, the *Census of Assam,*[6] conducted for the first time in 1881, describes that "The Miri, Dafla and Abor are names which have been given by the Assamese to three sections of one and the same race".

Thus, from the preceding accounts, both legendary and historical, it becomes crystal clear that the Misings belong to 'North-Assam Branch' group of Mongoloid races and they identify themselves as descendents of *Tani* whom they considered as the father of mankind.

SECTION-II

It has already been mentioned that history fails to furnish a comprehensive account of the origin and the early migration of the Misings in particular. Nonetheless, some fragmentary references to the North-Eastern Tribes can be found from the Aryan Vedic literature, Greek and Roman classical literature. Although, they do not contain any specific reference to the Misings in particular, these set of literatures contain some descriptions of the ethnic and cultural traits of those tribes basically identical with those of the present day Misings. Along with the Aryan advance into different parts of the country, the Mongoloid tribes happened to come into contact with them; and that is why in early Vedic literature, fragmentary references to the North-Eastern tribes can be found. Moreover, the accounts of early foreign travellers who either visited or heard of these regions also contain scant information of the tribe. Hence, such literary records are taken into consideration to make a general idea of the origin and early migration of the Misings.

The early people of the Brahmaputra valley and hill tracts of what is now Arunachal Pradesh were known as to the Vedic Aryans as *Kirata* long before Christ. According to Idnologist, the *Kirata* is the Sanskrit term which occurred first in *Yajurveda*, "indicated the wild Non-Aryan tribes living in the mountains, particularly the Himalayas and in the North Eastern areas of India, who were Mongoloid in origin".[8]

In Vedic literature, *Kirata* is mentioned as a cave-dweller. The *Atharaveda* refers to a *Kirata* girl who is said to have dug out a drug with shovels wrought of gold on the high ridges of the hills.[9] In the *Mahabharata Kiratas* are described as 'gold-like; *i.e.,* yellow in colour unlike other pre-Aryan people.[10]

The *Kiratas* are generally associated with the *Cinas* (Tibeto-Chinese). That these *Cina-Kiratas* included also the Misings can be presumed from the region which is pointed out as the habitats of those *Kiratas-Cinas*. In the early literature, e.g., in *Mahabharata* the *Cinas* and *Kiratas* are said to have surrounded the land of Pragjotisha.[11] *The Ramayana* mentions that the *Kiratas*, "with their hair done in painted top nots, pleasant to look upon, shining like gold, able to move under water, terrible, veritable tiger-man, so they are formed".[12]

The above account testifies that the *Cina-Kiratas* included alsot the Misings, the dwellers of Eastern Indian hilly regions, who were known to the rest of the country as early as the Vedas. *The Kalika Purana* (a 10th century work) interestingly speaks of the *Kiratas* as of "Shaven heads and yellow skins. They are strong, ferocious, ignorant and addicted to meat and drinks"[13] which are genuine indication of the Mising culture.

Other most important sources for the early history of the Misings are the Greek and the Roman Classical literature notably, Pliny's *Natural History*, Ptolemy's *Geography*, and the *Periplus of Erythrean Sea*, compiled before or after the Christian era. *The Periplus of Erithrean Sea* (1st Century AD) has recorded that the *Kiratas* had flat nose and extended their sway as far as Bengal[14] It is found in the record of Ptolemy a tribe known as Asmeraoei identified with the Misings [15] is the earliest record that mentions of the Misings. It is held on the basis of such identification that "some tribes had already settled in this land before the 1st century AD if not earlier".[16] Examining the Indian classical literatures S.K.Chatterjee holds that different branches of great Sino-Indian speaking people which had their settlement near the head-waters of the Yangtse-Kiang and the Hoang-Hu rivers to the North-West China, pushed South and West, probably from 2000 BC. "The North-Assam tribes of the Abors, Akas, Daflas, Miris and Mishmis" says S.K.Chatterjee "appears to come later and to have established themselves in the mountains to the north of Brahmaputra plains already in occupation of the Bodos".[17] It is therefore, evident from above facts that the North-Assam tribes including the Misings, have also settled in their present habitats since the beginning of the Christian Era.

The linguistic studies of the North-Assam branch language also gives us indication about the origin and migration of the Misings. G.A.Greirson on the basis of his linguistic study observed that North-Assam branch language is a connecting link of the Tibetans and Himalayan dialects with that of Kuki-Chin, Bodo, Naga and Kachin groups. He therefore concludes; "the home of North-Assam tribe may be considered as a backwater. The eddies of the various waves of Tibeto-Burman immigration have swept over it and left their stamp on the dialects".[18] The above instance indicates that the North-Assam tribes intermixed with various branches of Tibeto-Bruman language speakers and also migrated to their present habitats later than many other group of these language speakers. On the basis of his linguistic analysis G.A. Grierson even traces the migration of the Tibeto-Chinese Language speakers. G.A. Grierson writes;

"The first batch migrated during the pre-historic times; secondly, the Tibeto-Burmans migrated to Tibet and then to India, the period of which is unknown; thirdly, the Tai branch of Siamese-Chinese group migrated in about sixth century AD. Lastly the Kachin group who migrated in recent times".[19]

So, the above list of migration indicates that North-Assam tribes are included in the second wave of migration which took place between pre-historic and sixth century AD. It is therefore, certain that North-Assam tribes, including the Misings, have already settled in their present habitat since the beginning of the Christian era. It is interesting to note that there is striking similarity in some of the Mising words with the Chinese and Tibetans. The Chinese custom of performing the nine prostrations called *Kow-Tom,* has also been prevalent in same way among the Misings, which they term as *Kum-nam* (or *kum-to* in imperative sense). Likewise, Mising language has got lot of Tibetan roots. Bhikshu Kondinya has shown a few words having similar root for both the languages. LikeTibetan – *Mi* (Man), Mising – Ami, Tibetan-*Lak* (hand), Mising-*A:lak*, Tibetan-*Mik* (eye), Mising-*A:mik,* Tibetan-*Si* (water), Mising-*Asi,* Tibetan-*Lam* (path) Mising-*Lamtc* etc.[20] G.A. Grierson also writes that "The word *Mi-ri* (which only the first syllable is Tibetan, which means man) may possibly means nobleman".[21] According to L.A. Waddel also the term Miri is of Tibetan origin, which is equivalent to hill-man. He writes;

"The Miri are a typically Mongoloid people and called themselves Mi-zhiny or Mising, that is to say 'man of the soil or land' with the sense of native of the soil.... Doubtless they are so-called because they have retained the customs of their ancestors in the Upper Himalayas and South East Tibet......."[22]

It, therefore, appears that North Assam branch language including the Misings, has connecting link with the Tibetans and the Chinese. The impression on the language of Misings was probably left before or in the course of their migration to their present habitats.

The origin of the Misings may also be discussed from the stand point of physical anthropology. Considering the similarity of the physical features with that of Tibetan L.A.Waddel writes; "They have decided Mongoloid features so much so as to remind me in many ways of Tibetan and Lepchas"[23]. But according to G.S.Guha, many of the tribal population of North Eastern India, such as Mising, Naga, Bodo etc. are not true Mongoloid race unlike the Tibetan and Turki speaking people. He writes;

"The tribes living in the hills on the Northern and Eastern Frontier of Assam represent a separate type with head shape either wholly of with a tending to the dolichocephalic, the transverse diameter being narrower and occiput protruding somewhat. In the flatness of the nose, face, high cheekbones, oblique slit eyes and absence of hair on the face and the body,

they are however essentially Mongoloid (Dolichocephalic Mongoloid type) and must be regarded as different branch of that great race which entered from South-Western China."[24]

Therefore, it appears that North Assam tribes including Mising belong to Mongoloid (Dolichocephalic Mongoloid type) races. A somewhat similar type can also be found among the Tibetans, and has been reported also from certain parts of South-West China.

The other material cultures also indicate the origin and migration of the Misings. The North Assam tribes including Mising have also their own heirloom the precious bead known to them as *Tadok/Dokne* which, they price very much; and they use to purchase and sell it among themselves. Col. Dalton and some other authorities believe it to be Chinese origin.[25] Haimendorf observes similarity of the methods and beliefs associated with the sacrifice of animals by suffocation prevalent among the North-Assam tribes including the Misings, and the Amodopa tribes of Eastern Tibet, which he believes to be cultural dissemination from across the frontier.[26] It is apparent from the above instances that their material culture might have taken place due to intermixing with various human races in the course of their migration form South China to their present habitats.

We also need to trace out where the Misings came from and what route they followed in reaching their present habitat. In this connection it was pointed out earlier that the North-Assam tribes including the Misings, belong to Mongoloid race of mankind and the original habitat of these people appears to have been North-WesternChina covering the courses of the Yang-tsze-Kiang and the Huang-Ho river. Regarding routes of migration, authorities of various academic disciplines have pointed out the various routes of migration of the North-Assam tribes including the Misings, to their present habitation. G.S. Guha has concluded from his ethnological studies, that the Noth-Assam tribes represent a separate type and must be regarded as different branches of the great Mongoloid race which, entered from North Western China, and whose main body moved away towards Indonesia leaving a side stream in the Assam hills, such as that represented by the Miri, Bodo and Naga tribes".[27] From above it is clear that Guha has not pointed out the road through which they entered India, but stated that they were left in Assam Hills as a side stream.

P.C.Choudhury writes; "There are three or four routes of migration of human races into Assam; (i) The mountain passes of Tibet, Nepal and Bhutan; (ii) The route through Gangetic Valley and the Brahmaputra river from westwards (iii) By sea through the Bay of Bengal and Burma; and (iv) The passes of Assam and Burma".[28] He is of the opinion that the Alpines and the Mongoloid people entered Assam through these routes. Even he indicates that the North Assam tribes came from the North through the North Eastern routes. But S.K.Chatterjee is much more explicit in his description of the route that was followed by the North Assam tribes. He says;

"The Tibeto-Burman groups appear to have formed an area of dispersion in some tracts of to the east of Tibet and North East of Assam (The present day Chinese province of Sinkiang) from where they began to spread East and South. From this centre of dispersion, other Tibeto-Burman tribes took up trek into India, along the Brahmaputra river westwards. Some of them found homes in the mountainous tracts to the North of Assam where we find them in the Balipara Frontier Tract to the East of Bhutan as Abors, Miris and Daflas and in Sadiya Frontier Tract to the East of Mishmis".[29]

Thus, it appears that Chatterjee has indicated that that the North Assam tribes including the Misings, entered India through the North East corner of India after dispersion of the various waves of the Tibeto-burman immigrants somewhere in the Chinese province of Sinkiang. The above views of the eminent authorities, point out the fact that the North Assam tribes including the Misings as a separate and independent group of the Mongoloid races entered India through the North Easter corner.

It is evident from the above discussions that the Misings belong to the Palaeo-Mongoloid branch of great Mongoloid race of mankind, whose ancient civilization flourished somewhere in the upper courses of the Yang-Tsze-Kiang and Huang-Ho river valleys of North West China. From physical features, language and other cultural factors they are identified with the aboriginal tribes of Eastern Tibet. They have migrated from South China to the North Eastern regions of India through the meeting place of Eastern Tibet, South China and North Eastern India. They had to intermix with various human races, the eddies of which are evident in their language, physical features, cultures and traditions. The migrations of the North Assam tribes including Misings have taken place during the middle period of the pre-history and sixth century AD and their settlement in India has begun since before the first century of the Christian era.

SECTION-III

Although the Misings have no any own written documents of their origin and migration they possess a rich oral chronicles in the form of legend, myths, fole talk and folk songs which have been transmitted down from generation to generation. A legend, in which human generations are allowed to play freely, may however conceal a kernel of historical truth.[30] Elderly generations took them as actual happenings at certain point of time in the unknown past, and therefore moulded their inward mind according to the moral of the tale. Thus, social system rested on the gravity of these stories. Usually every tribe has a legend of its origin and migration believed by the succeeding generations as true. The legends of the Misings have been preserved through their age old traditions, and no traditions can be built on absolute untruth. Of course we may not accept the Mising legends or myths as historically true events, but they are also not necessarily untrue in every detail. These legends are part of their tradition which brings to recapture some unforgettable events by knitting a tale around them and then reflecting on them. So, in absence of written documents these oral chronicles could be used as a source materials to trace out their origin and early migration.

Origin of the Tribe

The Misings and its mountainous natives have a popular myth about the origin of the man in the earth. The Mising genealogical verse called *A:bangs** tells about the origin of the earth and life.

Sonaram Panyang, a Mising interprter, records a number of legends and myths of the origin of the Misings and the Adis. These myths throw some light on the traditional origin of the different sub-tribes of the Adis and the Misings. According to this tradition *Pedong-Ane* was prolific in procreation and gave birth to many sons. Some of them are *Do:mi,*

Do:pang, Do:shing and Do:bang. From *Do:mi* came the Minyangs, from *Do:pang* the Galongs and from *Do:shing* came the Misings.[31] The most popular and acceptable myth that is prevalent among the Misings is the mention of *Ke:yum* line of creation. However, this tradition is also prevalent among the Adis.[32] According to this tradition, in the beginning there was emptiness in this universe.

There was no shape or form, it was dark, there was no day or night; there was no land or water, not to speak of life. This state of first creation was known as *Ke:yum.* In simple meaning *Ke:yum* is nothingness (vacuum). Through cosmic vibration from *ke:yum* passed seven generations upto Sedi, in slow and steady succession as shown below:

From *Se:di* to *Tani* (first human being) it also took five generations. They believe that *Se:di* or the *Se:di-Me:lo* to be the creator or God. *Se:di-Me:lo,* created things from a mass of mud; light emerged, land, water and life came into being. Therefore the Misings and its allied groups considered *Sedi-Melo* as the creator or the God. From their union following generations proliferated to give birth to human beings (*Tani or Doni)* in the earth.

**Abangs* are verses of hymn of praise, worship to Gods and Goddesses, prayer to God for help, protection and blessings. The *Abangs* contain descriptions of social bindings and integration, origin of the living creatures, creation of Universe etc. The *Abangs* are the earliest known verbal songs of the community. Hence, these songs can be called as Historical songs or Poetical History of the community. These songs are transmitted from centuries past amongst the *Mibus.* The *Mibus* are considered as religious prophets of the community.

1. *Keyum (Yumkang + Kero)*
2. *Kasi*
3. *Siang*
4. *Abo*
5. *Bomuk*
6. *Mikseng*
7. *Sedi (+ Mc:lo)**

From *Pedong-Nane* all living creatures believed to have been propagated and in the last *Tani (Dani)* – the first man was propagated and *Tani* is therefore considered as the ancestor of the Mising and their allied groups. It is significant to note that they count their genealogies not from him but from *Pedong-nane.*

It has already been mentioned that *Pcdong-nane* was their progenitor. For example, *Pedong* begot *Do:sing, Do:sing* Mising as shown below in a family tree:

Pedong Nane

Dosing	*Do:mi*	*Dopang*	*Donga*
Mising	Minyong	Padam	Galong

The above account shows that in the Mising mythology *Ke:yom* is mentioned as the first in the genealogical line of creation. From *Keyum* to *Sedi-Me:lo,* the exact nature of the beings are very uncertain, but definite form took place from *Sedi,* hence they recognize *Sedi-Melo* as the creator. From Se:di five generations passed till *Pedong Nane,* the mother of *Tani,* (man) appeared. Hence, they trace their origin from *Pedong Nane.*

Early Home and Migration

According to a legend of the Misings, the ancestors of the Misings first lived with his offspring at a place called Killing-Kangey,[33] somewhere in the upper course of the Siang river. After passing many years there they moved downwards to the lower valley. The Misings, believed that when they migrated from Killing-Kangey they had to overcome a very rapid stream.

---

* '*Sedo*' and '*Melo*' (Sedi + Melo) literally signify the 'earth and the 'sky', but allegorically they are the creators of the universe; like Adam + Eve in Christianity and *Purush* and *Prakriti* of Vedantic philosophy.

7. *Sedi (+ Melo)**
8. *Dilling*
9. *Litung*
10. *Tuye*
11. *Yepc*
12. *Pcdong-nane or Pcdong-ane* (Perpetuating mother)

Only after days of prayer, propitiations to the deities by the *Mibu,* they finally found two very strong creepers climbing over a gigantic tree holding it erect near the rapid stream. It is also believed that only the Mili and Kardong clan of the Misings could cut the creepers and fell the tree across the banks of the stream. Finally, with these creepers they were able to corss the stream. These creepers are referred now as *Manying-Mankong* creepers. The Misings also believe that they came down from Killing-Kangey by two ladders called *avn KoLbang* (golden ladder) and *Murkong Kobang* (Silver ladder). Perhaps, the colour of the creepers were golden and silver in colour. From killing-Kangey, the Misings came over to Regi-Regam, then at Karko-Simong, Pega Selek, Agcha Selek and finally at Doyit-Pumi near present Sadiya.[34]

Regarding the routes they followed during their migration it is believed that the different groups migrated at different times and took different routes. As per legends, Mili, Kumbang, Patir etc. followed the old route of Adi Pasi and Mebo of Regamhills; Tayu-Taye, Taid and others took the Pangin-Pashighat route of Bapi Hills. Pait, Pawo and others migrated along the route of Torne and Jaging hills. The Shayang clan came down from Pesha-Shayang near present Dambuk of Dibang Valley District. Bori, Regon and Charo are said to have came down much latter. The Pegu, Doley, Kutum, Kuli are supposed to be the fore-runners of the other Misings, but the routes taken by them while migrating to the plains are not clear. However, the existence of a place called Pegu beyond Tayek in the upper region of Adi hills, and a lake known as Pegu-Siyeng near Karko till to day bear a palpable evidence that the Pegus had been there and took a route which was taken later by the Padams also while migrating down from Tibet.[35] They lived around Karko-Simong area for a considerable period before adventuring into he second wave of movement down along the Siyang valley.

It should, however, be mentioned that the real cause of their migration can not be ascertained at present. It must have been occasioned by some natural upheavals in their home land or by large scale racial movements set in motion by political happenings in those regions.

According to a legend prevalent amongst the Misings and the Adis "the Padams of Damro villge had some quarrel with the Minyongs of Sitang village and the Misings had aided the Padams. It is said that Padams did't know how to construct boats, therefore they requested the Misings to help them in constructing some boats. So the Misings built two big boats to cross the Siang river, because the Minyongs who were inhabited on the north bank had destroyed the bridge. When the victorious Padams were returning to their village, their boats were steered by two Mising men, namely, Lebang and Tumsik. Lebang intentionally crashed the boat against a big log that was floating there. Lebang's reason in capsizing the boat was due to the belief that if he did not sacrifice some Padams, the *Piyangs* (spirit of those person who were killed on war) of the Minyong people would not spare his own life.

The Padams, who came to know of the deceitful action of Lebang, were very much infuriated with the Misings. This episode resulted in the estrangement of the two communities. At the same time, the Minyongs were also extremely annoyed with the Misings because soon they also came to know that it was the Misings who had built and steered the boats which helped the Padams. The Minyongs too, thus became enemy of the Misings giving rise to internecine wars. Consequently after some time, the Misings were forced to move away from the vicinity of Padams and the Minyongs, the Misings first moved to a place near the confluence of the Lohit with the Dibang river.[36]

The above instances, therefore give some idea about their early home and migration. It can be assumed that their early home was located to the north of their present land which means somewhere in Tibet. It is to be mentioned that, according to the traditions, most of the Adis claim their origin from one race or tribe settled at Killing in the Bamo-Janbo country.[37] Moreover, Killing-Kangey is also variously called amongst the North-Assam tribes as Killing-Lidum, Killing-Litung, Lipin-Petkey, Teli-Lidung, etc.[38] The Killing-Kangey may be situated some where within or without the North Eastern boundary of Indian territory.[39] According to a version collected by Sachin Roy, the story of the migration of the Minyongs – (the allied tribe of the Misings) also starts from a place near about Telli-Lidung, somewhere in the upper course of the Siang river.[40] The Padams also place their origin near the source of Siang river. Therefore, it appears that all allied tribes of the Adis migrated from north of their present land which means somewhere in Tibet.

The stories of their migration give us some ideas of the directions and stages of their migration. Moreover, stories of the Padam, the Pasis and the Minyongs confirm the Mising migration that was followed by them at different stage. For example Padam story of the migration mentions that "at Killing-Kangey, where they (Padams) came across a group of people who identified themselves as Pegu and Doley. Finding inconvenient in living as close neighbours with the Bomis (now called Padams) the Pegus and Doleys vacated their land and moved out by following the course of the rivcer Siang towards the plains".[41] Moreover, "In the Yamne valley the Bomis found a number of Mising clans such as Dadi, Dai, nalem, Najong, Leying, Parak. Moying, Sayang, Donga, naro who moved out as the area became very thickly populated and followed the course of the river Siang towards the Plains".[42] According to the Pasi story of migration, when they migrated they corssed the place Pegu, which is situated at Karko area near Siluluak, and finally crossed the triver at Tayek.[43] As already stated the existence of place called Pegu beyond Tayek-Piago in the upper region of Adi hills, and a pond known as Pegu-Siyeng or Pegu-Sirung near Karko till today bear a palpable evidence that the Pegus had been there and took a route which was taken later by the Padams also while migrating down to lower valley. It is observed that the Padams, the Minyong and the Pasis, all of them crossed the Siang river at Tayek. Therefore, it appears that the Misings also crossed the river at Tayek-Piago before the Adis as they were the forerunners of the Adis. After crossing Siang river at Tayek-Piago, perhaps, they had spread up upto Damro and Dambuk area. It may be noted here that the Shayang clan of the Misings are believed to have originally inhabited in the Pesha-Shayang hills near Dambuk. Moreover, the Dambuk clan of Misings have migrated to the plains of Assam relatively recently from Dambuk area.[44]

Although at present it is difficult to identify many places mentioned in the early stages (*i.e.*, the stages beyond the present

Mising area) of their migation but places mentioned in the later staes can easily be identified. From the stories of their migration it is observed that their migration occurred group by group at different time. The Pagro group of the Misings, are the earliest migrants than other groups.[44] From the stories of their migration it becomes clear that during their migration the Mising had clashes with the various groups of the Adis. As such, the more adventurous groups had to accommodate themselves by moving furthr down and in doing so, those who set foot on the plains of Assam in search of fertile cultivable land, constiture the main bulk of the present Mising tribe of the Brahmaputra valley. Therefore, only a small number of Mising population are at present living along the foot hills belt of Siang, mostly in the East Siang district, adjoining the plains of Assam.

References

1. Census of India, 1961, Vol. II, Part V-A, p. 24.
2. G.A.Garierson, *Linguistic Survey of India*, Vol. III, Part-I, p. 572.
3. S. Dutta Choudhury, *Gazetteer of India, Arunachal Pradesh East Siang & West Siang Districts*, Itanagar, 1994, p. 30.
4. Alexander Mackenzie, History of Relations of the Government with the *Hills Tribes of the North East Frontier of Bengal.* (Calcutta 1984), chapter-VI.
5. W.W. Hunter, *A Statistical Account of Assam,* London, 1879, p. 220.
6. E.Stack, Miris, Daphalas and Abors. *In Report on the Census of India 1881, Assam,* Calcutta, Govt. Press, 1883, p. 86.
7. P.C.Choudhury, *The History of Civilization of the People of Assam to the Twelfth Century AD,* Guwahti, 1966.
8. S.K.Chatterjee, *Kirata Jana Kriti,* Calcutta, 1974, p. 84.
9. Sukla Yajurveda Vajasenayi Samhita, Book XXX, 16; V.V.4. 11, 1; of S.K.Chatterjee cit. p. 27.
10. Mahabharata, V, 548, cf. Chatterjee, *op. cit.,* pp. 31f.
11. Ch. IX, verse 51, 57, 69, pp. 2565-66, 11, 342f. Ref. T H.H.Wilson *Vishnu Purana,* (Cal. 1961), A list inserted in Bk. 111, pp. 156, -58162; *Mahabharata* (Hindi Edn. Gorakhpur) *Diovijaya Parva,* Ch. 26 Vs. 8-10, p. 743.
12. Kiskindhya Kanda, IV & V.V. 35.2.17; cf., Chartterjee, *op. cit.,* p. 3.

13. Panchanan Tarakaratna, *Kalika Purana,* (ed) Cal-1977-78, ch. 39; V. 104; *Kalika Purana,* ch. 39. V. 104.
14. W.H.Scoff, *The Principles of the Erythrean Sea,* Longsmen (London), 1912, pp. 46ff, 261.278.
15. E.B.Taylor, JASB, 1817.1.pp. 32f; P.C.Choudhury *op. cit.,* p. 84.
16. P.C.Choudhry, *History of Civilization of the People of Assam to the Twelfth Century AD.* (Guwahati-1987) p. 84; J.H. Hutton, Wildmen in Assam, J AS.B (New Series) Vol. XXVI 1031, Art. No.18.
17. S.K.Chartterjee, *The Place of Assam in the history and Civilization of India,* Guwahati 1970, p.9; JASB Vol. XV/NO. of 1950, p. 154ff.
18. G.A.Garierson, *op. cit.,* p. 572.
19. Imperial Gazetteer of India, Indian Empire (1881), Vol. 1, Chapter-VII
20. Bhikshu Kondinya, Mising Janajati (Hindi), New Delhi, 2, 1982, p. 6.
21. G.A.Garierson, *op. cit.,* p. 586.
22. L.A.Waddel, "A Note on the derivation of Miri", *Man,* II (56): 86.
23. L.A.Waddel, *The Tribes of the Brahmaputra Valley,* (1900), Delhi, 1975, p. 57.
24. G.S.Guha, *An outline of Racial Ethnology of India,* Calcutta, 1937.
25. E.T.Dalton, *Descriptive Ethnology of Bengal,* Cal, 1872, Group-I, Sect. 5(2), p. 28.
26. C.Von, Furer Haimendorf, *The Apa-Tanis and Their Neighbours,* London, 1962; Anthropos, Vol. 9 (1954).
27. G.S.Guha, *op. cit.,* p. 157.
28. P.C.Choudhury, *op. cit.,* p. 82.
29. S.K.chatterjee, *Kirata-Jana-Driti,* JRASB, XII No. 2. 1950.
30. S.Dutta Choudhury, *op. cit.,* p. 38.
31. S. Pa:nyang Kotaki, *Miri Jatir Buranji,* Dibrugarh, 1935, p. 6-30.
32. T. Nyori, *History and Cultures of the Adis,* Delhi, 1983, p. 33.
33. S. Pa:nyang Kotaki, *op. cit.,* p. 43.
34. N. Pegu, *The Misings of the Brahmaputra Valley,* Digboi, 1981, p. 30-40.

35. *Ibid.*, p. 31.
36. J.S. Bhandari, *Kinship Affinity and Domestic Group; A study among the Misings of the Brahmaputra Valley,* New Delhi, 1992, p. 251-52; N.C.Pegu, *op. cit.* p. 32-34.
37. T. Nyori, *op. cit.* p. 42; quoted from R.C.R. Cumming.
38. D. Doley, "History of Origin of the Tanis or Amis" in *The Misings: Their History and Culture,* (ed), J.J.Kuli, Guwahati, 1998, p. 31-32.
39. *Ibid.*
40. T. Nyori, *op. cit.* p. 40.
41. *Ibid.* p. 46.
42. *Ibid.*, p. 47.
43. *Ibid.*
44. J.S. Bhandari, *op. cit.* p. 28; N.C.Pegu, *op. cit.* p. 18.
45. N. Pegu, *op. cit.* p. 17.

7

Myth and Oral Tradition: Sources for Reconstructing Origin and Migration of the Tagins

Ashan Riddi

The English word myth came from Greece Muthos ('word' or 'speech').[1] Muthos in its meaning of 'myth' is the word for a story concerning gods and superhuman beings.[2] Event concerning the more remote periods often takes the form of a myth. Thaper states:

"Myth is in a sense a prototype history since it is a selection of ideas composed in narrative form for the purpose of preserving and giving significance to an important aspect of the past. Although myths cannot be used as descriptive sources on the past, their analysis can reveal the more emphatic assumptions of a society. Myth records what people like to think about their past and to that extent even some modern histories are not always free of an element of myth making".[3]

A myth "*is an expression of the sacred in words: it reports realities and events from the origin of the world that remains valid for the basis and purpose of all there is consequently, a myth functions as a model for human activity, society, wisdom and knowledge*".[4]

A myth, whether it's subject is the acts of deities or other extraordinary events, always takes us back ot *"beginning of all things"*; hence, the cosmology, the birth of the world, is a principle theme.[5] Myth is also defined as an utterance, often a tale recited in association with a religious ceremony. The myth involved archetypal or elemental character, themes and symbols. It focuses on the 'grand events' of the past-the creation of the world, the origin of man and gods, the justification of kinship.[6] It, thus, usually concerning some superhuman being or some alleged person or event with or without determinable basis of fact or natural explanation especially a traditional or legendary story that is concerning with deities or demigods and creation of the world and its inhabitants.

The creation of the earth, the sky, origin of human generation and migration of the Tagins are being recited by the *Nyibu* (priest) at the time of ritual ceremony. The *Nyibu* narrates the origin, migration and genealogy of the particular clan and family who performs the ritual.

Tradition is handing down of statements, beliefs, legends, customs, etc. from generation to generation by words of mouth or by practice. Thus, oral traditions are historical sources of a special nature. Their special nature derives from the fact that they are 'unwritten' sources couched in a form suitable for oral transmission, and that their preservation depends on the powers of memory of successive generations of human beings.[7] Though validity and reliability of the oral tradition as a historical source have been questioned and really pose problem for historians, "*the oral tradition is not necessarily untrustworthy as a historical source, merits a certain amount of credence within certain limits*".[8] For the Tagins who without are written records, oral traditions and myths form the main sources for reconstruction of their past.

Origin

The Tagins inhabited one of the most difficult terrains of Arunachal Pradesh. They tried to adjust themselves with nature and wanted to live in peace and free from diseases, sufferings and misfortunes. However, the natural phenomena remained mysterious to them. Their curiosity to know the source of the origin of this world must have resulted into various myths about the creation. There are various versions of the myths of creation.

One of these versions is:

The universe was an empty space. A figure appeared out of nothingness in that empty space. This figure was imagining being similar to human figure in male form. This figure was known to be KURIUM LULU.[9]

In another version, *Korium* and *Kolu* were two different figures that appeared out of nothingness in male and female forms respectively and were husband and wife.[10]

KURIUM-KULU wished that there be a universe in the nothingness. So he started creating various objects and images one after another. First, he created SECHI (the earth) and NYIDO or NYIDO-KOLO (the sky). Then he created DORICHEJI, DONYI, POLO and TAKAR. [11]

Dorichiji was created in the form of a human figure with highest degree of wisdom and knowledge. Though the *Sechi* and *Nido* were originated from *Korium* and *Kolu*, their relationship became unpleasant and they invariably started quarrelling. When the crisis was referred to *Dorichiji*, *Dorichiji* instructed *Chechinjerin* and *Dochinjerin* [two dwaft figures in human form believed to be originated in evolutionary process] to carry out dialogue on this problem. On the advise of *Dorichiji*, it was decided to separate the *Sechi* and the *Nido* permanently; the Sechi to remain on lower side and the Nido on above. To effect this decision *Sechi-Nido Kambe-Benam* [eitual ceremony] was performed and *Tatik* [frog] and *Tanu* [snail] were sacrificed.[12]

According to third version, *Kolu*, the wife of *Korium* gave birth to various bodies and images in the universe.[13]

According to fourth version, *Korium* and *Kolu* were soundless and boundless. That is why, the *Korium-Jiimi*, [jiimi means soundless] and the *Kolu-Jaama*, [jaama means boundless]. After, creation of *Sechi*, the earth, *Nido*, the Sky, *Donyi*, the Sun, *Polo*, the Moon and *Hai*, the River, and *Korium Dori*, the Dorichiji Korium and *Kolu* disappeared and remain permanently in *Jiimi-Jaama*.[14]

In a fifth version it is stated tht out of nothingness and emptiness of the universe, two forms known as *Korium* and *Kolu* came into being. They in turn bore three beings know as *Riumchinjerin, Riumsi* and *Riumdo*.[15] *Riumchinjerin*, eldest of the three, was endowing with wisdom and knowledge. Riumsi and Riumdo were extremely tiny at the time of creation. In myths, the smallness of *Riumsi* compared to *Rinikamchi* [small precious Tagin ornament] and that of *Riumdo* to *Tapo-Barnge* [Tagin ornament used for knotting the base of the necklace]. Within few days of conception, the *Riumsi* and the *Riumdo* began expanding swiftly creating crisis for space. The *Riumchinjerin* was greatly alarmed, as space was needed to contain different deities, spirits and other celestial and terrestrial elements. After a great deal of thought and deliberation, *Riumchinjerin* evolved a way out in which *Riumsi* and *Riumdo* were to be separate from each other. The separation of the two was effected through a Sechi-Nido Kambe-Benam [a ritual ceremony]. In the *Sechi-Nido Kambe-Benam, Sechi-ge-takri* (literary, earth's frog) and *Dote-ge-harchu* (kind of animal) were sacrifice to maintain peace, harmonry, and stability between Riumsi and Riumdo. This ritual put injunction on both Riumsi and Riumdo to observe 10 days *Iri* (religious taboo) in which both had to remain in virtual confinement and total inactivity. In the process of separation, *Ichi-Pinchi* (bat) came into being from the *Chekap-Dokap* (cleavage between Riumsi and Riumdo). On the fifth day of Iri, *Ichi-Pinchi*, instigated Riumsi that Riumdo was not observing the Iti and as such, it would be ridiculous for Riumsi to observe Iti. On hearing this, Riumsi became indignent and ceased to observe the *Iri*, while, *Riumdo* on the other hand continued to observe Iri religiously. Thus, *Rriumsi* despoiled and defied the religious obligation, incurring thereby Riumchinjerin's wrath, consequently the cursed *Riumsoi* underwent tremendous disorder within, in form of horrifying cyclones, eruptions and gargantuan floods taking the shape of mountains, valleys and rivers and became undulated. Hence, *Riumsi* became *Sechi*, the earth, *Riumdo* on the other hand complied with *Iri* and attained peace and stability thus, becoming the vast and peaceful *Nido-kol* (the sky). Therefore, the myth goes that other physical phenomena like *Dogum*, the thunder, *Doriak*, the lightening, *Bubhi*, the earthquake would not have come into existence but for the breach of the *Iri* on the part of *Riumsi*.[16]

With the formation of the *Sechi*, a need for light, water and computation of time arose. *Korium-Kolu* created *Donyi* (the sun), *Polo* (the moon) and *Hai* (the river). *Donyi* spread light; *Polo* gave a measurement of time and *Hai* provided water to the world of life form that was to take shape on *Sechi*. The *Takkar* (stars) evolved as daughters of Nido-Kolo. *Donyi* with its light is considering a female form and *Polo* with its measurement of time considered as male form. Hence, the name *Ayu-Donyi* (*Ayu* means grandmother) and *Atu-Polo* (*Atu* means grandfather) are for sun and moon in the Tagin mythology.[17]

After creating atmosphere conducive for life forms to take shape, *Riumchinjerin* adopted himself in two forms: *Sechi Cherichiji* and *Nido Dorichiji* who were to reside and preside over *Sechi* and *Nido* (earth and sky) respectively. *Cherichiji* and *Dorichiji* in unison produced *Si* a male spiritual form, and entrenched inside the *Sechi* to control the life that was to take on *Sechi*. *Si* became *Atu-Si* (grand Si). *Atu-Si* is believed to be residing in *Dachi-Lappi*, (a mythical place inside the *Sechi*). Now began the spiritual and physical dividion of *Atu-Si*. In the spiritual division, came the formation of different deities for each different form of life. From the lap of *Atu-Si* were formed *Doji* (land diety) and *Buru* (water deity). From *Atu-Si's* shoulder were formed *Pote-Hilo* (deity of prosperity) and *Bibu-Libu* (deity of well-being) and from bosom of *atu-Si*, Diri-Ane (deity of grain) Pane-*Mane* (the deity of wealth) and *Palo-Malo* (the deity of strength) etc. Simultaneously an equal number of malevolent spirits were formed out of the *Atu-Si like Maji-Yapom, Poru-Saru* etc. to counter the benevolent deities. In the physical division *Atu-Si*, was divided into three parts, each part assigned to each deity to reside and preside over. The *Dumpum* (head) portion was apportioned for Doji, the *Gara-Lepa* (middle) for human race to reside and that of lower portion for evil spirits. To demarcate and maintain the boundary of each part need to establish a body of judicial authority was felt. Hence, Dorichiji created a *Si-Moro* as the judge and head of the judicial authority to preside over when the need for justice arose. Even to this day, the name of *Atu-Si* and *Si-Moro* are invoked through ritual ceremonies to seek justice when denied in Tagin community.[18]

According to another version, after the separation of the *Sechi* and the *Nido*, the *Si* evolved out from the lap of *Sechi* followed by a number of benevolent spirits like *Pote, Hilo, Pirte*, etc., and equal number of malevolent spirits like *Maji, Yapom, Buru*, etc. In this evolutionary process, a female in semi-human from called *Sechi-Hinju-Thami* also originated. When she attained mellowness, she had contacted with *Seber-Dober-Bini* (male) and conceived. Finally, she laid two eggs, one in the first *Pikki* and other in second in the last Pikki[19] respectively. *Sele-Biyi* and Dole-*Biyi* (priests evolved from evolutionary process) consulted *Dorichiji* that what the eggs would be. *Dorichiji* informed that, the first egg would be the *Hai*[20] (the river) and the second would be the *Eji*[21] (the *Donyi*).[22]

Migration

Indeed, it is very difficult to arrive at any definite conclusion regarding the 'Tagins' original homeland, route of migration and date of their settlement at present place. However, there are some views on it, which need critical examination to draw the conclusion. Sachin Roy viewed that the Tagins are believed to have migrated from the Penzi a village in Tibet to Tadedage region.[23] However, he failed to mention how they migrated to the present area from Tadedage. M.L. Bose puts another view that the Tagins migrated from the Khams. Some Tagins are to be seen across that line in Tibet.[24] Bose seems to be very assertive about the place of Tagins migratioin and claimed some of the Tagins are found in Tibet, but has not mentioned about the route of migration. While, J.N. Choudhury wrote that the ancestor of the Tagins came from *Pui-Pudu* believed to be located in Tibet. From there, they came to Pumte and from there to Dibeh. *Abo-Tani* was the first to come and died at Nide-Lankin. Tagins moved from Dibeh to Nari and Nari to Nalo. In course of movement, their ancestors had crossed Subansiri and Khru rivers.[25] As per the oral traditions, *Abo-Tani* was common ancestor of Nyishis, Adis, Apatanis, Hill Miris, Tagins, and Mishings.[26] Therefore, as per this version all the *Tani* group of tribes must have migrated together to *Nide-Lankin*.

The Hill Miri tradition says that *Abo-Tani* with his seven sons used to live at the source of Subansiri River called Sipo-Rigo. They were always crying for food, so Abo-Tani with his wife fled away while the children were sleeping. Following the footprints of their parents, they moved down stream the river Subansiri. The eldest one went to plains; the second lived in foothills, the third settled near Panior River, the fourth stayed in Kamala valley, the fifth near Simi river, the sixth near Sigen and the last bother to travel was the ancestor of the Tagins.[27] As per this tradition, it seems that the Nyishis and Hill-Miris migrated down in course of Subsnsiri river from the Tagin inhabited place, but the Tagins never undertook the course of migration. The Bori myth says the Tagins were living in Gamen in Upper Siang district, but the Boris and the people of Payum drove them away.[28] This tradition believed that the Tagins migrated from upper Siang to the present settled area. Niranjan Sarkar points out:

The Tagins believe that like the Boris, Bokars and Ramos, they migrated from north to Mechuka area in West Siang District in search of cultivable land. They settled there and lived for some time at two places known to them as Gembu Kakaksiriu and Gine Gedunglingne. These places are believed to be somewhere in present Bori area. They continued their migration southwards....some of them....reached southern plain...They changed the direction of migration and came uphill by the banks of Subansiri till they reached present their habitant (sic) where their ancestor finally decided to settle.[29]

Like other *Tani* tribes the Tagins also claimed their origin from Tani/*Abo-Tani*[30] whom they regard as their ancestor. In the matter of genealogy, the Tagins have good memories and almost all elderly persons can trace their account from *'Tani'*, though they have different versions about the evolution of human among themselves. This may be recounted as follow:

After the creation of the *Sechi* (the earth) and *Nido* (the Sky) numerous spirits and organism-plants and living beings evolved on the lap of *Sechi*. In this evolutionary process, a female human figure was originated in Semi-spirit form.[31] The figure is believed to be created by *Si* (spiritual authority of the earth). She grew up without human partner, however, when attained maturity, she conceived through *Rilo-Rianso* (wind) and gave birth to *Tuni* and *Tupe*. *Tuni* was known to be *Tani* or *Abo Tani* and *Tupe* was known to be *Chene-Yapi* or *ane-Tapi* in complete human form and later on from their wedlock human race started on the earth.[32] Another version is *Si* created a female form called *Chetu; Chetu* in turn procreated three children in human form viz: two sons *Tuni* and *Tuki* and a daughter called *Tune.*[33] As there was no other human female, except his sister, *Tuni* married female of various objects and organisms such as leaves, tree frog, bird, etc., but no human offspring was born. With all futile attempts to create a human generation, *Tuni* consulted *Dorichiji* (God of highest degree of wisdom and knowledge) for solution. *Dorichiji* advised *Tani* to take egg of *Chei-Tashi* (Hen originated from the earth) and throw it on the abdomen of Tune. If the egg does not break any further action not to be taken, if egg bursts into loud, *Tani* can marry *Tune. Tuni* carried out the action without knowledge of *Tune*. Shocked at the bang of breaking egg thrown at her abdomen *Tune* jumped and embraced *Tuni*, thereby biological needs of body arose between them. Thereafter, both started as life partner and human races were born out of their wedlock.[34]

Another version is that, *Sechi* created *Chetu* (Tune), who was born *Poha-Tuni* (Tani in semi-spirit form) then from *Poha-Tani*, *Nigur* was born; from him Gurni from *Gurni*, *Nia-Tani* (complete human *Tani*) was born.[35]

According to oral history of the 'Tagins' migration, the Tani group of tribes migrated from the same place Ane Puii-Pudu.[36] From Puii-Pudu, the Dogin-Mole (migration) started via Esi-Naka, Uyi-Pere (exit), to Laru-Satu, Yagne Dibah (upward route), from this point, the different groups moved to different directions: to Hampu-Rialu, Ditir-Dinia and Dikur-Dirik (lift side of slope down and last visible mountain) the Adis and the Dodum, Dol and Dopum (Nyishis) moved toward Apa-Moya (dense forest), Ayu-Satu, (upward land), Diri-Dima (many mountains & Hills) and Lali-Lalen and Kara-Didi (mountains peak). And to the middle following the course of Sinik (Subansiri) the Tagins come down to Dibin-Disap (place imagined to be barren), from there to Pute-Gate and Reko-Gah (entrance to vegetation), then to Sokek-Geli (single entry point between two patches of landmass joined by branches of tree), and Nyprie-Sesso, (branch of tree that joined two patches of land at single entry point) and then to Pate-Yorja (elevated land slopingdown) and finally Rutu-hampu and Diso-Katu [37] (mountains in present settled area).

Another versin is that the Tagins migrated from Ane Puii-Pudu in Tibet to present area. From Ane Puii-Pudu, they moved to southward via Hini-Dali, than to Tato, than to Yapik than to Polo, and from Polo they moved westward via Mobuk from Mobuk to Moya, than to Lipi than to Kora and Banium and finally spread in present settlement area. [38] Nevertheless, some of the Tagins in and around Daporijo again moved upwards to upper course of Sinik (Subansiri) in order to search for a safer place away from their enemies.[39]

However, Mra and Na Tagins do not claim to be line of Abo-Tani as their ancestor, but from Nido (rain).[40] They migrated from Helujiang (Migyithun) via same route together with

Apatanis, but Mras stayed at Lemeking area whereas the Apatanis and Na Tagins proceeded downward. Apatanis stayed at Ziro, while Na Tagins returned back to present inhabited area.[41] The Mra and Na Tagins migrated from lower Tibet. The entire Tsari area, including Yume-Yuto and chikchak villages belong to the Na clan. The Tagins collected taxes from these places as war gratuity after they had suffered defeat from the Tibet.[42] Helu (Migyithun) in both banks of Gelen (Tsari Chue) belong to Mra Tagins and the Tibetan came later on, therefore, the Tibetan gave annual subsidy and twelve years compensation to the Mra Tagins.[43] Once, the Tagins ransacked Yume village of Tibet.[44] Still some of the Tagins are in Tsari area. In April 1956, Puri Taring (late) a Tagin leader of own clan in Helu/ Longju invited S.M. Krishnatry to establish Gyagars (Indian) influence at Migyithun. However, Krishnatry informed Puri Taring that the Indian Frontier does not cover Migyithun on Indian sides and they must better remain with Tibet. Then Puri Taring approached Krishnatry to rehabilitate his clan at Gilomo (hunting ground of Mra) in Indian side.[45] Puri Taring finally took settlement at Daporijo town. The Tagin villages like Longju/Helu in Migyithun area in Indian side have been reported to be occupied by the Chinese patrolling party.[46] Therefore, the Na Tagins and Mra Tagins were settled at Gelen (Tsari Chue) valley before migrating to present land and still some Tagins are said to be there.

Thus, according to the oral history of the tribe, they migrated from the South-Tibet. In any case, the Tagins along with other Tani group of tribes must have left Tibet before reaching of the Buddhism there, *i.e.,* 7th century AD as the tribes do not bear any influence of Buddhism and have retained their pristine way of life.

References

1. Kees W. Bolle, *"Myths: An Overview"* in Mircea Eliade, general Ed. *The Encyclopedia of Religion,* Macmillan Publishing Company, New York, 1987, Vol. 10., p. 261.
2. *Ibid.*
3. Romila Thapar *Ancient Indian Social history: Some Interpretations,* Orient Longman, New Delhi, 1979, pp. 294-95.
4. Kees W.Bolle, *"Myths: An Overview"* in Mircea Eliade, *Ibid.*

5. *Ibid.*, p. 262.
6. Romila Thapar, *op. cit.,* p. 295.
7. Jan Vansina 'Oral Traditional and historical Methodology' in David K. Dunaway & Willa K. Baum (ed) *Oral History an Interdisciplinary Anthology,* Altamira Press, Walnut Creek, London, New Delhi, 1984, (1996), p. 122.
8. *Ibid.*
9. Tapen Siga, 'Creation of Universe', *Dibe Nyeli, a* Souvenir on the occasion of celebration of the Si-Donyi, 1999, Tagin Si-Donyi Festival Committee, 1999, Daporijo, Arunachal Pradesh, p. 5.
10. Data collected from field.
11. Tapen Siga, *Creation of Universe, op. cit.*, p. 5
12. *Ibid.*, p. 1.
13. Data collected from field.
14. Data collected from field.
15. Tania Soki, Lardik Kare & Talum Dubi (ed) *Mythology of Si-Donyi,* Tagin Cultural Society, Daporijo, Upper Subansiri District, Aruanchal Pradesh, 2001, pp. 1-2.
16. Tania Soki, Lardik Kare & Talum Dubi (ed) *Mythology of Si-Donyi,* Tagin Culture Society, *op. cit.*, pp. 1-2.
17. Data collected from field.
18. Tania Soki, Lardik Kare & Talum Dubi (ed) *Mythology of Si-Donyi, op. cit.*, pp. 1-2.
19. Pekki, Cages in the back of the house for hen to lay eggs.
20. Hai, in the classical language for the river.
21. Eji, is also a classical language for the sun.
22. Tadi Riddi, *op. cit.*
23. Sachin Roy, *Aspect of Minyong Padam Culture,* North-East Frontier Agency, Shillong, 1966, p. 13.
24. M.L. Bose, *British Policy in the North East Frontier Agency,* Concept Publishing House, New Delhi, 1978, p. 16.
25. J.N.Choudhury, *Aruanchal Panorama,* Directorate of Research, Itanagar, 1992, p. 134.

26. Joram Begi, The Aruanchal Times, February, 24, 1997.
27. The Hill Miri tradition, in Verrier Elwin's *Myths of the North East Frontier of India,* North East Frontier Agency, Shillong, p. 116.
28. Bori Myth, in Verrier Elwin's *Myths of the North East Frontier of India,* North East Frontier Agency, Shillong, p. 108.
29. N.Sarkar, *The Tagins,* Directorate of Research, Department of Cultural Affairs, Govt. of Aruanchal Pradesh, Itanagar, 1999, pp. 1-2.
30. Legendary Ancestory of Tani tribes.
31. Tapen Siga, 'Creation of Universe', Monograph (unpublished), p. 2.
32. *Ibid.*
33. Mythology of Si-Donyi, Tagin Cultural Society, Daporojo, 2001, p. 6.
34. Tate Riddi, *op. cit.*
35. Interview with Takam Eke, Siyum, June, 13, 2001.
36. Place in their language imagined to be in Tibet.
37. Interview with Taru Bui (priest), Village Bui, January 27, 1997.
38. Interview with Tapak Hali, Dumporijo, July 7, 2001.
39. Data collected from field.
40. *Ibid.*
41. Narrated by Mra Tabe (late) in S.M.Krishnatry, *op. cit.,* pp. 1-176.
42. S.M.Krishnatry, *op. cit.,* p. 157.
43. *Ibid.*, p. 88.
44. *Ibid.*, p. 157.
45. *Ibid.*, pp. 157-158.
46. Data collected from field.

8

Sources of History of Arunachal Pradesh: With Special Reference to Apa Taniis

Pura Tado

Arunachal Pradesh has remained secluded from outside world for a long time. It was virtually cut off from other civilizations surrounding it due to lack of infrastructure of communications. The state government exposed the tribal societies of the state only in late fifties. Except for the Khamtis, Sherdukpens and Monpas, other communities living in Arunachal Pradesh do not have their own scripts. As a result, history of these indigenous communities can be reconstructed from their oral literatures, myths, social and political institutions, festivals and performances.

The Apa Taniis living in Ziro Valley of Lower Subansiri district of Aruanchal Pradesh is no exception. Their history can be reconstructed from their oral literatures, myths, legends, social and political institutions and festivals they perform and observe.

Oral Literature

The oral literatures of the Apa Taniis can be clubbed into two broad categories. They are:

(*a*) Mijih.

(*b*) Migung.

The *Mijih* consists of *Ayu* and *Barih. Ayu* is recited in Apa Taniis style of tune and tenor when the same *Ayu* is recited in Nyishi style of tune and tenor, it is called *Barih.*

Mijih throws light on the history of Apa Tanii society and its different social, political, economic and logal institutions and practices. It tells about the origin of everything from birth of the universe to social stratifications and organizations. It also throws light on the origin and functions of different social and political institutions and why need for them arose.

Each *Ayu* informs a particular aspect of Tanii society. It is like *Upanishads* of great Indian Epics. Thus, *Kolyung-Kolo Ayu* tells us about the origin of our earth. It describes the different stages of evolution of mother earth and how we human beings adapted as per evolving environment. Thus, different *Ayus* inform us about different aspects of history of the Apa Taniis.

The *Ayus* are further decided into *Asang Ayu* and *Aha Ayu*. *Asang Ayus* are more complicated and only matured persons could understand well. *Ayus* falling into this category are recited by those persons who know them completely. It is never left half recited. The belief is that the stanzas of the *Asang Ayu* has tantric powers like *mantras* of an Indian Tantrick. Unless it is recited completely, it will have bad effect on the person who recited it half.

Aha Ayus, on the other hand, can be recited at any time by anybody. It can be left half-recited also. There is no side effect whatsoever. These *Aha Ayus* tells about the performances and observations at mundance level. Hence they throw light on mostly social and economic history of the Apa Taniis. If one knows these *Ayus* thoroughly and analyse them properly, one can reconstruct the history of the Apa Taniis very well even if there is no written script.

These *Ayus* are recited during certain occasions, like festivals. Specially, the *Asang Ayus*, are recited during festivals like *Myoko*. Competition between two adults take place in reciting the *Asang Ayus* during festivals. *Aha Ayus* can be recited at any time and on any occasion. These are, usually, recited during working time in the fields where two adults or children compete. These *Ayus* are never recited deep inside the jungles. *Ayus* and *Barihs* are recited by male members only and never by women.

These *Ayus* are handed down from older generation to younger generation through a collective training when the children attain the age of ten (10) to twelve (12) years of age.

The children go to the house of the elderly in the evening after their dinner. They seat around the hearth and listen to the *Ayus* recited by elderly. The children listen to his tune, tenor and style of recitation of the *Ayus.* The elderly person recites the *Ayus* stanza by stanza and explains the terms used in the *Ayus.* This explanation is very essential as the language of the *Ayus* are in priestly language, much different from the ordinarily spoken language of the community. The elderly trainer tells how to question and answer the opponent. He tells all the tricks and problems of each *Ayus.* He also takes tests of the trainees by asking at random to recite a particular portion of a stanza of the *Ayu* being taught.

Migung

Migung literally means chronicle of events that is history. *Migung* is the oral chronicle of different types of wars between individuals, families, clans and villages or communities including disputes with Gods. It tells about their causes, responses of societies and the results of settlements of different types and nature. *Migung* also tells us about different social strifes and upheavals and resultant social formations and social and political alliances. It also chronicles incidence of famine and epidemics and their origin, cause and resultant social reactions and ultimate results.

Thus, *Migung* tells about the evolution of Apa Tanii society from its origin till date. *Migung* is the record not only of events but it tells about the causes and resultant reaction of the society and ultimate results. Thus, through *Migung* one can get fairly accurate idea about the sources of customary laws of the Apa Taniis.

Migung is sometimes called as *Paleh. Migung* or *Paleh* can be divided into two types corresponding to time periods covered. Thus, *Migung* is divided into *Ui Paleh* and *Supung Paleh. Ui Paleh* is the chronicle of events, when Abo Tani, the ancestor of Apa Taniis, lived with gods and Goddesses. *Supung Paleh* records the events when Apa Taniis lived with other human beings.

Myths and Legends

Another source of history of the Apa Taniis could be their myths and legends. Most of the myths relate of the exploits of *Abo Tani,* the fore-father of the Apa Taniis. These myths tell about the struggles and travails of *Abo Tani* when he lived with the Gods and Goddesses most of whom were his enemies. Myths surrounding *Abo Tani* includes his struggle to preserve and continue his race in enimical environments. It drove him to seek advice, make alliance with different Gods and Goddesses. This has resulted to certain festivals which binds society and promotes camaraderie among members. Likewise there are many myths surrounding Madam *Dolyang Chanjang* whose advice always saved *Abo Tani* from all sorts of difficult situations.

There are many legends in Apa Tanii society. They usually revolve around individuals like, Madams Paping Puming, Pame Pubyang, Ami Doriibo, Tabyu Yapih, Nanii solih etc. and men like Miido Hodre, Miido Byai, Miido Gorbii, Roring Kojin, Pato Dolyang etc. The behaviour patterns of these individuals which the legend tells give us faily a good idea about the history of the Tanii people of Ziro valley.

Moreover, every village and its clans have a legend which is called *Gontihnii* in Tanii which tells the history of their village. For example, Hija group of village has a legend (*Gontihnii*) thus – "Siilang Taru Paru Habii, Siikre Tasso Passo Habiila".

It means that the present village settlement area is known as Siilang and Siikre. It was full of thick wild creepers and after destroying them the land was occupied and the village was established. Likewise Hari group of villages boast about Killing and driving away of Pagang and Pali communities in thousands. Their legend says thus – "Pagang Lallyang Mi Pali Langngo Ni Panii".

Social and Political Institutions

Social and Political institutions of a community could be the source of history of that community. The *Gora* and *Buliang* are two such prominent institutions of the Apa Taniis. These social and political institutions usually evolve along with the development of a society. Hence, if we study these social and political institutions seriously and analyse them properly, we can know the history of that society.

Gora is an unique institution of the Apa Taniis. The *Gora* is composed of elderly persons who are well-versed in customs, practices and customary laws of the community. Their number is not very large. They are usually selected by the villagers unanimously. The *Goras* exist at clan level, at the level of many clans together and at village level.

Their main function is to arrange and perform common *pujas* of the clans and village. They give advance information throughout the village before performance of a *puja*. The *Goras* also arrange items offered to Gods and Goddesses in the puja. They also arrange the priest for the performance of necessary rituals. Usually, common *pujas* like *Myokung*, *Dree* and *Yapung* which are related to agricultural operations are arranged and performed by the *Goras*. *Goras* also enforce strictly, the observance of the *Anyodu* (period of abstinence from dong work). *Anyone* violating *Anyodu* is punished by imposing fines and if need be reperforming the community *puja*.

Resources for arranging the community *puja* is collected by the *Goras* from each household of the clans or village according to the nature and purpose of the *puja*. No household refuges the donation given for the *puja*. Moreover, there is no uniform item of contribution: Individual households are given freedom to give any item as per their convennience. Now a days, money has become the standard of contribution.

The *Buliang* is a politico-judicial institution of the Apa Taniis. The origin and history of the *Buliang* reflects the history of Apa Tanii community. There are oral literatures which vividly describe about origin, purpose, power and functions and finance of the *Buliang*. By studying and analyzing the *Buliang* one can have a fairly accurate history of the Tanii people.

The *Buliang* is a traditional self-govening institution of the Tanii people. They represent an *Uru* (extended family) at clan level, a clan at village level and whole village at comminuty level. Member of a *Buliang* is also known as a *Buliang*. It is a two tier organization. They are *Buliang* and *Miha Pillo*. The membership of the Buliang is hereditary. Usually powerful and wealthy families have contributed membership of a *Buliang*.

The *Buliang* has three functions. They are:

(*a*) Political

(*b*) Judicial and

(*c*) Social.

Whenever, there arises a situation which my create disharmony among villages within Apa Tanii community or with villages of other communities around Apa Tanii villags, the *Buliang* takes initiative to normalise the situation. Thus, whenever, peace and tranquility of the clans, villages or communities are likely to be disturbed, the *Buliang* takes the initiatives to restore it.

Likewise any dispute which arises and likely to disturb peace of the clans, villages or communities, the *Buliang* takes the initiative and arbitrates the disputes.

Certain socio-religious festivals cannot be performed without the permission of the *Buliang*. Thus, the most important community festival of Apa Taniis, the *Myoko* cannot be started without the permission of the *Buliang*.

In order to get rid of evil influences of evil spirits, the suffering family may call in *Buliangs* to his house and wine and dine them well. Likewise, barren couple the wine and dine the Buliang in their home to get a child.

Festivals and Performances

Festivals and performances of a community could be the source of its history. The Apa Tanii community performs three major festivals:

(a) *Myoko,*

(*b*) *Murung* and

(*c*) *Subuh.*

Myoko is performed by a group of *villages*. Therefore, Apa Tanii villages are divided into three group of villages for the purpose of celebration of *Myoko* festival. Thus, *Myoko* is performed by a group of villages each year. *Myoko* performing villages invite the non-performing villages to pertake their hospitality. Ceremonial gifts are given. Competition of *Ayu* and *Barih* takes place. Social relations are renewed with gifts to children and elderly persons. Whole social organizations and life of Apa Taniis can be studied thoroughly through *Myoko* festival.

Another important festival of the Apa Taniis is the *Murung*. It is performed by an individual family and shared by all the households' of Apa Tanii community. Every household helps the performer of *Murung* according to his family relationship with him. The near relatives give more help than the distant relations. If one observes carefully the stages of performance of *Murung* festival and hears the recitations, one can have a fairly good idea about history of the Apa Taniis.

Subuh is another festival of the Apa Taniis. It is performed by an individual but helped by near relatives and shared by everybody. This festival also throws light on the evolution of Apa Tanii society.

Social Customs and Traditions

Social customs and traditions could be another source of history. These have arisen to meet the needs of a society placed at a particular environment of that time. The Tanii society is no exception. It is loaded with many social customs and traditions. These are the bone and flesh of customary laws which organize and govern society at different occasios and needs of the time.[1]

Government Reports and Documents

For periods covering after 1945 we may refer to some governmental documents for supplementing the available traditional sources of history for Apa Tanii society. Prof. Christopher Von Furer Haimendorf was the first scholar to study the Apa Tanii society and their way of life systematically beginning in March 1944. The following reports, Diaries and books by him may be consulted.

1. Diaries of Travels in Subansiri Region (Shillong, 1945).
2. Ethnographic Notes on Tribes of Subansiri Region (Shillong 1947).
3. The Apa Taniis and their neighbours (London, 1962).
4. A Himalayan Tribe: from cattle to cash (New Delhi, 1980).
5. The Highlander of Arunachal Pradesh (New Delhi, 1982).
6. Himalayan Adventure: Early Travels in North East India (New Delhi, 1983) and
7. The Himalayan Barbary (London, 1955).

One may also go through Mrs. Ursula Graham Bower's book – The Hidden Land" (London, 1953), for glimpse into Apa Tanii history.

Verier Elwin's following books may also give some ideas about the history of Apa Taniis.

1. Democracy in NEFA (Shillong, 1965).
2. India's North East Frontier in the Nineteenth Century (Oxford University Press, 1959).
3. Myths of the North East Frontier of India (Shillong, 1958).
4. A New Book of Tribal Fiction (Shillong, 1970).

Reference

1. The article is based on participant observation as the author belongs to Apa Tanii Comminity. The author took training in reciting *Ayu* when he was in primary school at his village.

9

Geneaology as a Source of History: A Case Study of the ApaTaniis

Nani Bath

History is about remembering the past. It is essential to remember the past in order to understand the present and to plan for the future. The safest way to remember the past is to trace our geneaology. This paper is an attempt to trace the geneaology of the Apa Taniis and to verify whether it serves as a source of social history.

Recovery of history is an important marker of a culture. History is recovered orally and through written records. Oral history and social memory are our living contacts with the past.[1] In a tribal society, which has no writing, sources of history are limited to people's memory. These memories are passed down from generations to generations. Prof. Blackburn has identified four major areas of memory and oral history in Apatani society: 1. ritual; 2. objects; 3. oral traditions; 4. ordinary memory of past events.[2] I would include geneaology as an aspect of oral traditions. Genealogies, Prof. Romila Thapar writes, relate to the past and claim to be records of succession.[3]

Geneaology is helpful to the individuals and the society in many ways. It is through geneaology that the society can be constructed or reconstructed. It helps an individual to identify his root and himself.

The Apa Taniis count geneaology on all occasions. The priest invokes the spirits of our ancestors for the well-being of the society and clan members. The rituals associated with this are know as *Ayo-Ashi Menii* in Apatani dialect. Geneaology helps an individual identify the group from which bride can be taken or the group to which bride can be given. Interestingly *Anchal* segments are distributed on clan lines. Each clan has one or two *Anchal Samiti* members. A clan will have number of *Gram* members corresponding to the number of lineages. Generally a clan consists of four or five lineages and hence four to five *Gram* members will be represented in the *Panchayati Raj* Bodies from that clan.

One's geneaology helps a man trace back his migration route. "Geneaologies are obtained encapsulations of the migration and movement of peoples in time".[4] For instance, the Galos know which forefather lived at which place in the course of migration. The Galos called the system as *Doko-Kalam Ruman.*[5] The Apatanis of Arunachal Pradesh, as the legends say, come form a land vaguely located in the north known as iipyo *Supung.*[6] This place is probably located near Tsangpo river of China. The people who settled in the villages of Hija, Dutta Mudang-Tage and Michi-Bamin are said to have migrated from *Tapang Tale* (an area east of the Apatani Valley) by crossing Kuru river. The ancestors of the villages of Hari and Biila believe to have migrated viz *Pepu-Sala,* an area north of the present valley, and the people of Hong claim to come viz *Naring-Ako,* northeast of the valley. They are supposed to have crossed the Kalam river.[7]

The chronological arrangement of genealogies provides the dimension of the measurement of time.[8] This is possible through genealogical calculations to know which ancestors lived in which century. The Galos can trace back up to thirty-five generations, counting from ancestors *Jimi.* This means, they remember the name of a forefather who lived in 10th century AD if average generation gap is taken to be 30 years.[9] However, the present author could not gather information beyond 28th generations of the ancestors of the Apatanis.

The Apatanis were originally settled in seven traditional villages – Hari, Biila, Hija, Hong, Michi-Bamin, Mudang-Tage and Dutta. These villages are believed to have been named after seven brothers. Kalung, Reru and Tajang were born to Biila. Kalung has six clans (brothers). Reru and Tajang consist of seven clans each. The Nani-clan of Reru is further subdivided into five lineages.

The following is the diagrammatic representation of the clans of Biila village:

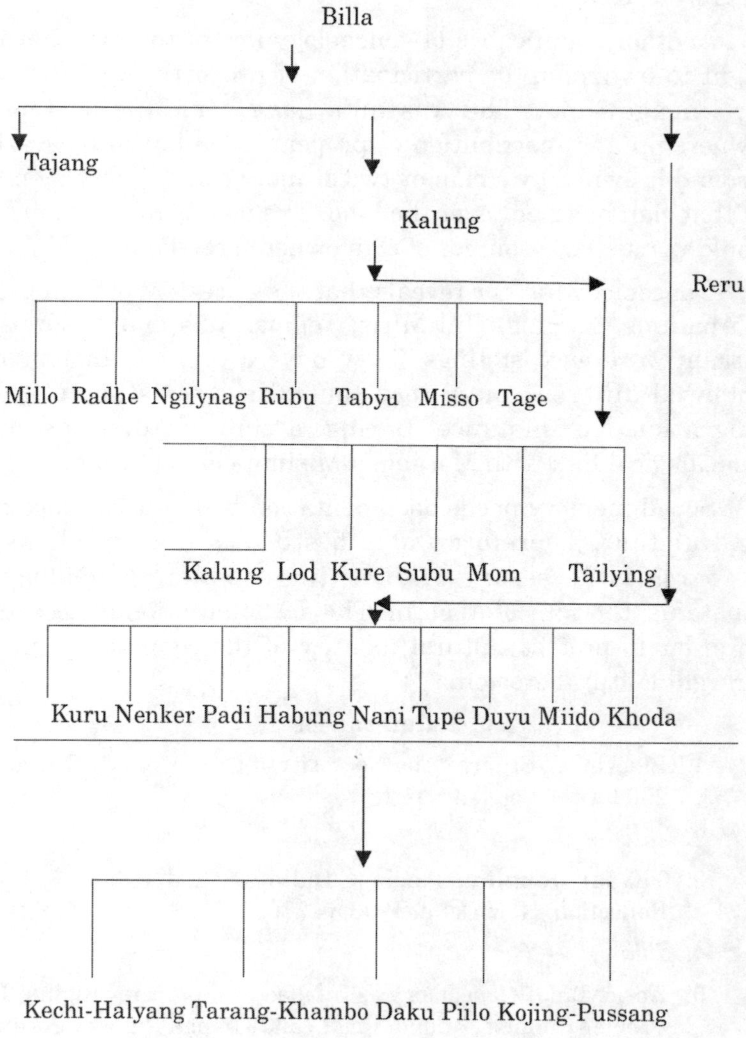

Tupe and Miido clans of Reru no more exist. Padi and Habung, and Kuru and Nenker are 'borther-clans'. The brother-clans share the blood of sacrificial pigs and they do not intermarry. Nenker-clan of Reru is considered as the oldest clan and hence believed to be the eldest son of Reru. Similarly Tabyu clan of Tajang is the oldest one. It is difficult to identify the father of Biila and to ascertain whether Billa was the brother of Hari or Hong.

Another significance of geneaology lies in the fact that the right to ownership or participation of property can be proved by lineage links. The Apatanis have a unique system of ownership and distribution of property. The burial or grazing ground is owned by a clan or two or more clans. Every member of that clan has right over the land. The members of other clans couldn't use the resources of clan owned forestland.

Geneaology further reveals that the ancestors of Tani group – Apatanis, Nyishis, Hill Miris, Tagins, Adis and Mishmis of Assam were once siblings. They have a common history but followed different migratory routes in later stage of their migration. For instance, Boring, a clan of Adis, has close genealogical link with Morang, a Mishmi-clan of Assam.

Social memory needs documentation before it becomes dim and distant. Therefore indepth study and comprehensive research is necessary to draw the complete genealogy of Apatanis, the sons of Abotani. The documentation is necessary in order to protect cultural identity of the community and to prevent cultural erosion.

References

1. Blackburn, Stuart, "The Necessity of Oral history", Guwahati, 2002, Dree Souvenir, p. 1.
2. *Ibid.*
3. Thapar, Romila, "Ancient Indian Social History", Some Reflection, New Delhi, 1996, p. 286.
4. *Ibid.*
5. Karlo, Tado, 'Geneaology as Intellectural property Rights: Tani People's Context', human Rights and Human Rights Education, A.K. Singh (ed.), Itanagar, 2002, p. 241.
6. Haimendorf, C.V.F., 'A Himalayan Tribe from Cattle to Cash, New Delhi, 1980, p. 13.
7. *Ibid.*
8. J. Vansin, 'The Oral Tradition', London, 1965, p. 102, as cited in Thapar, *op. cit.*
9. karlo, Tado, *op. cit.*

10

Pre-Historic Sources of Arunachal Pradesh

Byomakesh Tripathy & Ramesh Chandra Joshi

Introduction

Arunachal Pradesh, earlier known as NEFA (North East Frontier Agency), got its statehood on 20th February 1987. It is lying between 26° 30' N to 29° 30′ N latitude and 91° 30′ E to 97° 30' E longitude covering an area of 83743 sq. kms. It has an international border with Bhutan to the west (160 km), Tibet and China to the north and north-east (1,080 km) and Myanmar to the east (440 km). Southern part is delimited by national boundary with Assam. The capital of the state is located at Itanagar. It is named after Itafort meaning fort of bricks built in 14th century A.D. There are 16 districts *viz. Tawang, West Kameng, East Kameng, papumpare, Lower Subansiri*, Upper Subansiri, *East Siang, West Siang, Upper Sinag, Dibang Valley, Lower Dibang Valley, Lohit, Changlang, Tirap*, Kurung *Kumey*, and *Anjaw* with head quarter at Tawang, Bomdila, Seppa, Yupia, Ziro, Daporijo, Pasighat, Along, Yingkiong, Anini, Roing, Tezu, Changlang, Khonsa, Laying-Yangte, Hawai respectively.

The population of Arunachal is 1,091,117 (census 2001). It is scattered over 12 towns and 3649 villages. The State has the density of 13 persons per sq. km. There are 26 major tribes and a number of sub-tribes inhabiting the area. Most of these communities are ethnically similar, having derived from a common stock but their geographical isolation from each other has brought amongst them certain distinctive characteristics in language, dress and customs.

The Monpas, Sherdukpens, Membas and Khambas who live

in the high mountains along the northern borders follow the lamaistic tradition of *Mahayana* Buddhism. Khamptis and Singphos inhabiting the eastern part of the State are Buddhists of *Hinayana* sect. Galos, Adis, Akas, Apatanis, Nishis, Mishmis, Mijis, Wanchos, Tangsas etc. worship Sun and Moon God named as *Donyi-Polo*. The Noctes practice elementary form of Vaishnavism. The important festivals of Arunachal Pradesh are *Mopin, Solung, Nyokum, Lossar, Si-Donyi, Boori-boot, Dree, Reh, Sipong Yong, Chalo-loku, Kshyatsowai, Tamladu, Sarok, Nichido, Sangken, Mopin, Oriah* etc

Physiography

Altitude in the state is ranging in between 120m to 7079m above mean sea level. Physiographically it may be divided into four divisions *i.e.,* the Himalaya, Mishimi hills, Purvanchal Hills and Foot hill Plain. A brief description of each physiographic division is as follows:

Himalayan mountains are further divided into four regions *i.e.,* Tythes, Great, Lesser and Outer (Siwalik). The dividing lines in between two divisions are thrusts and maintain specific individual physiographic characteristics. In the extreme south, plain area is separated from the abruptly rising Siwalik Hills (Outer Himalaya) by the Foot Hill Thrust (FHT). Uneven topography, dendritic and parallel to sub parallel structurally controlled drainage pattern, swift-flowing consequent streams and deep valleys of antecedent rivers are the main geomorphic characteristics. The height of Outer Himalaya is ranging in between 120m to about 800m above mean sea level. The important localities in the lower part of this region are Pasighat, Likhabali, Kimin, Itanagar, Balijan, Ramghat and Bhalukpong. Lesser Himalaya is separated from the Outer Himalaya by Main Boundary thrust (MBT). This thrust zone is marked by very wide valleys, characterized by fans and cones of landslide debris, recent to sub-recent fault and triangular facets on spurs. The Lesser Himalaya is made of Precambrian and Paleozoic sediments over thrusted by vast thick sheets of metamorphic rocks injected by Precambrian - Paleozoic granites. The height is ranging in between 900m-3500m. The main localities of this region are Seppa, Tenga valley, Bomdila, Kalaktang, Ziro, Raga, Tamin, Daporijo, Mengia, Along, Kaying and Boleng. Maximum settlement concentration of Arunachal Pradesh is found in this region. Great Himalaya is separated by main Central Thrust from the Lesser Himalaya in the South. The height of this range is from 3000-6000mts. Taksing, Limking, zoirang and Nacho are the main localities of this region. Because of cold climate and less fertile soil population density is very low. It is made up of high grade metamorphic rocks that are extensively injected and migmatised by mid tertiary granite. It is characterized by extremely rugged and youthfull topography, sharp peaks, deep gorges with vertical to convex wall and very steep gradient. Tethys Himalaya is separated by Trans Himadri Thrust from Great Himalaya in the south. In this region height is ranging in between 3000-7000 meter. Bumla, Tefhngla of Twang district, Migyetung pass, Tung pass of upper Subansiri and Tunga, Lemdo pass of West Siang are situated in this region. Mishmi Hill is delimited in west from the Himalayan ranges with a Tuting -Tiding Thrust. In the south it is separated by Mishmi thrust from the Purvanachal Hills. In the east it is continuing to Myanmar. The rocks are made of metasedimants of Precambrian age with younger mafic and acidic intrusive. The height ranges in between 2000 to 6000m. above mean sea level. Main rivers of this area are Lohit, Dibang and Siang rivers. The important localities of this region are Anini, Hyuliang, and Walong. Changlang and Tirap district are made of sedimentary rocks and known as Purvanchal Hills. This range is extending from North to south and extends through Nagaland and Mizoram. Mishmi Hills are found in Dibang, Lohit and Anjaw district height is found more than 4000 mts. These hills are made of metamorphic rocks consisting gneiss and schist. The ranges are older than Purvanchal hills.

The main rivers which are draining this area are Siang, Dibang Lohit, Subansiri and Kameng. Siang (Dihing) river originates from Kailash Mansarower range and flows about 1600 km in Tibet. Taking 'U' shape turn at Namcha Barwa hills which height is 7748 mts. It enters in Arunachal Pradesh. Dibang (Sikang) river is draning Mishmi Hills and passing through Sadiya, debouches in Brahmaputra river. Lohit river originates from Nyimo Chomo Mountain range of Yunan Province of China where it is known as Rangto Chhu flowing towards south east, enters in Arunachal Pradesh and passing through Hauliang meets in Brahamaputra river.. Subansiri river originates from Tibet where it is known as Tsari Chhu, flows through India and meets with Brahamaputra near Dulung Mukh Localities. Kameng river one of a main tributaries of Brahamputra, flows in the western part of the state. The catchment area of this river system is about 9860 square kilometers. In general climate of Arunachal Pradesh is humid sub-tropical characteristised by high rainfall and high humidity at sub-Himalayan belt, the temperate climate at lower Himalayan region. During winter higher ranges of the Himalaya experience snowfall. Rainfall varies from 1000mm in higher reaches to 5750mm in the foot-hill areas. The minimum temperature is around o° C in winter months in Bomdila and Tawang whereas it rises to 35°C (during summer months) in Namsai and Tezu areas of Lohit district. The state is rich in its abundance species of flora and it varies from open scrub (grass land) to alpine forest in the greater Himalayas. This diversity of topographical and climatic conditions has favoured the growth of luxuriant forests which are home to myriad plant and animal forms adding beauty to the landscape. Soil characteristics vary from place to place with the change in altitude, parent material and climate. In general soil texture is sandy to loamy in the hills and clay to sandy clay along the rivers valleys and foot hill plain.

Geological Set-up

Tethys Himalaya includes Lum La formation consisting inter bedded schistose quartzite and biotite schist, marble, grayish green coarse crystalline. This formation is underlain by Se La group. It is exposed in Tawang-woming La Section (Kumar, 1997). Great Himalaya is made of high grade metamorphic green schist to amphibolite facies rocks. These rocks are found around Se La Pass, higher reaches of Kamala River, upstream of Taliha and Yapuik (Kumar, 1997). Main Central Thrust (MCT) and Lumla formation are separating this unit in south and north respectively. In the east these rocks are delimited by Tidding Suture. Main rocks are gneiss, schist, quartzite and migmatites. Lesser Himalayan rocks are named as Bomdila Group which is further subdivided as Khetabari, Tenga and Chilliepam. Khetabari formation comprises sericite-quartz, phyllite,schist, quaratzite graphitic phyllite with bands of marble and calc-silicates. Lower part of Chilliepam Formation contains basal oligomictic conglomerate followed by quartzite with thin bands of dolomite, black phyllite and dolomite. Upper member includes carbonate with phyllite. Dirang Formation unconformably overlying the Bomdila group in south and truncated in north by the MCT. It includes garnet-muscovite-biotite schist, flaggy and platy garnet-quartzite, intrusive biotite augen gneiss, schist and quartzite. Gondwana rocks are found to be uncomformably lying over Bomdila Group along south. It includes conglomerate, sandstone/quartzite purple shale, diamictite, dark grey feldspathic sandstone and grey to black carbonaceous shale with lenticular coal beds, basalt, andesites, acidic ruffs, and lapillis. Lithological sequence of the Outer Himalaya in Arunachal Pradesh is grouped into three rock stratigraphic units which are from bottom to top Dafla, Subansiri and Kimin formation roughly corresponding to the Lower, Middle and Upper Siwalik of the Western and Central Himalaya. The main rock types are conglomerate, sandstone and shale.

The rocks of Mishmi group are exposed over large part of the Dibang and Lohit district in the eastern Himalaya (Singh and Choudhary, 1990). In this area all litho-units are trending NW-SE and dipping towards NE. It includes meta-sediments and associated granite gneiss, granodiorite and granite with mafic and untramafic intrusive.

In Purvanchal Hills the deposition known as Jaintia Group is further divided into two formations *i.e.,* Langpar and Sylhet. Langpar formation is made of shale and sandstone with calcareous matter. Sylhet formation is unconformably overlain by the sequence consisting the Disang and Barail Group. It is made up of limestone, sandstone and carbonaceous shale. The age of Disang and Barail Group sequence is estimated as Middle Eocene to Oligocene.

Disang Group comprises grey shales interbeded with mudstone and sandstone. Barail group is divided into three formations *i.e.,* Laisang, Jenam and Tikak Parbot. Laisong is named after Laisong locality in the Jenam River comprises very hard grey thin bedded sandstones alternating with sandy shales, occasionally carbonaceous with thin streaks of coal. The Laisong grades upwards into more argillaceous sequence of alternation of buff bluish green and grey coloured sandstone, sandy shale, carbonaceous shale, and often iron stained shale are known as Jenam Formation. It also comprises thin coal seams. Jenam Formation grades into overlying Tikak Formation made up of hard, ferruginous massive sandstones with subordinate shales in upper Brahamaputra Plain and Purvanchal Hills.

The Tipam Formation is conformably overlain by the Girujan formation. It comprises grits with lenses of conglomerate and sandstone with minor shale. It is unconformalby overlain by the Namsang formation in upper Assam. At places the Namsang is not developed, the Girujan is overlain by the older Alluvium. The Girujan formation is absent and are immediately lying to south-east of Bramaputra river between Tengaghat and Jorhat but thickness out south-eastwards and in east where it is about 2000m thick in the Kumchai well in Arunachal Pradesh. Namsang Formation is unconformably overlaying the Girujan Formation. It includes a sequence of soft sandstone with thin clay beds and lignite conglomerate. It contains beds of grit and conglomerate in upper part, including small pebbles of sandstone, and rarely small fragments of jasper. Dihing Formation is unconformably overlying the Namsang Formation as observed in the Dihing river section. It comprises a 250-300m thick sequence of pebble bed with clays.

Pleistocene Environment – Ice Age in Arunachal

The Pleistocene epoch called the 'Age of man' which saw the origin and evolution of man during a time ranging from 2 million years to 10,000 BC is known to be a geological period of severe climatic fluctuations of alternating cold and dry periods due to lowering and rising of earth" temperature. The effects of these climatic fluctuations, consisting of four main glacial advances with three intervening warm interglacial periods, covering the entire Pleistocene epoch, could be established with the help of geomorphological features in the glaciated and periglaciated regions, founal successions, sea leval fluctuations, marine geology and marine organisms. Ever since penck and Bruckner established the four fold succession of Pleistocene glaciations in the Alpine regions of Europe in 1909 with the help of glacial moraines and river terraces observed in four Alpine streams – Gunz, Mindel, Riss and Wurm, this scheme served as a model of establishing glacial and interglacial climatic cycles in northern hemisphere. The entire climatic phenomena of the pleisterine epoch are collectively known as Ice Age. (Sankalia, 1974).

In the tropical regions of the world, there was, however, no permanent snow cover on the entire land surface. Here the effects of Pleistocene glaciations were observed in higher altitude. Helmut de Terra and T.T. Petterson tried to establish that the Pleistocene glacial and interglacial phases had left their marks in Kashmir and in the potwar plateau and the Kashmir glacial cycles were in many ways comparable to those of Europe. (Deterra & Petterson 1939). As in case of northwestern end of the Himalayas, the northeastern end was also affected by Pleistocene glaciations as revealed from the geological study of H.H.Godwin – Austin in Naga Hills. (Austin, 1975, 209-13). As far as northeast is concerned Siwalik fossils are reported from Garo hills. Tripura has also yielded Siwalik mamals. It was only in 1974-75, the first ever vertebrate fossil *i.e.*, the molar of Bos has been unearthed by the Geological Survey of India, from the upper tertiary horizons of Eastern Himalayas within Arunachal Pradesh. This evidence is noticed in the Ramghat area of the lower Subansiri district. The discovery is of considerable importance establishing the continuation of western Siwaliks, as the probable habitation of the area of the Hominids and Paleolithic men. (Jaswal, 1976). The evidences of Siwalik fauna in Garo hills and Tripura, being taken together, may suggest the migration of these elements from Arunachal Siwaliks to those places or vice versa towards the end of the Miocene period. Bopardikar and his team, who surveyed the Daphabum area of district Lohit, have reported about high terraces around Wakro, between Halaikrong and Hawai on Lati river, and in various parts of the area (Bopardikar, 1972). It is believed that a detailed examination of the area between Wakro and Lungsi on Kamlang and between Hawai and Hayuling would yield concrete information for the study of terrace formations and early Stone Age industries in this area. However, the story of Early Stone Age (Paleolithic) man in Arunachal, in spite of its great prospect, is still an uninvestigated subject.

Arunachal: Ethnological

The ethnographic accounts of the tribes of the state – their origin, migration and affinities are a less investigated subject so far. However, ethnographic acconts of a number of tribes can be utilized to link up Arunachali culture with prehistory. The state is the home of more than hundred tribes and sub-tribes, who are affiliated to the so-called "North Assam group of Tibeto-Burmese group of language". With regard to their racial affiliations they have been described as Indo-Mongoloid, proto mongoloid, Paleo-Mongoloid and so on. It is evident from the Somato-Scopic characters that the people of the state show characteristics of the Mongoloids. In metric characters, the people are short or below medium in stature. In finger ridge pattern, most of the population shows similarities with the Bodo population of North East India. In anthropometry, however, almost the entire population maintains a distance from rest of the northeast, which may be explained by their geo-political isolation for a petty long time (Goswami & Das, 1990). A study of the origin and migration of the area reveals that the tribes of the central part like the Adis, the Mishmis, the Tagins, the Nyishis, the Apatanis and other migrated from some parts of southern Tibet. The *Mahayana* Buddhist tribes of the state like the Monpas, Sherdukpens (western frontier), Membas, Khambas in (northern frontier) are also said to have come from Tibet but definitely later than the central Tani tribes of the state. The other Buddhist group belonging to *Theravada* Buddhism migrated from Burma to eastern part of the state only in late medieval period. Tribes like the Tangsas, Wanchos, and the Noctes are said to have migrated from Burma, after the coming of the Ahoms to Assam in early 13th century AD. It seems the first migration to the area took place in central part of the state. (Choudhury, 1983). Prof. S.K.Chatterjee while speaking on the Sino-Tibetan Mongoloid expansion, writes: "The area of characterization for the primitive Sino-Tibetan speech appears to have been north western China between the Huang-Ho and the Yangtsze Kiang Rivers". He further mentions that the Mongoloid tribes from Western China speaking forms of Sino-Tibetan speech appear to have been pushing south and westwards from their original home land in prehistoric times. Anthropologists have thrown light on the close parallels between the cultures of the tribes of central part of Arunachal with those of Indonesia, Borneo, Laos and other parts of Southeast Asia. It is also opined that the tribes of present Arunachal Pradesh with their variation of so-called Mongoloid characters had a Southeast Asian origin and their migration to their present area of dispersion took place from that direction in prehistoric times (Choudhury, 1983). However, if we support the above hypothesis, it is difficult to co-relate the myths and legends of various central tribes, regarding their coming from Tibet through the northen frontier of Aruanchal. Whatever may be the fact, through the traditional routes and mountain passes of the Arunachal hills, India maintained contact with Tibet, China, Burma and Thailand from prehistoric period and thus the Eastern Himalayan state therefore, holds the key to study the East-West cultural contacts that are known to have persisted since the prehistoric period.

Findings of Pre-Historic Tools

The study of Prehistoric archaeology in the state of Arunachal had its genesis in the latter part of 19th century, when Lubbock reported a light green jade celt of Neolithic period, which was collected from Namsang in the Tirap district. (Lubbock, 1867, 822). E.H.Steel in 1870 described three more neolithic Celts from the same Namsang area. The first piece was of greenish jade stone, while the second piece was of the same material but smaller in size; the third one being made of a soft white stone having brownish yellow on its outline. (Steel, 1870, 267-268). In 1871, John Anderson collected a huge tool-kit of neolithic implement from the Mishmi hills of Arunachal. (Anderson, 1871, 410-415). Around 1917, Healy of Geological Survey of India said to have collected a curvilinear facetted tool made of streaked and mottled jadeite, from within the boundaries of Arunachal (Raiker & Chatterjee, 1980). R.D. Banarjee, the first Indian Scholar of study the prehistoric remains of Arunachal in 1924-25, described a stone edze found on the left bank of the river Dihong in a village called Mebo in the district Siang. (Banarjee, 1924-25, 102). During 1933-35, J.P.Mills and J.H.Grace surveyed the Sadiya Frontier Zone and collected more than a dozen of Neolithic tools. J.P. Mills collected in 1933, a curvilinear facetted tool, a rounded buttaxe, a tool having bifacially ground median edged type and two tools of unifacially ground edge type. J.H.Grace credited to have recovered a curvilinear type facetted tool of bone and another of black basalt, gneisses an unifacially ground edge tool, a bifacially ground median edge type tool and two curvilinear type, one of limestone and another of jadeite. In all, as many as seventeen specimens are reported from the sadiya frontier zone and all of these stone tools are now preserved in the pitt rivers museum, Oxford. The first report of this collection was made by Professor A.H. Dani (Dani, 1960: 60-62). Later on this collection was studied by Sharma (Sharma, 1980). Many of the implements in this collection are made of different varieties of jadeite, which is not locally available in Arunachal. Rest of the implements are made on a variety of locally available rocks such as sandstone, basalt, gneiss, schist and talcose with serpentine views. Technologically, there are (i) chipped and edged ground axes (ii) pecked and edged ground axes (iii) fully ground tools. Some implements of Jadeite were initially shaped by sawing technique. Typologically, there are two dominant types in this collection viz. Stone axes with lenticular cross section and quadrangular type with rectangular cross section. The minor types are hog backed type of celt and slender chisel of jadeite. (Ibid.).

After Independence, due to the untiring efforts of various researchers, Neolithic tools are reported from the nook and corner of Arunachal Pradesh. These are found as surface finds in areas now inhabited by communities like Monpa, Sherdukpen, Khowa, Miji, Aka, Nyishis, Tagin, Hill Miri, Apatani Memba, Khamba, Bokar, Adi, Mishmi, Khampti, Singpho, Nocte and Wancho. Neolithic celts have also been reported from the areas inhabited by the Sulungs. (Stonor, 1952, p. 50). In 1969-70, Y.A. Raiker found three triangular ground axes and one bar type polished broken celt during excavation at Bhishmaknagar in the district Lohit without stratographic context. (Raiker & Chaterjee, 1980, pp. 5-1). In the same year, the first scientific survey for prehistoric remains was undertaken by B.P. Bopardikar of Archaeological Survey of India and his team in district Lohit. Daphabum area of Lohit district was explored with a view to trace habitational site of primitive man and to determine relation between western and eastern Himalayan glacial and glacio-fluvial phenomena and formation of terraces of stone age industries. Among ten sites surveyed in this area, prehistoric antiquities were found only in three sites namely Kale, Techum and Glow. Neolithic tools classified as shouldered axes, chisel, triangular axes, and splayed axes were noticed, besides a few artifacts like choppers, hand axe, cleavers, scrapers, flakes, points and core, indicating a pre-neolithic phase of culture in Arunachal Pradesh. (Bopardikar, 1972, 5-8). Professor M.C.Goswami and his associates published a report of a collection of 18 neolithic celts from the Kameng district of Arunachal (Goswami et. al., 1972: 29-35). This neolithic collections consisted of shouldered celts, trapezoidal, triangular and splayed axes, are said to have preserved in the Anthropology Department of Gauhati University.

D.K.Duarah (1979: 13-14) reported for the first time neolithic celts from the Kamala valley in Lower Subansiri district, which prompted scholars to carry out extensive exploration in different parts of the Kurung and Kamala valleys. (Ashraf,1990: 16-41). During the survey, the researcher found a chipped cum polished neolithic axe at Sangram, a 'T' shaped cylindrical stone hammer at Vigo, two stone axes from Taram, a shouldered celt from Lia, a double edged waisted bald from Mindung and a rectangular (elongated) axe, waisted blade, round scraper, hammer, chisel etc. from Taba. The first prehistoric excavation in Arunachal which was undertaken at parsi-parlo by Ashraf during 1982-83 (Ibid.) revealed a single culture. The aceramic neolithic stage is characterized by scrappers and large cutting tools with the rudiments of pecked and ground techniques. It is interesting to note that the ground and pecked (Polishing) technique, one of the hall marks of neolithic tradition took its birth during the phase. The ceramic neolithic stage is characterized by the occurrence of pecked and ground stone implements, waisted blade/axe and facetted tools with hand-made pottery. The ferrolithic stage is nothing but a continuation of the preceding phase but it witnesses the use of iron implements. The stone implements of this phase are round butted pecked and ground celts. Six basic rock types were used by the Kamla valley people as raw materials for their tools and these are sand stone, basalt, schist, quartzite, griciss and jadeite. Most of the tools of Kamla valley were made through pecked and ground technique. However, in some cases flaking or chipping technique is also not uncommon. The majority of tools whether flaked or ground possesses convex cutting edge with plano-convex, bio-convex and rectangular cross section.

Niranjan Sarkar in 1982 published a report of 12 neolithic celts and some broken pieces of celt, which he has collected from different parts of the State. (Sarkar: 11-25). These tools were noticed from the areas inhabited by Aka, Sherdukpen, Monpa, Miji, Tangsa, Khamba, Memba, Digaru Mishmi, and Khampti. These antiquities were in the form of shouldered celt, but axe, facetted celt, tanged axe, chisel and celts of more of less triangular and subrectangular shape. These tools are mainly made of shale and jadeite, though majority of these are of jadeite. Most of these tools were probably used as hoe-blade and axe-blade. Most of the ethnographic mesium of Arunachal locating in the district headquarters possess a number of Neolithic tools of the area. Of late; many neolithic tools are reported from foothills areas of Arunachal and other parts of the State. Even in or around the capital city of Itanagar, a few neolithic tools have been recovered.

Analysis of Archaeological Data

Although Early Stone Age cultural relics have been found in adjoining regions in Burma (Movius, 1949: 32977), and in the Garo Hills of Meghalaya (Sharma, 1980), Arunachal Pradesh is yet to have this type of Stone Age material except at Daphabum area and in Kamla valley and as such no clear cut picture on the Paleolithic period is known to us. Evidence of Mesolithic culture, dating from about 8000 BC to 4000 BC. as found in Indian context is also not available from the state. However, at Daphabhum area, in various places pre-neolithic tools were recovered. Unifacial and bifacial chopper of Alubari, few ovates from Kale, one Unifacial chapper and a flake from Tawling, proto handaxe from Teehu, Cleavers from Kale, side scraper on flakes from Glow, points on flakes, broad rectangular flakes, paralles sided flakes, cores, cylindirical core from different parts of Daphabhum area reveals that this area was inhabited from the Paleolithic times. (Bopardikar,1969). In Kamla valley of Lower Subansiri district, a typical power Paleolithic chopper has been recovered (Ashraf, 1990). Here it may be mentioned that the excavation at the site Parsi-parlo in Kamla valley area, has yielded scrappers and large cutting tools, typical pre-neolithic tools with the rudiments of pecked and ground techniques, though the tool kits is essentially a paleolithic one. It is interesting to note that ground and polishing technique, one of the hall marks of Neolithic tradition, took its birth during this phase. This phase may be considered as a transitional phase between old and new Stone Age cultures in the area. Thus the site of Parsi-Parlo provides example of evolving of pre-neolithic tools to tools of Neolithic period. Of late a few pre-neolithic tools are collected from Doimukh area, which are preserved in state museum, Itanagar. A beautiful stone artifact typotechnologically belonging to the middle Paleolithic industry is also recovered from Itanagar area. Y.A.Raiker has mentioned about a few microlithics from some parts of Lohit area. However, paucity of extensive study in this regard, makes it difficult to understand the pre-neolithic culture of Arunachal Pradesh.

In the absence of contextual and other artifactual data, there remains one kind of archaeological material *i.e.,* the stone tools, through a systematic analysis of which some attempts could be made to reconstruct the neolithic period of Arunachal. Here it can be mentioned that except the excavated remains of Parsi-parlo, all the neolithic stone tools found in the state are of surface collection without any stratIgraphy. The assemblage of neolithic tools reveals an innate relation in material and form to the geological and geographical conditions of the area. The raw materials consist of flat slabs, probably collected from stream beds. They were chosen for the purpose, because there was actually very little need for prior chipping or flaking and grinding or smoothing of these slabs. By slight battering or hammering and grinding of the edge either on one side or both the sides, they can be turned into tools. Locally available rocks were used generally for making stone tools. However, Arunachal presents neolithic material of a rare rock which is foreign to the state as well as to India as a whole. It is Jadeite, a variegated brightly coloured rock of very high quality, which occurs in plenty in China. The nearest source of these rock is Yunnan in South-West China. Infact, the prolific use of Jadeite in preparing tools in Arunachal strengthens Arunachal's links with Yunnan. The findings of kamala valley, particularly 'T' formed type cylindrical stone hammer is unique in Northeast region, while the constricted blade is an innovation of Szechwan stone Age culture of eastern China (Chieng, 1942 & Chang, 1977). The occurrence of this extraneous cultural material in Arunachal is therefore highly significant so far as human migration and cultural diffusion in Arunachal is concerned.

The manufacturing techniques of Arunachal stone implements are of two types. Majority of stone tools were manufactured by applying a technique called packing, as a primary shaping process of the tools, the other technique, *i.e.*, technique of grinding being confined only for preparing and sharpening the cutting edge. A typological analysis of Arunachal neolithic reveals that majority of the tools are of tanged or shouldered type of stone tools, which is more eastern Asiatic in character because this type of tools are very rare in other parts of India beyond north east India and is a characteristic type fossil of eastern Asiatic and Pacific Neolithic culture spreading from North China through South East Asia and North East India to New Zealand (Sharma, 1998). Other dominant type are stone axes characterised by triangular shape with a tapering but end regarding the origin of smoothed stone axes of India. Wheeler (1947-48: 295) and Worman (1949: 199) are of opinion that the distribution of this neolithic traditions shows a northeast to southwest orientation. In his latter work, Wheeler (1959-89) has not only maintained his former position but also has gone a step further by specifying the route through which the tradition is believed to have come to India from China. He refers that the route passed through Yanze Valley, Szechwan and upper Burma to Northeast India. Similar view has also been maintained by E.C.Worman (1949: 199), who writes "India smoothed stone celts of Neolithic type, regardless of their cultural affiliation appears to have derived from the eastward". He also argued that Northeast India served as a corridor through which neolithic tradition from Eastern Asia entered India. Arunachal, situated on the mountain wall dividing India and Burma, played the role of contact zone between western and eastern cultural tradition in prehistoric times. Earlier, scholar believes that Neolithic shouldered celts were cut by metal wires to obtain the angles and were possibly copied from metal prototypes (Dani, 1960). However, it has now been demonstrated that shale and sandstone can be cut by a shell piece or silvers of bamboo, and as such knowledge of metal need not be assumed for the manufacture of shouldered celts (Thapar, 1985).

Though neolithic tools are found in good numbers, pottery of the period are few and during the exploration of Kamla valley, plain (thick and coarse) ware, stamped (grid pattern) ware and irregular corded wares were noticed. All the potsherds were coarse in texture and hand-made. A few potsherds were also noticed during the excavation at parsi-parlo. These potsherds were having shapes like rounded bottom without furned rim, with stamped-honey comb design, rounded bottom splayed out rim with square grid design, plain ware and a small piece of cord impressed potsherd. Typologically, these ceramics tallies with that of neolithic pottery of Assam, recovered from surface collection and stratified deposit. (Sharma, 1967: 126-128). Here it may be mentioned that the findings of shouldered celt in associating with the cord marked pottery have a wide distribution in East and Southeast Asia.

In the absence of sufficient data, exact parallels with cultures of other region can not be established. Nevertheless, the Neolithic assemblage of this Northeast including Arunachal region has been compared with the late Bacosonian of Southeast Asia which revealed significant influence from Sichuan and Yunnan (Sharma, 1981: 41-52). That there is unmistakable evidence of Chinese Neolithic over Arunachal is clearly demonstrated by the presence of Jadeite neolithic objects in the State. The jadeite neolithic axes are rare material and are typical products of Chinese neolithic in their typotechnological characteristics the typical quadrangular shape, the technique of pecking, the specialized method of working jadeite invented in China and above all the availability of this rare rock in that country. The jadeite axes of Arunachal may be comparable to those from Honan, Shensi and Kansu province of China (Anderson, 1943, 261-262). This presupposes that the Arunachal jadeite axes were most probably derived from Northwest China. The history of migration of Mongoloid population from the headwater of Hwang-Ho and Y ang-tiz e kiang into Arunachal and Northeast India, as known from literature, could be attested by archaeological evidences.

Material Culture and Beliefs

No direct evidence for the domestication of animals and plants has so far been obtained but from the circumstantial evidence, it can be inferred that slash and burn and shifting cultivation must have practised during this period. Since the available technology was incapable of improving the yield, shifting cultivation was the most expedient solution to the problem. The stone axes would have been used for forest clearings with a view to farming. Probably the people were crude agriculturist, practising shifting cultivation by using fire as the chief means of clearing land and stone holes for finding the young plants and weeding the grasses. Probably spices of rice and millet, which are native plants of the area were grown. Further, the population must have depended to a great extent upon the almost inexhaustible source of forest products, a practice still current among the present inhabitants of the area. No structural remains or any other evidences such as post-holes etc. are found in the excavation at Parsi-Parlo, which shows that it was an open-air campsite. The neolithic people would have lived either in huts, which were built exclusively out of perishable materials or in natural shelter in Arunachal. The people inhabited the highlands and high slopes for the production of cereals. However, the neolithic people of Arunachal had learnt the idea of producing pottery though these were only handmade. Besides, we are in dark as to how they made their living and what type of material culture they had.

The neolithic celts of the region are associated with various myths and beliefs of the local people. These beliefs have a similarity with that of the Burmese and other people of the Southeast Asian countries. The local people cherish neoliths as charms and occasionally use them as amulets to ward off different kinds of calamities and evils. The collectors believe them to have fallen from sky with thunderbolt and these are dropped generally on the ground in the vicinity of dormitories or struck the house. The Monpas, Sherdukpens and Khambas believe that the deities hurl these thunderbolts from the sky to strike the evil slints. Another belief prevalent among the Mijis, Akas, Gallongs and Khamptis is that the deities hurl these from the sky to punish men and creatures guilty of acts offensive to the deities. The Khambas and the Tangsas, on the other hand, have firm belief that the deities hurl these to the house of a man to punish him for committing some sin. Even the Digaru Mishmis, Tangsas and Wanchos avoid a house struck by thunderbolt. Infact, majority of tribes of the state have their own belief and faith regarding these stone tools. (Sarkar, 1982), which are quite interesting.

Megalithic Remains

Erection of megalithic (great stone) monuments as memorial stones and customs of megalithic burial chambers are prehistoric customs dating back to New Stone Age. Though megalithic burials in South India belong to the Iron Age (100 to 300 BC), in many parts of central, eastern and north eastern India, it is of prehistoric as well as recent period, as the prehistoric tradition still survives as living tradition in many pockets of eastern and north-eastern India, Scholars like J.P.Mills (1939), Gurdon (1914), Hutton (1929), Haimendorf (1946), and many others have worked on megalithic remains of North East India. However nothing is known about the megalithic remains of Arunachal Pradesh. Y.A.Raiker has discovered a megalithic site at Jamiri in East kameng district (Raiker, 1979). Raiker had found three pairs of upright stones on the separate spots of the village, Jamiri. The first pair of stone was noticed in the courtyard of jamiri chief and next pair was located about 30 mtrs. east from the first pair, the third pair of stone and other stone remnants were found about one km. south-eastern direction from the village. Raiker mentions that the last pair of stone was comparatively lower than former and some stone blocks near by it have contained a number of undeciphered script: The remains are said to be of dolmens types. Nothing more is known due to absence of excavation in the site. However it has to be admitted that the megalithic remains of the state are till not adequately known to us.

Authors and Date

The wide distribution of neolithic tool points to the once widespread neolithic culture in Arunachal. But we can not clearly say who were the neolithic people and whether or not they were ancestors of present local inhabitants of the state. However, findings of the first ever vertebrate fossil *i.e.,* the molar of Bos from the upper tertiary horizons of Eastern Himalayas *i.e.,* from Ramghat area in Arunachal along with a few Paleolithic tolls from Kamla valley and Daphabhum area, some tools of pitts erstwhile Arunachal, now preserved in pitts river's museum displaying Mesolithic traits, findings of microliths in district Lohit, all point to the fact that people lived in this area in pre-neolithic period. The combined evidence of ethnology and archaeology make us to believe that the pre-neolithic people in Arunachal belonged to the same ethnic stocks as were responsible for the contemporary cultures of other parts of Northeast India, Burma, South China and Southeast Asian countries. They could have been the Austiric speaking people who are supposed to have lived here till their dispersal or miscegenation with later Mongoloid immigrants of Northeast India who penetrated from China and Southeast Asia in the neolithic period (Das, 1984 & Sharma, 1984 b). Mortimoer Wheeler also ascribes the authorship of neolithic people to an early wave of people, entering Northeast from Burma around the 1st millennium B.C. (Wheeler, 1959), practising a rudimentary type of agriculture.

As far as the date of neolithic culture in Arunachal is concerned, we are handicapped due to the paucity of scientific dating like C_{14}, TL dating. Prof. H.D. Sankalia has postulated two phases of Neolithic culture for Assam, the earlier being ascribed to $\underline{C}$ 5000 BC and the later to $\underline{C}$ 2000 BC (Sankalia, 1981 p.1-6). However, Alchins have rightly warned that "In assigning any sort of date to the neoliths of Assam, two things need to borne in mind: (a) the lower limit must be considered as relation to Chinese Neolithic and may be of unexpected antiquity; (b) the Assam hill are tribal areas down to the present and stone tools may well have persisted in use until very late times (Alchins, 1968, p.172). This observation holds good regarding the Neolithic culture of Arunachal too. Here it may be mentioned that in nearby state of Tripura, neolithic tools are dated to *c* 1500 BC by C_{14} method (Sharma, 1991, p. 52). Even the findings of a piece of iron from the Ferolithic phase along with neolithic tools in the uppermost phase during the excavation at Parsi-Parlo, do indicate a date not before 1000 BC. Taking all these dates into consideration, we may tentatively argue that the probable date of neoliths of Arunachal are most probably contemporary with the dates postulated for latter neolithic of Assam by Prof. Sankalia. However, more spade work is needed to explore and excavate various stone age sites of Aruanchal in a scientific way to have a clear picture of prehistoric archaeology and its allied problems.

References

1. Alchin, Bridget and Alchin Raymond (1968), The birth of Indian Civilization, Pelican Harmonds Worth.
2. Anderson, John, (1871), The Stone Implements of Yunnan etc. Report on the Expedition to Western Yunnan via Bhamo.
3. Anderson, J.G. (1943), "Researches into the Prehistory of the Chinese", Bulletin Museum Far Eastern Antiquities Stockholm, 15, pp. 1-34.
4. Ashraf, A.A., (1990), Prehistoric Arunachal (A Report on Archaeological Exploration and Excavation at Kamla valley etc.), Directorate of Research, Govt. of Arunachal, Itanagar.
5. Banerji, R.D., (1924-25), Neolithic Implements from the Abor Country, Annual Report, Archaeological Survey of India, new Delhi.
6. Barua, K.L., (1939), "Prehistoric Culture in Assam", Journal of Assam Research Society (JARS), Vol. 7, No.1 pp. 6-18 & No. 2, 35-41, Gauhati.
7. Bopardikar, B.P., (1972), "Prehistoric Investigation – Daphabhum Scientific Survey Expedition (NEFA)" in Archaeological Congress and Seminar Papers (ed) S.B. Deo, 1-8, Nagpur University, Nagpur.
8. Chang, Kwang Chih, (1977), The Archaeology of Ancient China, 3rd edition. New Haven: Yale University.
9. Chiang, Te-K'un, (1942), The "Lithic industries of Prehistoric Szechwan", Jwcbrs (Journal of West China border Research Society), Vol. XIV, p. 1-16.
10. Child V.G., (1951), Man makes Himself, The Thinkers Library, London.
11. Chaudhuri, P.C., (1944), "Neolithic Culture in Kamarupa", JARS, Vol. XI, Nos. 1-2, 42-47, Gauhati.
12. Chowdhury, J.N., (1983), Arunachal Pradesh (From Frontier Tracts to union Territory), New Delhi, Cosmo Publications.
13. Dani, A.H., (1960), Prehistory and protohistory of Eastern India (with a detailed account of the neolithic cultures in mainland Southeast Asia), 60-62, Firma K.L. Mukhopadhyay, Calcutta.
14. Das, B.M. (1984), "Some aspects of physical Anthropology of Northeastern India" in Tribes of Northeast India (ed.) S.Karotemprel, pp. 39-57, Shillong.

15. De Terra, H. and T.T.Paterson, 1939, Studies on the Ice Age in India and associated human cultures: Washington D.C: Carnegie Institute.

16. Goswami, M.C. & P.B.Das, (1990), The people of Arunachal Pradesh – A physical survey, Directorate of Research, Itanagar.

17. Duarah, D.K., (1979), "Neolithic Celts from Subansiri District, Arunachal News", Aug, Vol.No.8-9, 13-14, Directorate of Research, Govt. of Arunachal, Shillong.

18. Goswami, M.C. *et. al.*, (1972), "A typological study of some prehistoric tolls from the Kameng district of NEFA (Arunachal)", Journal of Assam Science Society, XV (1), 29-35.

19. Grierson, G.A., (1901), Linguistic Survey of India, Vol. III, Tibeto-Burman Family, Part-I, Gazette Office, Calcutta.

20. Hutton, J.H., (1928), "Prehistory of Assam", man in India, 8 (4): 228-232, Ranchi.

21. Joshi, R.C. and Rawat A.S. (2001). Morphotectonic observation along Main Boundary Thrust in between Dikrong and Ranga River, Eastern Himalaya, Arunachal Pradesh, Technical Project Report, submitted to Dept. of Science and Technology, Govt. of India, New Delhi, p. 91.

22. Jaswal, I.J.S., (1976), "Search for Early man in Northeastern India", man in India, Vol. 56, 276-277, Ranhi.

23. Kumar, Gopendra, (1997), Geology of Arunachal Pradesh, Geological Society of India, Bangalore, p. 217.

24. Lubbock, Sir John, (1867), The stone Age – Stone tools in Upper Assam, Athenaum, No. 2069, June 22, p. 827, London.

25. Mishra, V.N., (1964), "Neolithic Problem in India" in V.N.Mishra & M.S. Mate (ed.), Indian Prehistory, Deccan College, Pune.

26. Movius Hallam L., (1948), "The Lower Paleolithic Cultures of Southern and Eastern Asia", Trans Amer. Pho. Soc., 38: 329-93.

27. Raiker, Y.A., (1979), "Megaliths at Jamiri", Aruncahl News, vol.8, Sep. No. 6, p. 5.

28. Raiker, Y.A. & S. Chatterji, (1980), Archaeology in Arunachal Pradesh, Directorate of Research, Govt. A.P., Shillong.

29. Sankalia, H.D. (1974), Prehistory and Protohistory of India and Pakistan, Post-graduate and Research Institute, Deccaan College, Pune.

30. Sankalia, H.D. (1981), "From History to Prehistory in Assam" in cultural contours of India (part-II) ed. V.S.Srivastava, pp. 1-6., Abhinav Publications, New Delhi.

31. Sarkar, N, (1982), "Neolithic Celts from Arunachal Pradesh", Resarun, Vol.VIII, No.2, Directorate of Research, Govt. of A.P., Shillong.

32. Sharma, T.C. (1967), "A Note on the Neolithic Pottery of Assam", Man, n.s. 2, No. 1, 126-128, London

33. (1980), "Prehistoric Archaeology in Northeast India – A Review of Progress" in Eastern Himalaya (ed) T.C. Sharma & D.N. Majumdar, 102-135, Cosmo Publication, New Delhi.

34. (1981), "The Neolithic Pattern of Northeastern India" in Madhu: Recent researches in Indian archaeology and art history (ed), M.S.Nagaruja Rao, 41-52, Delhi, Agam Kal Prakashan.

35. (1984a), "Northeast India in Prehistoric Times" in Tribes of North East India (ed) S. Karotemprel, 1-28, Firma K.L.M., Calcutta.

36. (1984b), "Recent Advances in Prehistory and Archaeology of North East India", Presidential Address, XI, Annual Conference of ISPQS, Gauhati.

37. (1991), "Prehistoric situation in Northeast India", in Archaeology of Northeastern India (ed) J.P.Singh and Gautam Sengupta, 41-58, Har Anand Publications, in association with Vikas Publication House, New Delhi.

38. (1998), "Prehistoric and Archaeological sources for the History of Nagaland", Bulletin of Assam State Museum, No. XIV, 19-35, Directorate of Museum, Gauhati.

39. Singh, S. and Chowdhary, P. K. (1990). "An Outline of the Geological Framework of the Arunachal Himalaya", *Journal of Himalayan Geology*, Vol. (2) Dehradun, pp. 189-197.

40. Steel, E.H. (1870), Celt found among the Namsang Nagas, Proceeding of Asiatic Society of Bengal (PASB), 267-268, Calcutta.

41. Stonor, C.R. (1952(, The Sulung Tribe of the Assam Himalayas, Anthropos, Vol. 47, p. 50, London.

42. Thapar, B.K., (1985), Recent Archaeological Discoveries in India, UNESCO, Paris & the centre for East Asian Cultural Studies, Tokyo.

43. Wheeler, R.E.M., (1947-48), Brahmagiri and Chandravali – Ancient India, 4, 180-310 A.S.I., New Delhi.

44. (1959), Early India and Pakistan, Thames and Hudson, London.

45. Worman, E.C., (1949), "The Neolithic Problem in the Prehistory of India", Journal of Washington Academy of Science, 39 (6), 181-201, Washington.

11

Excavated Sites of Arunachal Pradesh

Byomakesh Tripathy

The North East Frontier State of Aruanchal Pradesh is the meeting ground of various cultures, since early period. Geography has undoubtedly played an important role in the flourishing of distinct cultural heritage in difference parts of the state. One can locate Buddhist heritage – both of *Mahayana* and *Hinayana* affiliations in western-northern and eastern frontier of the state; in the foothills, influence of Brahmaputra valley culture can be discerned. Where in the central part of the state, the heritage of the Tane people is preserved by a number of tribes, following their indigenous faiths and beliefs system. It is to be noted here that in the foothills area of the state, a number of archaeological sites are being explored and excavated by the research department of Arunachal Pradesh after independence. In this paper, an attempt has been made to present the archaeological findings of all the excavated sites of the state, as a source of the history of Arunachal Pradesh.

Bhishmaknagar

The archaeological site of Bhishmaknagar[1] is located about 29 km east of Roing, Lower Dibang Valley district, on a plateau like land in the foothill area. The Research Department of NEFA, excavated the site in 1969-72, which yielded remains of a fortress, pottery, terracotta art object, decorative tiles, inscribed bricks, etc.[2] The mountain provides natural defence on three sides and the construction was made in such a way, to prevent any southern aggression and hence, the fort took an elongated semi-circular shape. The earthern rampart is about 4.5 mts high and 6 mts. in width and continues for more than 5 kms with occasional gaps. The fort has an extent of approximately 10 sq. kms. In the centre of the complex, remains of a brick built structure, may be a part of palace, can be identified. It has a plinth area of 1860.52 sq. metrs. The central structure is having three halls, the extension rooms and six entrances. A stone wall of a height of 1.5 meter surrounds the building; the remains of which are still identified. The brick walls of the palace is about 1 meter high. The base of the exterior of the building is covered with an offset of the bricks, while the walls stand almost on a natural soil. Tiles with decorative motifs were fixed on the innerside of the boundary walls. No brick soiling is noticed on the floor. On the eastern and western sides of the fortress, two impressive gates are found. The western gate is larger having two rooms attached to it, while the eastern one has only one room. The direction of the gate is significant, as an early straight entry through them is blocked and a left turn made necessary. However, the condition of both the gates are highly dilapidated. The western gate is facing the north, while the eastern gate is facing the south.

The assemblage of Bhishmaknagar pottery can be broadly divided into two types – one having made out of well-levigated clay and the other one of a coarser variety. The ceramics are basically red in colour and wheel-turn, unknown to this region. The important shapes are bows, dishes, dish on stand, spouted vessels, jar, decorative finials etc. These wheel-turned and fine potteries bear close affinity with the potsherds excavated from Ambari site in Gauhati, of *c* 10th -12th century AD. Among the terracotta objects, horse, elephant, tiger, plaques having animal and floral design, roof tiles, etc. have been recovered. A number of inscribed brick tiles have come from the excavation. The tiles depict two combating tigers on one side and on the other side, two elephants facing each other. A few tiles are having the depiction of two combating lines in stylish form with an inscription, written around the animal motifs in Bengali-Assamese script of medieval period in Sanskrit language; it goes likewise *"Japatta Sri Sri Laksmi Narayanam"*.

Explorations in the area, have also unearthed a single piece of inscribed brick with depiction of lions, a broken piece of tiger having prominent teeth, a terracotta deer plaque etc. In 1905, T. Bloch, trekking along the outer wall of the fortress, made an archaeological exploration of the area and collected some tiles bearing carving of animals, birds, human figures, floral and geometric motif. [3] The Assam State Museum houses a few terracotta sculptures noticed from Bhishmiknagar. These include a male figure in standing posture, a human figure in walking attitude, two warriors, a male and a female standing and a rowing scene. Infact rowing scene depicted in sculpture is extremely rare in Northeast India.[4]

The architecture of the fortress indicates to a well laid out plan and high degree of expertise. The pottery and terracottas of the site reveal the cultural contact of the area with Brahmaputra civilization.[5] Hannay even believes that the specimens of earthern wares discovered from the ruins of Sadiya (including Bhishmaknagar) bears close affinity to those found in Gangetic Valley.[6] The short inscription mentions the popularity of Visnu worship at least during the period in the adjoining region. Here it may be mentioned that Hannay during his exploration of Bhashmaknagar area, came across a sculpture of Krishna, a fine specimen of the early medieval sculptural art.[7]

The ruins at Bhishmaknagar is believed to be associated with king Bhishmak of the *Mahabharata* fame as the local people, the Idu Mishmis have a tradition that king Bhishmak and princess Rukmini hailed form Mishmi hill region. However, this seems to be a later tradition. As regards the authorship of Bhishmaknagar fortress, it is definite that the site belongs to early medieval period and most probably constructed by the Pala or Chutiya rulers of Assam between *c* 11th to 13th centuries AD.

Rukmininagar

About 12 kms north of Roing in the Lower Dibang Valley district, a hill fort in found known as Rukmininagar fort extended over two Idu Mishmi villages of Chidu and Chimiri.[8] The earthquake of 1950 however, have completely destroyed the remains of the fort of Chidu village. In 1973-74, excavation by Directorate of Research, Govt. of Arunachal Pradesh, have unearthed two brick built rooms, measuring 10m x 10m and 10m × 12m, the brick structure upto plinth leval is still existing. Exploration in subsequent years have traced out another debris of brick on the northern hill of Chimri village. This site is called as *'Rukmini Nat'* in local language meaning bricks of Rukmi or the palace of Rukmini. The place is associated by the local people with the Krishna and Rukmini legend of the *Mahabharata* fame. Large number of Potteries, red in colour, wheel-turned, with good texture and made out of well levigated clay, are noticed. The shapes of the potteries, their types, manufacturing technique etc. are comparaele with those of Bhishmaknagar. A date of *c* 10th – 12th century may be ascribed to the fort.

Sivalinga Temple

The Site of *Siva-Linga* temple is located about 8 miles north east of Paya inspection bunglow, on the way from Sadiya to Tezu. It is hardly 5 kms from the site of the famous *Tamresvari* temple of Sadiya. During excavation at the site in 1965-1966,[9] two brick built structures were unearthed. A solid cube of 0.915 meter enshrising a huge *Siva Linga* made of granite, of 1.06 mts high and a little away, another cylindrical foundation of 1.20 mts diameter were noticed. Together, these structures have been identified as part of a Siva temple, of medieval period. The bricks used are well burnt and larger in size as comparable to those of Bhishmaknagar. The site way is dated to *c* 14th – 15th century AD. A new construction has been made on the debris of old temple. The excavation reveals that Brahmanical culture flourished in the foothill area of Lower Dibang Valley of Aruanchal Pradesh.

Vijoynagar Stupa

Vijoynagar is an outpost in the eastern most corner of the Changlang district of Arunachal Pradesh, near the Indo-Myanmar border and 145 miles from Margherita in Assam.[10] Exploration and excavation of the site was undertaken in 1971 by Y.A. Raiker of Research Department of Arunachal Pradesh. During exploration, a brick structure (a *stupa*), locally called as *Kangmu*, came to the limelight. It was an octagonal edifice. The monument is heavily damaged. It seems that the *stupa* had an octagonal base with relief designs or, and the central tumulus bult over it.

An imaginative reconstruction makes the excavator to believe that originally, the *stupa* must have been a massive pile composed of a conical structure, superimposed on an octagonal base. The octagonal platform, about 2.13 m high, is said to be horizontally divided into three zones, the lowest one broadest at the bottom (2.44m), rises in five diminishing ting terraces. Over the lower terraces, one can notice the slender most middle portion (1.62m wide) while the upper zone is said to have widened out in the extending tiers. On the frontal portions of the octagonal platform, roseets marks have been introduced in base relief. Further, on each of the eight corners of the platform, seated on Semi-circular bases are small solid domes and in between these corner members, can be seen similar domes placed on Vshaped seats. The excavator is of the opinion that most probably, there were sixteen miniature domes in the original stupa as a whole. The central tumulus of the *stupa*, which is completely lost at present, was probably a conical super structure, wich was crowned by a tapering finial ending either in multi formed umbrella or a pointed one. According to the excavater, originally the *stupa* could have been 8m high. The whole edifice is a brick structure with an external plaster in lime concrete.

The excavation has yielded few flat images of Buddha, made of quartz amber, steatite, clay besides of small metal images of alloy mainly of lead numbering fifty, which are very significant findings. These images which are now preserved at Jawaharlal Nehru State Museum, Itanagar can be categorized into two groups – the larger ones have a replica of the *stupa* on the reverse and the smaller ones bear a pointed vertical column at the back. One interesting point to observe in these images is that all of them have the curious horn like protuberance on the crown of the head, tapering to a point, which is typical of images from Burma and Siam. Besies, a few potsherds and an octagonal silver coin of Ahom king Gaurinath Singha (1780-1797) are being reported from the site.

As a whole the structure lacks uniformity and the execution reflects imperfect in many respects. The whole edifice is a modest work of architecture. The structure is made of bricks with external plaster in lime concrete. The *stupa* is of *uddeshika* type and stylistically may be compard with the medieval *stupas* such as that of Himawza and Pagan of Burma and adjoining Thailand area.[11] It is believed that while the Khamtis migrated from upper Burma to their present settlement in Lohit area, they settled for sometimes at Vijoyanagar (earlier called *Khomong*) in late 18th century and to cater their religious need, they built this modest but very important *stupa*. The findings of the Ahom silver coin from the excavation do indicate that when the Ahom currency was in use, the Buddhist *stupa* site of Vijoyanagar was a living center and the piligrims of Assam used to visit the sacred site. Taking all the above things into consideration, the *stupa* may be assigned a date of late 18th century AD.

Ita-Fort

The Itafort, from which the modern name Itanagar originated, is an important medieval archaeological site of the state. The earliest refernce to remains of Itafort is noticed in the writings of B.C.Allen in the Lakhimpur Gazeetter of Assam of 1901 which mentions that in the valley of Barapani, about two days journey from Harmoti garden into the Nyishi country, there are the ruins of an old city. He further narrates that two brick walls about one metre in breadth run parallel to one another at a distance of about a mile.[12] Captain G.S.Lightfoot, the then Political Officer, visited the Ita area in 1929 and 1941, but did not mention anything about the Itafort ruins.[13] In 1942 D.N.Das had visited the site and tells us about a fort on Hita, where in ancient times a refugee king from Assam built the fort.[14] Later on the Research Department of Arunachal Pradesh, has surveyed, and excavated the remains of the fort. The excavation was undertaken earlier by Y.A.Raiker (1974-77), followed by D.K.Bora (1996).[15]

This monument, which is in ruins at present, is the part of a big fort complex. It is a brick built fortified area of an irregular shape, partly man-made and partly natural. It is enclosed by natural ridges and brick ramparts, closing the western and eastern flanks. To the north and sourth are the ridges and steep cliff, affording adequate defence to the fort. Of the two ramparts, the western one runs for almost one and a half kilometer long. The eastern rampart is having only one gate, while the western one has two gates. The average width of the rampart is 1.5 mtr and the original height could be of 5 mtr. In the north and sourth, irregaluer steep ridge of more than a kilometer length each, provide natural defence. The area of more than a square kilometer, thus fortified, is sloping from south to north.

Three gates of varying sizes are noticed in eastern, southern and westen directions. The eastern gate, the highest point of the fort is heavily damaged one. Built on stone masonary, this gate overlooks Doimukh in the Dikrong valley. The southern gate facing Gohpur and Ramghat area in the sourth, is built largely in bricks and with limited use of stone and stone slabs. Animated and floral designs were used for the doorways. The southern gate, most probably being the main entrance to the fort, was heavily built having provisions for round the clock sentry. Two cells on either side of the interior face of the southern gate were probably used for the sentry. Of these two cells, the left one had an opening passage with corridor parallel to the wall of the gate. Most probably high wooden doors were fixed at the gates, which have perished so far. The eastern gate probably remained close unless situation demanded, otherwise, as one does not find any provision of sentry, as noticed near the southern gate. The western gate faces the river Senkhi and the ruins at the gate reveals that comparatively less defence arrangements existed in this area. Out of the three gates, the eastern and the western gates are so strategically located that one can have a commanding view of Assam plain below. From the southern gate, one could command a view upto Gohpur Ramghat and Pisoka, which definitely would have helped to detect any attack from these area concerned.

No standing structure of any sort is noticed inside the fort area. However, scattered brickbats in various parts of Itafort area provide some ideas regarding ruins of some medieval settlements inside the fort. The fort is built of bricks as well as of stones. The bricks are of variety of sizes, including the ornamental bricks. The stones used are mainly sand stone. The bricks used are typically medieval and a few of pre-Ahom period as well. One of the significant aspects is that no binding material such as lime mortar was used except the mud. The entire brick rampart laid on mud mortar, tells the story of a developed engineering feat. Iron clamps and nails were used in the construction of fort.

Among other remains, mention may be made of a few potteries recovered from the site. The pottery from Itafort site is of a coarse variety and is heavily damaged; shapes like bowls, pots, spouted vessel etc. can be identified. A piece of pottery (spout) unearthed from the site, has a large content of kaolin in it. It may be mentioned here that kaolin pottery is one of the basic characteristics of medieval pottery of Brahmaputra valley.[16] The fort belongs to the category of forest (hill) fort and has an elongated semi-circular shape as prescribed by Kautilya in his Arthasastra.[17] The remains of the fort indeed provides an idea of the development of the fort architecture in the foot hills of Arunachal Pradesh.

There are no literary or archaeological evidences, which provide information about the date and the builder of the Itafort. Scholars generally ascribe the Itafort to one Ramachandra, a king of Jitari dynasty, who is said to have constructed the fort in between 1350 to 1450 AD.[18] Some other scholar believe that the Itafort was built by the Ahom king Chakradhvaj Simha in 1668 AD.[19] However, amidst different opinions, it may be certainly told that the fort was constructed during 16th -17th century, as a scrutiny of archaeological data makes us to believe.

Malinithan

The historical site of Malinithan is located in the foothills of Likabali sub-division of West Siang district of the State.[20] The site is on a hillock of about 21 m height that overlook the mighty Brahmaputra, flowing about 5 kms away. The site was noticed by an Assistant Political Officer of Sadiya region W.H. calvert, who visited the Abor hill in the years 1936-1939. Subsequently after independence, Sri Dharmeswara Baruah, the Base Superintendent and Sri B.C.Bhuyan, Political Officer visited the ruins of Malinithan. L.N.Chakraborty, the then Director of Department of Research, NEFA administration, for the first time made an intensive field survey of the area in 1968 and during 197-72, excavated the site, unearthing more than hundred masterpieces of stone images of Hindu Gods and goddesses along with beautifully decorated plinth of temple, which reveal the plan of a full fledged Brahmanical temple complex of early medieval period. The second phase of excavation is still progressing on the site.

The excavations conducted in the first phase, have yielded bases of three temples, aligning in the east-west direction. The first base, located in the eastern most flank, arranged in a rectangular plan on a slanting position. The second base is larger in size and unique among the prevailing types in the site in the sense that it has three unequal rectangular plans, which may be identified as the *Mukhamandapa*, *Antarala* and *Garbhagriha*. The plan of the temple in east west direction, approximately measures 31 m in length and 10.30 mts in breadth. Adjacent to the north of the *Mukhamandapa*, can be noticed a base of miniature temple, which was perhaps the place, where the Nandi image was installed. The *Mukhamandapa* is connected with two flight of steps from its western and eastern arms respectively, which were probably used for entry and exit. The *antarala* is in a dilapidated condition and some of its courses of stone blocks reveal outer façade carvings in the form of scroll creepers and geometrical designs. The garbhagriha like the other two buildings is built of stone with geometrical, and scroll designs etc. From the smaller peripheries of the temple bases, it may be observed that provision of the circumbulation was kept around the ground level of the temple. Architecturally, the temple plan follows the *Nagara* school of temple architecture of medieval period and has similarity with the temple plans of Da-Parvatiya temple near Tezpur, Guptesvara temple of Singri, and of Madan-Kamadeva temple near Baihata Chariali of Guwahati, all in Assam.[21] Asmanya architecture was followed in construction of the temple. The masons had adopted dryasylar masonary technique. There is total absence of bricks in the site, which distinguishes it from other archaeological site of the state. The plinth had *Ratha* design, a common architecture feature in Orissa style temples. Iron clamps, nails and pins were used. Stone beams were placed horizontally and above it a *sikhara* like super structure or the temple had a shrine superimposed by curvilinear *Sikhara* with a square astylar *mandapa* with pyramidal roof of horizontal tiers. The third temple base is noticed in the extreme western boundary from the main temple base and at a distance of 200 mts from the main temple site. The temple base is arranged on a rectangular plan but it is completely damaged during the laying out of a road. During the second phase of excavation, another base of a temple, some architectural fragments, and one stone drainage system has been unearthed.

During the excavations a number of Brahmanical sculptures are noticed; which includes that of *Dwarapala*, Guardian deity, scenes from social life, erotic scenes etc. An icon of Durga of late medieval period is worhipped in the modern temple in the site. She is in *tribhanga* posture, standing on her *vahana* lion, below her feet lies, the decapited head of buffalo from which neck, emerges the demon *Mahisasura*. The lion is shown holding the right elbow of *Mahisasura* by its claws. She is shown trampling the demon with her feet. The deity holds *trisula*, rosary, discuss, dagger and other attributes in her hands. Among other icons of *Devis*, a solitary icon of *varahi* and a few images of *sarasvati* and Lakshmi are found: A few saivite sculptures like those of *Siva Linga*, Siva, Nandi Bull are also noticed. A Sivaicon in *tandava* pose is an interesting specimen of the site. A fine image of *Nandi* Bull is carved seated on a crouching posture on a plain pedestal. Other *parivardevatas* of Siva such as Ganesha and Kartikeya are also represented in the site. Some fine images of Ganesha in sitting, standing and dancing postures are yielded from the site. A dancing Ganapati icon of granite is a fine specimen of medieval period and an independent image of Kartikaya, seating on *ardhaparyankasana*, with his *vahana* peacock is a prize specimen of the site. A solitary icon of Krishna and Radha is depicted on a corner pillar stone. Two images of Brahma with Savitri and Sarasvati on both sides are also recovered. One of the finest surya images of northeastern India, on a chariot, with various attendant figures like those of *Mahesvati, Nikshuba, Rajni usha, Pratyusha, Danda* and *Pingala* is also found. An icon of Indra on his *vahana Airavata* (elephant) is another fine piece of art. A few *rishis*, figures of *gandharvas, vidyadharas*, and social scenes of erotic sculptures also deserve our attention. The erotic sculptures explain the influence of tantricism in this region. The stone sculptures of the site could be divided into two categories, considering the raw materials and stylistic idiom. The first category of sculptures are made from granite, and a few sculptures like the big image of surya, Ganesha, Kartikaya and Indra belongs to this category and the second category of sculptures are made of sand stone, from which most of the sculptures of the sites were prepared. The best example of this category is the large size image of *Nandi* Bull and the presiding deity, Durga in the modern temple of Malinithan. Some of these images have stylistic affinities with

Orissan School of art and the Pala art of Bengal. The lion on elephant motif and the hairdress of various sculptures point to the influence of Orissan art. Here it may be pointed that during early medieval period. Assam had cultural interaction with Orissa[22] as well as Bengal.

On the whole, it can be mentioned that the architecture and sculptural tradition of Malinithan bears evidence of contact between various groups of people, having different cultural traits – indigenous and external. The relics give definite evidence of contact between various peoples, of the contribution of architects, sculptors and masons, who came to the foothills of Arunachal and Assam from time to time from the neighbouring states of the country. Stylistically, the ruins can be dated to *c* 10th – 12th century AD.

Naksaparvat

The site Naksaparvat comes under the Seijosa circle of East Kameng district and lies 27 km to the north of 52 NH at Biswanath Chariali in the Sonitpur district of Assam.[23] The site is located on the left bank of the river Borgang. The archaeological site of Naksaparvat was first visited by Late R.M.Nath in 1948, who published his observation on the Naksaparvat ruins in his book 'The background of Assamese culture'. In 1973, Sri G.C. Talukdar, published a short article on the ruins of the site in Arunachal Review. In 1978, D.K.Bora of Research Department of the State visited and explored the site. During his exploration, he noticed that the Naksaparvat was surrounded by a rampart and scattered with a number of fallen structures with stone pillars. The archaeological excavation was undertaken by D.K.Bora and his teams during 1985-1991. This is the only site where horizontal excavation has been undertaken in the state so far.

The archaeological site has an upper settlement and a lower one, as known from the surface findings and during excavations. The upper settlement of Naksaparvat is fortified by a rampart, partly of earth and partly of stone. The whole area within the fortification was taken for excavation by grid method. Each name such as NAKSA-1, 2, 3, and so on. Altogether at 24 places, which had ruins lying scattered over them, is subjected to excavation. The settlement pattern of the site exhibits two distinct types of rampart – (i) the settlement of the Royals (upper settlement) and (ii) the settlement of the common people or upper lower settlement. The upper settlement, perhaps the settlement of the Royals, is surrounded by two distinct ramparts, one of earth and the other made of sand stone blocks. The earthen rampart covers the western and northern sides of the settlement. A wide rampart has also been noticed as an extension of the northern rampart. The present height of rampart is about 1.5 mts, and its length is 620 mts. The stone rampart is in the form of a thick wall, made out of sand stone blocks. This defensive wall was constructed on the southern part of the site and in the south-western corner, a passage is noticed between the earthen and the stone rampart, which was most probably connecting the upper settlement with the lower settlement of the common people. The length of the stone rampart is about 230 mts. Just below, on the southeastern corner of the upper settlement, a large rectangular pond where a soak pit or sedimentation tank is noticed, which perhaps acted as a filtering device against the inflow of hilly water. Another pond is located outside the rampart to the north.

The lower settlement area, covering about four hectares of land, belongs to the same age as that of upper settlement. The excavator has noticed remains of ordinary hut, made of perishable materials almost over the ground and hence, believe that the area was inhabited by the common people. A factory of blacksmith is identified in the lower settlement area.

During the excavation, two different types of house remains are encountered. One was the piled houses, which were constructed with perishable materials like bamboo and planks, supported by long wooden beams and secondly the normal houses with floor of bricks bats and pebbles, the top was covered with mud plaster. Sometimes, floor having a brick platform or with a floor of undressed stone blocks are also noticed. Superstructure of the houses at the site was of perishable materials.

The site has yielded a good amount of pottery, stone sculptures, iron objects of household implements and weapons, etc. beads, glass objects, bangles, a number of engraved stones and a solitary silver coin. The pottery of the site is both wheel thrown and handmade; the percentage of handmade pottery is minimum. However, these handmade potteries are kiln-burnt.

The wheel turned pottery is of red slip in surface treatment, and well levigated and somewhat weathered. The shapes noticed in the pottery are those of storage jar, vase, pitcher, cooking pot, bowl, long necked pitcher, etc. A few stone sculptures, twenty in numbers, are yielded from the excavated site. Among them are eight columns of fine-grained sand stone, having engravings of figures, such as, human, plants, animals, birds, reptiles etc. The engravings are bold, simple and crude and represent socio-cultural-religious life of the people. The physiognomy of the people as represented in sculptural art reveals mongoloid feature. The male figure represents warrior sometimes with a dagger or club in his one hand or engaged in wrestling; some figures of dancing male are also identified. Female in sitting posture, with a sword, in standing posture, holding a lotus in one of her hands are also found. A few specimens of art of the site are preserved in state museum, Gauhati. These are specimens of tribal art of medieval period. The building materials *i.e.,* the stone bear some engraved symbols or markings on its body, with both geometric and non-geometric figures, which are more or less hieroglyphic in character. As many as 40 different types of symbols like a bow with an arrow or a triangle with a pair of antennae or a set vertical strokes etc. are encountered at the site. The excavator believes that these are the identification marks denoting or segregating different groups of masons amongst themselves.

A few beads only seven in numbers, made of stone, glass and terracotta are noticed. The site has yielded a large number of Iron objects in the form of household implements, weapons, house-building materials etc. The weapons include offensive objects like different types of arrowhead, spearhead, pointed rods, etc. A few glass objects, similar to those of Ambari findings, have been excavated, from strata, of late medieval period, associated, with the Mughal glazed ware.[24] A solitary silver coin was unearthed from the upper settlement, which belongs to the Nawab of Bengal. The obverse and reverse of the coin is impressed in Persian script. On the obverse, it is written *"Aas sultan-e-Alam Samuddin (Samsuddin) Abul Majaffar Shah Alam"*, and on the reverse is *"Tow sad Samsuddin Al Alam Ahed Attacha"*. This Muslim coin would have come to the site, from the neighbouring area of Biswanath, which was the scene of contest between Ahoms and the Mughals from 16th century onwards.

On the basis of stylistic consideration of stone sculptures and other antiquities from the site, it can be dated to the 15th – 16th century AD. The site is a single culture site and for the first time, provides an idea of socio-economic-cultural life of the foothills people of Arunachal. The excavation is of immense importance for the study of medieval life of the people of Arunachal, as other medieval sources of the state like the *Buranjis* do not provide enough materials for the reconstruction of medieval society and economy of the state.

Parsi-Parlo

The site of Parsi-Parlo is noticed in the Kamla valley during 1979, in the district of Lower Subansiri. The site was excavated during 1982-1984.[25] This is the only prehistoric excavated site of a single culture, (Neolithic culture), which can be divided into aceramic Neolithic, Neolithic and Ferrolithic phase. In the aceramic phase, tool kits are essentially Paleolithic, represented by scrappers, large cutting tools with ground and polished technique (which is a hall mark of Neolithic age). The phase is considered as a transitional phase between Paleolithic and Neolithic age. There is a complete absence of pottery in this phase. The aceramic stage is characterized by the continuation of the preceding phase, but without scrapper, large cutting tools. Pottery appeared in this period, having square grid and honey comb, beater impressed design. The ferrolethic phase saw the continuation of Neolithic tools, but it witnesses the use of iron implements. A single piece of iron implement in the form of a blade of a scraper is recovered from the site. Pottery noticed in this phase are like those of ceramic stage. No structural remains are noticed, which point out that Parsi-Parlo was an open air camp site. The pottery are of rounded bottom without turned rim, rounded bottom with splayed out rim, or rimless bowl, with cord impressed square grid and honey comb design.

The most interesting aspect of Parsi-Parlo is the occurrence of an iron tool in the site. It is not known whether the technology was a local innovation or had been brought from the neighbouring area. The occurrence of iron provides a date of *c* 1000 B.C or less to the upper phase of the site and as such the site may be given a time period of *c* 1500-1000 B.C.[26] or less. However, we can not rely on a single piece in the state. But the remains of the site prove that in the state, Paleolithic tradition developed to the Neolithic tradition through aceramic and ceramic Neolithic phase which perhaps succeeded by Iron Age.

Conclusion

A survey of the excavated sites indicate that the antiquities recovered provide an idea of the history of the state from prehistoric to late medieval period. The remains of the foothills are influenced by Brahmaputra valley culture. However, the ruins at Naksaparavat reveals the blending of indigenous and Brahmaputra valley culture. So far, excavations are limited, for which no comprehensive knowledge of the sites is known to the scholars. It is hoped that future explorations and excavations in a scientific way, would throw new light on the history and culture of the state.

References

1. J.F. Michell, The North East Frontier of India, New Delhi, 1973, pp. 64, 115-116.
2. Y.A. Raiker, Bhishmaknagar: A Forgotten Chapter in the History of Arunachal Pradesh, Arunachal News, Vol. 1 (2), March, 1972, Shillong, pp. 31-36.
3. T. Bloch, Report of the Archaeological Tours in Assam, Jan-Feb, Calcutta, 1905.
4. R.D.Choudhury, Archaeology of the Brahmaputra Valley of Assam, New Delhi, 1985, pp. 167-168.
5. Rajatnanda Dasgupta, Art of Medieval Assam, New Delhi, 1982, p. 92.
6. S.F. Hanney, "Notes on Ancient Temples and other Remains in the Vicinity of Suddiya, Upper Asam", Journal of Asiatic Society of Bengal, Cal. 1848, June, pp. 466-67.
7. *Ibid.*, pp. 471-72.
8. Y.A. Raiker, "Rukmini Nati: The Widening Horizon of Bhishmaknagar, Arunachal News, 3 (7), October, Itanagar, 1974, pp. 2-6.
9. L.N. Chakravarty, "Early History of Lohit District", Resarun, 4 (1), Jan-Mar, Itanagar, 1978, pp. 1-6.
10. Y.A. Raiker, Vijaynagar: "The Forgotten Khomong" (a small booklet) published by Research Department of Arunachal Pradesh), Shillong, 1974.

11. Rajannubhab Damrong, History of the Buddhist stupas in Siam, Bangkok, 1926.
12. B.C. Allen, Assam District Gazetteers, Vol.VIII, Calcutta, 1905, p. 99.
13. G.S. Lightfoot, Extracts from the Tour Diary of Political Officer, Balipara Frontirer Tract from the Month of March-April, 1941
14. D.N. Das, "Ruins of Mayapur", Journal of the Assam Research Society (JARS), Vol. III, Gauhati, 1949.
15. D.K. Bora, History and Archaeology of Itanagar, Itanagar, 1996, pp. 21-24.
16. N.P. Choudhury, Historical Archaeology of Assam, New Delhi, 1985.
17. P.C. Choudhury, The History of Civilization of the People of Assam, to the twelfth century AD, Guwahati, (Revised, Third edition), 1987, p. 272.
18. *Ibid.*, p. 292.
19. Lila Gogoi, The Buranjis-Historical Literature of Assam, New Delhi, 1986, p. 55.
20. L.N. Chakraborty, Malinithan: Heritage of Arunachal Pradesh (ND), published by Director of Information and Public Relation, Arunachal Pradesh Administration.
21. P.C. Sarma, Architecture of Assam, Delhi, 1988, pp. 134-35.
22. B. Tripathy, "Orissa and North East India – A study in Cultural Interaction", in A.C.Pradhan et. al. (ed.), Utkal Hisotical Research Journal, vol.XVII, Bhubaneswar, 2004, pp. 45-53.
23. D.K. Bora, *et. al.*, Medieval Life at Naksaparvat, Itanagar, 1997.
24. T.C. Sharma, "Excavation at Ambari (Guwahati), its problems and prospects" in J.B.Bhattacharjee (ed.), Proceedings of NEIHA, Shillong, 1990, pp. 21-24.
25. A.A. Ashraf, Prehistoric Arunachal, Itanagar, 1990, pp. 37-40.
26. T.C. Sharma, "Prehistoric Situation in North East India", J.P. Singh & Gautam Sengupta (eds), Archaeology of North Eastern India, New Delhi, 1991, pp. 41-58.

12

Sources of Economic History of Arunachal pradesh

J.B. Ganguly

Economic history of any territory should indicate the economic well-being or problems of its people in the past and changes thereof over the chosen period of time. In a developed monetized economy such changes are quantified in the estimation of the growth, stagnation or decline in the gross domestic product. GDP measures the value of total production of goods and services and earnings from external trade. For simple, non-monetized barter exchange economies or for economies having both barter and monetized exchange transaction systems, statistical estimation GDP and its change over time is extremely difficult and imprecise if at all.

The process of production of goods and services entails application of human labour power and non-human energy available and mobilized resources and capital goods. The volume of output is determined by not only the quantum of employment of labour, capital and resources but also the productive efficiency of labour which is a function of technology of production, health of labour, working conditions, motivation of labour to produce more, and the entrepreneurial efficiency. Technology is developed and adopted by human beings whose ability to innovate technology depends on the level of development of the human resource itself. And education, training, experience, culture, ideology, etc. largely shape the potential of human resource.

In pre-market economies, growth of population itself, results in increased investment of working capital in the sense that the households are compelled to cut short the leisure time of its members to be able to produce more to feed increased number of mouths. Therefore population growth up to a certain limit promotes growth of output of goods and services. Therefore as a surrogate for measuring economic growth, the population growth may be enumerated.

Economic history should explain the structure and performance of economies through time. This structure is exemplified by the political and economic institutions, such as, property ownership system, political set up, demography, technology and ideology. Any change in any one or more than one element of the structure may cause a change in the performance of the economy.

In the absence of a fully monetized system of transactions, economic growth may be ascertained by estimating population growth, capital formation, technological change and what Fernand Braudel has termed as portrayal of material life of people, in other words, the structures of every day life, which indicates the limits of the possible. The language of economic science deals with to 'transparent visible realities' about 'production, exchange linked to rural activities, to small shops and workshops, to banks, exchanges, fairs and (of course) markets'. 'But there is another, shadowy zone, often hard to see for lack of historical document, lying underneath the market economy: this is that elementary basic activity which went on everywhere and the volume of which is truly fantastic. This rich zone, like a layer covering the earth, may be called for want of a better expression *material life or material civilization*'.[1] This includes foods of the masses, drinks, stimulants and drugs, houses, interiors of houses, costumes, fashion, sources of energy, metallurgy, transport, money, etc. These facts about the life of the tribal people of Arunachal Pradesh in the Pre-colonial and colonial period need to be noted for they represent the varied dimensions of their social and economic conditions in these periods. These facts would throw light on the limits of the possible level of economic development.

In the pre-colonial period most of the tribes, but not all, were in the pre-literate stage who do not have any written records of their origin, migration, productive activities, technology, size of population, etc. But oral traditions, folklores, song folk tales told at the time of performing *pujas* and festivals, etc. may provide some insights into their structures of everyday life and productive activities. These facts, of course, would need to be compared with other sources, such as, historical accounts of the neighbouring kingdom, namely, the Ahom *Buranjis*, accounts of travellers, etc. The tendency of glorifying the past on the basis of mythologies must be shunned as this will cause loss of objective narration of the reality.

Growth of population may be estimated by ascertaining the changes in the number of villages and migration of tribal households concerned, using up of forests in the process of shifting cultivation etc. During the colonial period annual administrative reports have accounts of the people, their customs, agricultural produces, cottage industries, the land system, natural resources, law and order situation, natural calamities, inter-tribal and tribal-British relations, educational and health care facilities, etc. Besides, some travellers, ethnographers, missionaries, planters, et. al. also wrote about the people, their profession and activities, etc. Since 1871, the work of compilation of decadal census of population began in the country. Population censuses for this part of the country were also conducted though not on an exhaustive basis and results were included in the reports on the censuses of Assam. These reports not only indicate the territorial spreads and size of population but also people's occupations or means of livelihood, education, health conditions, etc. Other official publications of that period include gazetteers, statistical accounts and survey reports. These publications are helpful in constructing the history of the people of Arunachal Pradesh, no doubt, but these official texts must be critically examined and compared with other historical evidences.

Local tribal economic histories may be constructed by meticulously and methodically analyzing and evaluating comparatively by referring to general historical developments, accounts of migration pattern, ways of life, relations with the plains people, land management system, control over access to productive resources like forests, water bodies, etc. may be compiled. The questions that require to be resolved may be: (i) when did the tribe concerned started using iron tools in place of Neolithic tools; (ii) when and why could a tribe take to sedentary terrace cultivation in place of shifting cultivation and what was the change in land ownership system; (iii) when did a tribe learn about and acquire firearms for use and what were the social, economic and cultural impacts of this development, etc.

In the pre-colonial period several tribes carried out trade with not only the neighbouring tribes but also Tibet, Bhutan, Assam, etc. Details about such trade and its contribution to development of technology, acquisition of new consumption and capital goods, etc. need to be portrayed.

Some of the tribes collected rent from the neighbouring foothill villages in Assam later came to be known as the *posa* system. Details about the practice and its magnitude and impact on the economy of the tribe should be objectively analyzed.

The system of slavery as one of the means of labour was prevailed among some of the tribes. The truth about this system particularly the master-slave relations having an impact on the productivity of labour needs to be brought out. Some of the tribes took to opium consumption. When and why was this habit acquired and what was the resultant impacts on their health, productive ability need to be bought out.

Reference

1. Fernand Bruadel, Civilization and Capitalism, 15th –19th Century, London, 1986, p. 25.

13

Ahom Documents and their Importance as Source of History of Arunachal Pradesh

J.N. Phukan

Geographically the territory of Arunachal Pradesh is mostly hilly and lies immediately to the east and north of Assam. The three districts of Arunachal viz. Tirap, Changlang and Lohit lie to the east, and the rest are to the north of Assam. Assam and Arunachal had been and still are close neighbours. Naturally, therefore, it could be well-imagined that those who lived in the immediate vicinity or near the border of the two contiguous units had some sort of relations between them irrespective of the political power or powers that held sway over these territories. And this situation must have been going on since the time of human settlement along the bordering region of Assam and Arunachal Pradesh. The history of relations between Assam and Arunachal Pradesh thus goes back to many centuries past. But not much detail is known about the actual relations and the people involved in such relations before the thirteenth century.

But from the early thirteenth century AD we possess firmer evidences about the people of Arunachal and their land in the Ahom documents. I would, therefore, confine myself to these Ahom documents as source and their importance in reconstructing the history of Arunachal Pradesh.

The Ahom Documents

The Ahom, a Tai people who came from Mong Mao in Yunnan to the Brahmaputra valley in the early thirteenth century, had with them a system of keeping records of events concerning their king and the kingdom. The recording of events continued all through the Ahom rule of six hundred years. Such records constitute the bulk of the Ahom chronicles generally known as *Burnajji*. *Buranjis* are a mine of information of various happenings that took place during the period from the early thirteenth century to the early nineteenth century. As the Ahom were *Tai* speaking people and had their script, all early Ahom chronicles were written in the *Tai* (Ahom) language only. It was since about the beginning of the seventeenth century that chronicles were also compiled in Assamese language, and at the same time the compilation of chronicles in Ahom language continued till the end of the Ahom rule in 1826. Today we are thus in possession of chronicles in two languages – Ahom and Assamese. Information contained in the *Buranji* is considered reliable and trustworthy. A good number of chronicles of the Ahom period are available to us. Of these several Assamese language *Buranjis* and one Ahom language *buranji* (in original text in Ahom with English translation) have already been published. In addition to chronicles, the Ahom rulers had issued a good number of inscriptions in several languages. All these constitute the Ahom documents.

Although the Ahom documents are primarily concerned with the Ahoms themselves and their kingdom, occasional references often with some details about the people living in the hills surrounding the kingdom are come across from time to time. In this way the Ahom documents contain information of the Arunachal Pradesh or its people as well. In the absence of information in the Ahom documents we would have been much poorer in our knowledge of Arunachal and its people during the medieval period. The Ahom documents are therefore invaluable source for reconstructing the history of Arunachal.

It must, however be noted that information about Arunachal Pradesh or its people appears in the Ahom documents only in connection with activities of the of Arunachal people having bearing on the Ahom kingdom. Therefore such information or accounts of Arunachal are by no means systematic and complete. But all such information as found in the Ahom documents is highly valuable for two reasons (i) its trustworthiness, (ii) absence of other source.

Ahom Document as Source for Arunachal History

For a better understanding of the Ahom documents as source of history of Arunachal Pradesh, the land, viewing from the Assam side, may be arranged as follows: (1) the extreme eastern part comprising of the Patkai region, (2) the north eastern and central region comprising the territory roughly lying to the east of the Bharali river and (3) the western region lying to the west of the Bharali river. The extreme eastern region came in close contact with the Ahom since the early thirteenth century whereas the northeastern and central sectors became coterminous with the Ahom kingdom during the reign of king Siu-hum-mong (1497-1539) who annexed the Chutiya kingdom of Sadiya and the land of the Bhuyan chiefs. The western sector touched the boundary of the Ahom kingdom from the time of Ahom occupation of Darrang and Kamrup during the seventeenth century.

Seen in the light of the expansion of the Ahom kingdom, the eastern sector of Arunachal *i.e.,* the Patkai region had its longest period of contact with the Ahom, and hence more information about this sector can be expected in the Ahom documents. But in the western sector there was the shortest period of contact between the Ahom and Arunachal and hence less amount of information in the Ahom documents.

The Patkai Region in the Ahom Documents

The Patkai region of Arunachal Pradesh finds its earliest mention in the Ahom chronicles for the fact that the route followed by the Ahom to the Brahmaputra valley passed through it. But finding the valley around a lake called Nong Jang at the southern face of the Patkai Pass, the Ahom settled there for a few years and then turned into an Ahom colony under the charge of a governor. From the account given in the chronicles, it can be known that before reaching the Nong Jang Lake, he passed throught the country of Myen, identified as Naga. There were also Naga villages in the hills around the lake who confronted the Ahom but were ultimately defeated and made submission. The villages mentioned in the chronicles were Kha Ru Khu, Pung, Kang, Ti Thang, Bing Lao, Lal Te Ma, Lan Pang Kaw, and Ta Riu. On further advance to the Doi Kao Rang (now called Patkai), in the Upper and the lower range there were six Naga villages the name of which are given as Pa Puk, Teng Kham, Khun Khat, Khun Tang, Tang Ching and Ja Khang. At first they refused to submit and fought stubbornly. After a severe fight, they were defeated and were given a very harsh treatment was given to them. Seeing this other Naga villages in the neighbourhood submitted (the names and number slightly vary in different chronicles. (For details, Ahom Buranji = AB, 45; Deodhai Assam Buranji = DAB, 7-8; Satsari Assam Buranji = SAB, 46; Purani Asam Buranji = PAB, 46; Assam Buranji found in Sukumar Mahanta's family = ABSM, 6).

The Ahom settlement in the Khamjang valley continued under a governor throughout the Ahom period. The retention of this place was necessary to keep the route open that linked Assam with the Tai states to the east. The Patkai region and its people are recorded in the Ahom chronicles at different times on different occasions (AB, 52, 54, 83, 92, 134-39; PAB, 50; ABSM, 8, 9; DAB, 13, 15, 32-33, 40, 47-48; ABKTP, 18; ABD, 4-5; ABD, 4-5).

The North Eastern and Central Region

In this region lived the Mishmi, Mishing, Adi, Nyishi. The Mishmi appears as *"Michimi"* in the Assamese language chronicles, or *'Naga Michimi'* and *Mi-si-mi* in the Ahom documents (chronicles and inscriptions), are first mentioned in the Snake Pillar Inscription found near Sadiya (now in the Assam State Museum, Guwahati) in connection with a royal proclamation of king Siu-hum-mong (1497-1539). In this document they were asked not to cross the Dibang river to the other side, and to supply annually (to the Ahom government), a certain amount of *Kong* (poison). This is a very important document which provide us information on Mishmi territory to the west, their product, and relation with the Ahom government. In the Ahom chronicles references to them are not many. (ABHKB, 46; AB, 231-33, PAB, 160-62).

The Mishing appear in the Ahom documents as Miri, Sadiyal Miri, Chutiya Miri and Kha Kang Lai. The earliest reference to the Miri (Mishing) appears in the reign of Siu-seng-pha (1603-41). Thereafter they are recorded in the Ahom documents in a number of times. (ABHKB, 40; ABKTP, 32; ABD, 9-10, 32; AB, 153-54, 192-94, 267; PAB, 160-162; TB, 24-25).

The Nyishi Bagni appears as *Chungi Dafla* or *Pachima Dafla* in the Assamese language chorinicles, and *chungi* in the Ahom-language chronicles. They are mentioned in the chronicles a number of times. (DAB, 54-55, 82-83; ABSM, 48, 80, 124-25; PAB, 73, 162-64; BHKB, 40; AB, 132-36, 192-93, 219, 340-41; ABD, 31-32, 62, TB, 95, 98-100, 128-29, 141-43).

The Khamti

The Khamtis are latecomers to Arunachal Pradesh. They came sometime during the middle of the 18th century from Khamti Long in Burma, and settled near Sadiya. They appear in the chronicle when they caused trouble. (TB, 120, 147-48; AB, 364-65; SAB, 95-97).

The Bhutias

The people living in the hills on the western section to the north of Assam are generally called by the name Bhutia, which includes for our purpose Monpas and others. They appear in some chronicles towards the end of the seventeenth and the eighteenth centuries. (TB, 95, 151-55, 167-69, 179-81, JB, 152-58).

For utilizing the Ahom historical documents as source of history of Arunachal Pradesh, the information may be classified under several heads.

1. Various occasions, or events which led to recording of Arunachal Pradesh or its people in the Ahom documents. These may be raid, primitive expedition, collection of articles, *posa*, sending of emissary etc.
2. The date of such occasions in terms of reigning king in Assam, or year, month and day, if recorded.
3. Proper names of particular tribe, sub-tribe, clan, hills, rivers or stream, places (in term of geography) of villages and persons.
4. Arrangement of *Pal-sewa & Posa, of duar,* raising of rampart (*garh*).
5. Reference to polity in terms of *gam, raja,* village headman.
6. Products of the hills such as methun (bon fontalis), deer–hunting dog, *miri-jim* (a kind of blanket), *gartheon* (a kind of herbal root), *bih* (poison), *mishimi-teeta,* etc.

One of the problems is the proper identification of proper names, for, many of these appear in Ahom/Ahomised or Assamised forms. However, the information from various *Buranjis* if critically evaluated would through new light for the study of medieval history of Aruanchal Pradesh.

Some Ahom Documents

- Ahom Buranji (AB), ed., and translated into English by Golap Chandra Barua, first publisjed 1930.
- Assam Buranji found in Sukumar Mahanta's family (ABSM), ed by S.K.Bhuyan, first published 1945.
- Assam Buranji ed. by S.K. Dutta (ABD), first published, 1938.
- Deodhai Assam Buranji (DAB), ed. by S.K. Bhuyan, first published 1938.
- Assam Buranji by Kasinath Tamuli Phukan (ABKTP), first published 1844.
- Assam Buranji by Harakanta Barua (ABHKB), first published 1930.
- Satsari Asam Buranji (SAB), ed. by S.K. Bhuyan, 1964.
- Tungkhungiya Buranji (TB), ed. by S.K. Bhuyan, 1932.
- Jayantia Buranji (JB), compiled & ed. by S.K. Bhuyan, first published 1937.
- Snake Pillar Inscription in the Assam State Museum, *Annual Report of Archaeological Survey of India*, 1924-25.
- Besides the above there are other chronicles in the Ms in the Department of historical & Antiquarian Studies, Guwahati.

14

Sources of the History of Arunachal Pradesh: The Ahom Chronicles

I.S. Mumtaza

The Ahoms, who came to the Brahmaputra valley from Mong Mao-Lung in southwestern China in the early part of the thirteenth century, were the first, in the North East India, to introduce the system of recording their activities. From the time Siu-ka-pha left his native place, they recorded each stage of their march and occurrence, and also the people they came across or loss of any followers. This system they assiduously continued throughout their long rule of six hundred years in Assam and thus developed historiography of Assam. It is the Ahom chroniclers or record keepers, both officials and non-officials, who possessed a keen sense of history and wrote detailed account of happenings and political upheavals of the kingdom. The Ahom rulers and high officials as well employed chroniclers and court historians, who maintained profuse records of their activities, very often in systematic way, whom they came into contact, and thus recorded their historical and chronological order. In addition to these, they used to note down, whatever they could collect information about people or tribes with whom they came into contact, and thus recorded their historical anecdotes and chronological account of events. The Ahom age thus produced a good number of chronicles bequeathing to posterity a rich treasure of historical literature. These literary records are valuable source materials for reconstructing the history of the region as a whole and also constitute an important source history of individual tribe in the neighbouring hills. Like many other tribes in the North East India, the tribes of Arunachal Pradesh, too, do not have any old written documents of their won. But the Ahom chronicles constitute the most valuable as well reliable single source for the reconstruction for the history of Arunachal Pradesh particularly the period before the coming of the Europeans to the region. The present paper is an attempt to delineate the references to the tribes of Arunachal in the Ahom chronicles, which are valuable in the reconstruction of the history of Arunachal Pradesh.

The earlier literary records of the Ahoms are found in Tai, the original language of the Ahom. With consolidation and expansion of their kingdom in the valley of the Brahmaputra, the Ahom adopted local language *i.e.,* Assamese. Thus records were compiled, in addition to the Tai language, in Assamese too. Some of the chronicles have been published under different titles, such as, *Ahom Buranji,*[1] *Deodhai Asam Buranji,*[2] *Assam Buranji,*[3] *Purani Assam Buranji,*[4] *Assam Buranji,*[5] *Tungkhungia Buranji,*[6] *Assam Buranji,*[7] *Satsari Asam Buranji,*[8] *Asom Buranji Sara,*[9] *Assam Buranji,*[10] Kamrupar Buranji,[11] *Jayantia Buranji,*[12] *Tripura Buranji,*[13] *Asamar Padya-Buranji,*[14] *Kachari Buranji.*[15]

Although the relations between the hill people of the northern hill range (modern Arunachal Pradesh) and the plains people of the Brahmaputra valley have been existing since time immemorial in the absence of extensive historical literature it is difficult to know about them. It is the Ahom chronicles, *i.e., Buranji* of the Ahom; that occasional mentions have been made of the relations of the Ahom government on the one hand and the different tribes living in the hills around the kingdom on the other. The frequent references indicate that socio-economic relations of the systematic nature did take place along the passes in the foot hills that were created by the numerous river that came down the hills. The hill tribes normally came down along the courses of rivers to the plains and thus established a relation, and went back after a sojurn. Traditionally such passes are known as *duar* (door) in eastern India from Nepal eastward and it is through these *duars* that the people of Bhutan and present Arunachal Pradesh have been interaction with the plains people since long past. There were many such recognized *duars* between the Ahom territory and the hills of the tribes of Arunachal Pradesh. From the point of debauchment of Jia Dhansiri into the plain to Doimukh there were as many as nineteen *duars* linking these two territories.

The Patkai region of Arunachal Pradesh had great strategic importance to the Ahom rulers. It was through the Patkai that they came to the Brahmaputra valley and it was this route through which they had maintained their relations with other Tai rulers of Upper Burma and Southwestern China.[16] In order to ensure the safety of this route the Ahom rulers were ever vigilant and took prompt action to quell any disturbance in this region. Although the Ahom came into contact with the tribes of the northern hill range in the first quarter of the sixteenth century, after the annexation of the Chutiya Kingdom,[17] the *Buranjis* are silent on their relation for about next one hundred yeas. From the reign of Siu-Seng-Pha (1603-41), better known as Pratap Singha, after the occupation of the territory up to the Barnadi, we found a continuous relation between them. To maintain cordial relation with the inhabitants of these hill ranges, the Ahom rulers adopted the system then prevailing and gave it a definite shape, which was afterwards termed as *posa*. One of the terms of the *posa* was that the hill tribes were allowed to come down once in a year through particular *duar* to collect their necessary articles, and go back after a sojourn. In return the tribal chief with whom the *posa* was settled had to render his allegiance through *pal-seva* to the Ahom ruler. The hill tribes strictly adhered to the terms and conditions of the *posa* as well as by the Ahom government in the frontiers. Any violation was considered by the Ahom rulers as defiance of the allegiance and hence was controlled promptly.

The *buranjis* also record a number of clashes occurred between the Ahom army and the tribes right from the very beginning of the Ahom rule. A few instances are given below. During the reign of Siu-Sen-Pha (1439-88), the Tangshu Naga of the Patkai region came down to the plains pretending friendship and attacked some villages, but they were quickly repulsed and the guilty were severely punished.[18] During the reign of Siu-Pung-Mong alias Chakradhvaj Singha (1663-69), the Miris (Mishing) made a raid and killed two Ahom subjects residing adjacent to their hill. The Ahom force sent in 1655 against them defeated and killed three hundred Miri and also burnt twelve of their villages. The Miris then agreed to pay to the Ahom king an annual tribute of bison, horses, tortoises, sword etc.[19] Pratap Singha settled *posa* with the chiefs of the tribes inhabiting in the present-day Arunachal Pradesh and raised rampart (*garh*) and assigned separate routes for each tribe.[20] According to *Assam Buranji* (ed. By S.K.Dutta), Siu-Tan-Pha alias Siva Singha (1714-44) constructed an embankment for the Daflas (Nyishis) along the foot of the hills inhabited by them as a protection against future inroads by these "turbulent and restless mountaineers"[21].

Although sporadic clashes of the Ahoms with the tribes of present Arunachal Pradesh took place, the former considered the hills the safe refuge and shelter whenever serious danger threatened their lives by the invaders from the west. In 1563, when the Koch army approached the Ahom capital; king Siu-Kham-Pha (1552-1603) left for the hills of the Patkai and took shelter there till the return of the Koch army.[22] In 1662, during Mir Jumla's Assam invasion, Siu-Tam-La *alias* jayadhvaj Singha (1648-63) left the capital and took shelter in the Patkai region.[23]

References

1. In Tai language, Trans into English and ed. by Golap Chandra Barua, Government of Assam, 1930.
2. Ed. by S.K. Bhuyan, Department of Historical and Antiquarian Studies (DHAS), 1962.
3. Ed. by S.K. Bhuyan DHAS, 1960.
4. Ed. by Hemchandra Goswami, Kamarupa Anusandhana Samiti, Guwahati, 1922.
5. Ed. by S.K. Dutta, DHAS, 1938.
6. Ed. by S.K. Bhuyan, DHAS, 1963.
7. Kasi Nasi Nath Tamuli Phukan, Calcutta, 1906.
8. Ed. by S.K. Bhuyan, Gauhati University, 1974.
9. Ed. by P.C. Choudhury, DHAS, 1964.
10. Harakanta Barua Sadar-Amin, DHAS, 1962.
11. Ed. by S.K. Bhuyan, DHAS, 1958.
12. Ed. by S.K. Bhuyan, DHAS, 1964.
13. Ed. by S.K. Bhuyan, DHAS, 1938.
14. Ed. by S.K. Bhuyan, DHAS, 1964.
15. Ed. by S.K. Bhuyan, DHAS, 1964.
16. *Deodhai Asam Buranji,* p. 9, 19-20, 52-55, 97, 106-290.

17. *Ahom-Buranji,* pp. 54-57; *Deodhai Asam Buranji,* 4.
18. *Ahom Buranji, p. 52; Deodhai Asam Buranji,* p. 14; *Assam Buranji* ed. S.K.Bhuyan, p. 7, *Assam Buranji* by Kasi Nath Tamuli Phukan, p. 7; *Assam Buranji* by Harakanta Barua, p. 21.
19. *Ahom Buranji,* pp. 192-94.
20. *Ahom Buranji* by Kasi Nath Tamuli Phukan, p. 32.
21. E.A.Gait, *A History of Assam,* 1963, p. 21.
22. *Ahom Buranji,* p. 86; *Deodhai Asam Buranji,* p. 45; *Assam Buranji* ed. S.K.Bhuyan, 33.
23. *Ibid.* pp. 168-72; *Assam Buranji* ed. S.K. Bhuyan, p. 79, *Purani Assam Buranji,* 123.

15

A Few Assamese Sources for the Study of the History of Pre-Colonial Arunachal Pradesh

Jahnabi Gogoi

Assam is bounded on the north and east by the state of Arunachal Pradesh. Most of its ethnic inhabitants bear social, cultural, racial and economic relations with the peoples of Assam. It is therefore natural that those people drew attention of the early writers of Assam as and when they came to be associated with some stray or regular incidents that occurred in the state. Existing records show that tribes able to find places in the early records of Assam, are the Akas (Hrussos), the Daflas (Nyisis), the Miris (Misings), the Misimis, the Singphos and the Khamtis. The present paper will be an attempt to discuss few such sources which refer to the three major tribes of the eastern frontier of Assam, viz, the Daflas (Nyisis), the Singphos, and the Khamtis.

The Nyisis, are the most referred tribe in the early literary sources of Assam. The Assamese chronicles called *Buranjis* which are the official records of the Ahom kings making records of almost all events relating to the state, make mention of this tribe while narrating the events that took place since the early 16th century when the Ahom power extended to the north bank of the Brahmaputtra – their territory touching the foot hill areas of the present Arunachal Pradesh.[1] Of the numerous chronicles so far published, mention may be made of the *Deodhai Asam Buranji*, edited by S.K.Bhuyan, and published by the Department of Historical and Antiquarian Studies, Government of Assam, Gauwahati.[2] This chronicle in its published form is a collated form of several chronicles of which the first is called *Deodhai Asam Buranji*[3] P.C. Choudhury, the Director of the DHAS, writing the Preface to the second edited of the book comments "*The Deodhai Asam Buranji* is one of the earliest publications of the Department. The original manuscript, written in Tai-Ahom language, of which the present publication is but the Assamese translation in prose, covers the period from the beginning or the origin of the Ahom royal family to the accession of Jayadhvaj Singa. It goes to the credit of the editor that in order to make the narrative somewhat complete, he has incorporated useful information from a number of other original manuscripts bearing on the social life of the said ruling dynasty."[4] This chronicle records the clashes between the Ahoms and the Nyishis inhabiting the area near Sala during the rule of the Ahom king Pratap Singha (1603-1641). The cause of this clash is mentioned as attempt of the Daflas to make plunder in the villages of the foot hill areas.[5] The next reference is made to them during the rule of Styingpha *alias* Nariya Raja on the same context. This time they are mentioned under the name *Chungi*.[6] It is stated that the Ahom general this time defeated the Nyisis and raided their villages so that they finally came to terms and accepted Ahom vassalage.[7] This chronicle also records the origin of the Chutiyas and their state formation process in Sadiya region.[8] It appears that the Chutiyas were once hill tribe living in some areas presently covered by Arunachal Pradesh before they formed their state in the valley. If this is to be believed then this chronicle may be treated as one of the original recorded sources for the study of the early social changes of some of the tribes of the northern hills.

Another chronicle, entitled *Asam Buranui* (obtained from the family of Sukumar Mahanta), published by the DHAS and edited by S.K. Bhuyan, mentions that during the invasion of the Ahom kingdom by the Koch king Naranarayan (1540-1587) in the year 1562, the Nyisis joined hands with the Koch forces against the Ahom.[9] It is to be noted that this is the earliest reference of the Nyisis found in any written record in Assamese. The joining of the Nyisis with the Koch forces invading Assam indicates that the tribe under reference was primarily concerned with the nearest territories bordering their settlement for gathering items of livelihood which had become almost impossible after the tract had come into the possession of the Ahoms. Naturally, the Ahoms had very strained relations with Nyisis from the very beginning of their extension of power to the north bank.

Another *Buranji* titled *Tungkhungiya Buranji* compiled by Srinath Duara Barua, a scion of the Ahom aristocracy, throws much light on the history of the Nyisis, the Singphos and the Khamtis. Compiled by an eye-witness and an eminent participator of events, Srinath Duara Barua, this Assamese chronicle provides invaluable information for historians to study the history of Assam from the time of accession of the Ahom king Gadadhar Singha in 1681 to 1806—a period of 145 years of Tunghungiya dynastic rule in Assam.[10] According to S.K.Bhuyan, its editor, "chronicles of the later period of the Ahom rule being comparatively rare, the above *Buranji* proved a great revelation to me specially as it was compiled by an eminent Ahom official and noble.[11] The actual manuscript chronicle entitled *Tunkhungiya Vamsavali* caused to be compiled by Srinath Duara Barua, consists of history of fifty five years only, from 1751 to 1806. The history of the period from 1681 to 1751, and from 1806 to 1826 has been collated from two *buranjis,* viz, the *puthi* recovered in 1912-13 by Late H.C.Goswami from the Bengenaati *Satra* ... and another manuscript chronicle discovered by me (Dr. S.K. Bhuyan) in 1915 in the go-down of the American Baptist Mission, Guwahati....I have also given an account of the events of the ten years prior to Gadadhar Singha's accession narrating the circumstances which led to the ascendancy of the *Tungkhungiya* family: this chapter has been collated from the above two *buranjis* and several other chronicles.[12]

As indicated in the title, the chronicle throws much light besides the dynastic history of the *Tungkhungiyas,* on various other aspects, such as the great Moamariya revolt, relation of the Ahom Government with the British, the influence of the ecclesiastical authorities over the state, Ahom government, literature and culture, and also throws accurate side lights on some of the tribes of present Arunachal Pradesh, such as the Nyisis, the Khamtis, the Singphos and the Nagas.

The chronicle records that during the Moamariya revolt in Assam (1769-1806) the Nyisis along with their subordinate Assamese *paiks* called *Daphala Bahatiyas* gave much trouble to the Ahom Government. It is recorded in the chronicle that during the reign of Gaurinath Singha (1780-1795), when the Ahom Prime Minister Raj Mantri Purnanda Buragohain shifted the capital from Rangpur (Sivasagar) to Jorhat (Dichoi Nagar) due to its occupation by the rebels, and the king left for shelter at Guwahati, the Niysis took advantage of this situation and caused much trouble on the north bank.[13] The chronicle mentions that during this time some of the Nyisis came to the Prime Minister at Jorhat and pretended to request for a commander to guide them to fight against the Moamariyas.[14] The Buragohain Prime Minister being pleased on their way of approach presented them with numerous articles including golden bracelets and instructed them to go back to their place and remain ready to start for Rangpur, the Ahom capital, which was then under the occupation of the rebels.[15] The Prime Minister then sent the Charing Raja with some men to the north bank to lead the Nyisi force.[16] But to his astonishment he found that the Nyisis in combination with the Misings refused to obey the orders of the Charing Raja, nor they accompanied them to Rangpur.[17] So, the Charing Raja returned to Jorhat and reported it to the king.[18] It appears that the Nyisis who were always in search of opportunities to raid on the villages on the north bank, did not like to lose this golden opportunity when the Ahom forces were at their worst of strength. There are several other reference to the Ahom-Nyisi conflicts during the period of the last phase of the Moamariya revolt.[19]

The chronicle further informs us that the *Daphala-Bahatiyas*, a class of Assamese peasant *paiks* acceded by the Ahom government to the services of the Nyisis,[20] played significant role in the later phase of the Moamariya revolt. These disgruntled slaves of the Nyisis, because of their forceful separation from the society and families, were more friendly with their hill masters than to the Assam king.[21] The confusing situation created on the north bank near Tatibahar and Japaribhita by the Moamariyas was taken advantage of by them and they added much force to the already matured movement of the Moamariyas. Their participation in this phase of the movement has been recorded in details in this chronicle. The chronicle records that the *Daphala-Bahtuyas* joined hands with the Moamariyas and caused much havoc to the villages compelling the inhabitants to flee from their homes seeking shelter elsewhere.[22] The nature of their movement has been described in this chronicle as follows: "At Japaribhita, the Moamariyas and the *Daphala-Bahariyas* have created houses of cloth or tents, and behaving as rebels they have recruited volunteers. They are parading with fans made of peacock feathers, and are causing panic in the country by extortion and plunder".[23] The *Bahatiyas* did not remain content with this movement alone; in the year 1796 they organized a revolt under their leader called Phopai on the same place near Baskata.[24] During this movement they also imported *Barkandaz* soldiers from Bengal; but were finally defeated and Phopai was killed. [25] This was the last movement of the *Bahatiyas* recorded in the chronicle. It is to be mentioned in this connection that those *Daphala-Bahatiyas* who identified themselves with their hill masters, gradually got assimilated with the Nyisis, and by assuming all culture of the tribe they erased their paternal life-styles. Today their identity can no longer be traced out although elements of their Assamese culture might have been still there in their way of living. If this is well-researched a chapter of the social formation of the present Nyisi tribe of Arunachal Pradesh will be an interesting chapter in the history of this state, and about socio-cultural relationship between the peoples of the two important states of the Northeast.

The Nyisis, however, did not give trouble to the Ahoms always, nor the Ahom state adopted stern measure against them at all times. Although the *Tungkhungiya Buranji* did not mention such friendly relations between them, other chronicles recording events on other occasions, mention that king Pratap Singha, introduced the *Posa* system whereby he allocated certain territories on the foot hill areas to the Nyisis and a few other raiding tribes, such as the Nagas and the Akas (Hrussos), from where they were allowed to collect certain products, such as, rice and fish, which were indispensable for their living.[26] This Ahom king also built a line of fort and a road-cum-rampart along with Niysi hills in order to prevent them from committing raids in future.[27] He then made some provisions whereby the Nyisis had to offer certain items of their products to the Ahom king annually, such as *Manjit* and *Jaka* and *Methun*.[28] This policy of conciliation and appeasement adopted by Pratap Singha had good results later. It is recorded that since then till at least the time of the Moamariya revolt when the Assam state was ruled by a series of weak rulers, the Nyisis maintained friendly relations with the Assam king. The chronicle records that when King Rudra Singha (1696-1741) prepared to invade Bengal in 1713-14, he was greatly encouraged and helped by the tribes, mainly the Nyisis, by supplying him with men and materials.[29]

The Singphos, who form one of the numerous tribes of present. Arunachal Pradesh, are also mentioned in this chronicle. This chronicle, however, has not mentioned the period in which the Singphos entered the Indian border from their original homeland at Burma, present Myanmar. But it records how they too, like the *Daphala-Bahatiyas* and their hill masters, took advantage of troubled situation in Assam during the Moamariya revolt and attacked it. It is recorded that in the year 1723 Saka (1801 AD) the Moamariyas revolted at Bengmara who were defeated by the royal forces forcing them to retreat to Namrup where they, in combination with the Singphs, again fought the Ahom forces.[30] Here the Moamariyas being defeated again, the Singphos pretended to be submissive allowing them to collect certain items, such as, men, cows, buffalo, copper, brass and cloth.[31] After a few years, in 1806 the Singphos along with the Moamariyas and the Khamtis, another tribe of this region recently entering the Indian border from Burma, attacked the neighbouring regions in Assam.[32] It is recorded that this time king Kamaleswar Singha (1795-1811) sent forces on both river and land to fight the invaders.[33] The Singphos did not leave their attempt to invade the Assam territories even after that. The chronicle records that during the Burmese invasion when king Chandra Kanta Singha left his capital, the Burmese and their compatriots the Singphos, began to plunder the Assamese villages in ways beyond description[34] and captured and took hundreds of Assamese as slaves to their place.[35] The chronicle futher describes that unable to bear the recurring inroads of the Singphos, the Assam Prime Minister Purnananda Buragohain, in order to placate the Singpho leader Bichanong, had presented him with a girl-Rangili of an Ahom aristocratic family together with numerous slaves and servants.[36] Bichanong in his turn presented this girl to the Burmese king Bodowpaya to strengthen his friendship.[37] Purnananda's policy of appeasement, however, did not succeed to suppress the Singphos. The chronicle records that till the year 1825 the Singphos along with the Burmese plundered the villages when Captain Neufville suppressed their bostility and procured the release of six thousand Assamese captives who had been carried off by the Singphos and their Burmese allies.[38]

The records of this chronicle are corroborated by evidences from other chronicles too. For example, the *Satsari-Asam Buranji* [39] records that in the year 1719-20 Saka, the Sengphalringam or the Singphos invaded Assam[40] Although in the first instance, the Ahom soldiers could not make much headway against them who fought with canon, but soon they gave way, and the Ahom soldiers obtained from them many articles like men, cow, buffalo, duck, fowl, paddy etc.[41] This is further corroborated by evidence from another chronicle – the *Ahom Buranji,* written in Tai-Ahom language.[42] This chronicle mentions that the Singphos entered Assam for the first time in the year 1795-96 when Sengphalarningam Lanao entered into the Assam territory with an army.[43] The *Satsari Asam Buranji* informs about the Khamtis too. It is stated that in the year 1721-22 the Khamti king Burha Raja, the Barchiringiya Kacharis, the Pani Nara, the Phakials, the Miris (Misings), the Misimis, the Tekela Nagas, the Muluks and the Abors (Adis) attacked the Sadiyakhowa Gohain and killed him[44] In retaliation to this incident the Ahom forces invaded their territory and defeated them and captured the Khamti Burha Raja, some Phakials, Naras, Muluks and others and brought them to the capital.[45] The Assam king, however, did not order to kill them; rather he ordered them to be established in different places of the state, at Dichoi (Jorhat) and Baruarani, the Nagas at Nafaduar, the Muluks at Marangi and the Pani Naras at Titabar.[46] This is also corroborated by the *Ahom Buranji* referred to above.[47] It is interesting that at present there is no trace of those rehabilitated peoples captured in the Khamti war. Like the case of the *Daphala-Bahatiyas*, it is probably not improper to argue that the present Assamese society at Jorhat and few other neighbourings areas contain the blood and culture of those people although no statistical account or census report have ever mentioned them as distinct tribe in the last century.[48]

Another group of early Assamese literature containing reference to the hill tribes of the north is the set of Vaishnava literature consisting of the religious and biographical works. While religious works consists mainly of the *Bhagavata* translation by Sankardeva, his *Kirtanghosha,* and the *Namghosha* of Madhavdeva, the biographical group consists mainly of the *Charit Puthis* of the Vaishnava saints. In the *Bhagavata* translation Sankardeva mentions various tribes of the northeastern part of India of whom he specially mentions the *Kiratas* (Mongoloid tribes of the northeast). Kacharis, Khasis, Garos, Miris (Misings), Ahoms, Muluks, Kuvachas or the Koches, Mlecchas or the Meches and other impure (?) tribes.[49] Many writers believe that the Muluks are a branch of the Singphos.[50] Such reference indicates that those people were known to the people of the valley since early times. Similarly, Madhavdeva also mentions Misings among other tribes.[51] Of the *Charit Puthis* the most voluminous is the *Katha Guru Charit* or the *Guru Charit Katha,* a biographical work written in prose about the last part of the 18th century.[52] This while narrating the early life and works of Sankardeva, makes mention of the Dafla raids (*Dafala maran*) on various times due to which he had to shift from place to place in search of security.[53] The first one was about the year 1521-22. As a result of such raids many traders and craftsmen had to leave their home on the north to the western part of Assam.[54]

Another source of information in Assamese language about the Khamtis, Singphos and the Nyisis, and of course, about the Garos, Nagas, misings, the Akas (Hrussos) and Mishimis is the *Orunodoi,* the first Assamese monthly, published by the American Baptist Missionaries from Sivasagar in the year 1846 edited by missionary Dr. Nathan Brown. The monthly published a series of articles containing history and culture of those tribes in its different editions in the years from 1846 to 1849. Those articles were in fact adaptations from the records of Captain Butler given in his *Sketch of Assam*[55] Those were written by one called As, meaning Anandaram Dhekial Phukan (?).[56] one may derive important and interesting information about the living style and cultural pattern of those tribes at the time under reference.

Haliram Dhekial Phukan in his *Assam Buranji*, published in the year 1829, and written in Bengali has also made certain important references regarding those tribes. This work has been treated by most historians as equal to an early chronicle, for it was written by an Assamese gentleman during the period when Ahom rule was till not totally rooted out in Assam. This work mentions that in the Abor country *i.e.,* the territory of the Adis copper is available.[57] It informs further that the Singphos and the Nagas captured the people of Assam and sold them in Mungkong *i.e.,* Burma during the period of the Burmese rule in Assam (1818-26).[58] Dhekial Phukan further informs that after the British East India Company had taken over Assam, many Assamese peasants fled to the Singpho country to evade heavy burden of taxes imposed by the British, because there was no system of payment of taxes in the Singpho dominated territory.[59] As for the political life of the tribes under references (Khamti, Singpho, and others) Dhekial Phukan says that those tribes were divided into different clans and they have no supreme kings of their own; they were ruled by their chiefs.[60]

Thus, from the above it can be said with much certainty that Assamese literature of middle ages form a set of genuine source materials to study the history and culture of the northeastern hill tribes in Middle Ages in particular, and of their present times in general. If properly studied, they may reveal to a large extent the process of the growth and development of their society in historical perspective. The above is only a short and brief account of preserved and published sources about a few tribes in a language which was and is still known and spoken by most tribes of the northeast. Assamese folk literature may be another group of important sources to study the history of the hill tribes besides many legends, traditions and folk tales prevalent among them. The academics in Arunachal and the neighbouring states naturally need a class of researcher who should be well-versed in the language and literature of the neighbouring state of Assam.

References

1. Suhungmung Dihingia Raja (1497-1539) was the first Ahom ruler to have extended his territory to the north. It was he, having extended his territory to north of the Brahmapurra, took census of the population in the year 1510 See E.A. Gait, *A History of Assam*, 2nd edn. Reprint, 1981, Guwahati, p. 82.

2. Here the 3rd edn., 1990, has been used.
3. Preface to the 2nd edition.
4. 3rd edn., Guwahati, 1990, p. 45.
5. p. 90.
6. *Ibid.*
7. pp. 193-212.
8. First published in 1945. Here the 3rd edn., (1988) has been used.
9. p. 32.
10. pp. Preface to the 2nd edn., Guwahati, 1964, pp. iv-xxii.
11. *Ibid.*
12. *Ibid.*, p. v.
13. p. 124.
14. *Ibid.*
15. *Ibid.*
16. *Ibid.*, p. 125.
17. *Ibid.*
18. *Ibid.*
19. pp. 125ff.
20. S.K.Bhuyan, *Swargadeo Rajeswar Singha,* Guwahati, 1975, pp.
21. *Ibid.*
22. *Tungkhungiya Buranji,* p. 94.
23. *Ibid.,* p. 140.
24. *Ibid.*
25. *Ibid.*
26. *Ibid.*
27. *Assam Buranji* by Harakanta Barua, 2nd edn., Guwahati, 1962, p. 40.
28. *Ibid.*
29. *Ibid.*
30. *Satsari Assam Buranji,* 2nd edn., Guwahati, 1964, p. 151.
31. *Tungkhungiya Buranji,* (Ass), p. 144; Eng. p. 147.
32. *Ibid.*

33. *Ibid.*, p. 186 (Ass); Eng. p. 192.
34. *Ibid.*, Eng., p. 194.
35. *Ibid.*
36. *Ibid.*
37. *Ibid.*
38. *Ibid.*
39. *Ibid.*, (Eng), p. 194.
40. *op. cit.*, p. 176.
41. *Ibid.*
42. *Ibid.*
43. *Ahom Buranji,* pp. 176f.
44. *Ibid.*
45. *Ibid.*
46. *Ibid.*
47. *Ibid.*, p. 177.
48. *op. cit.*, pp. 364f.
49. The Census Report for 1872 mentions that the people in the Khamtis in the Sibsagar District numbered 21 only, See W.W. Hunter, *A Statistical Account of Assam,* Vol. I, reprint, Delhi, 1990, p. 236.
50. M. Neog, *Sankaradeva and his Times,* Guwahati, reprint, 1998, p. 75.
51. W.W. Robinson, *A Descriptive Account of Assam,* Reprint, New Delhi, 1975, pp. 371ff.
52. Neog, *op. cit.*, p. 75.
53. U.C. Lekharu, Pathsala, 15th Reprint, Guwahati, 1987, pp. 44, 339, 465.
54. *Ibid.*
55. *Ibid.*
56. *Ibid.*
57. Haliram Dhekial Phukan, *Assam Buranji,* Calcutta, 1929, pp. 108.
58. *Ibid.*, p. 74.
59. *Ibid.*, p. 75.
60. *Ibid.*, pp. 73f.

16

The Posa System: A Historical Analysis

Sristidhar Dutta

The *posa* system occupies a very important place in the medieval history of North East India with continuation of its importance upto the British colonial regime. It is, of course, understood that the study of the *posa* system with its various aspects like the system itself and its origin, its role in the socio-economic life of the people of the Hills and Plains, as an instrument to know about the agricultural and other products of the areas under *posa*, as a diplomatic device of the ahom regime, the British policy of its continuation of course with change in the mode of its operation for colonial capitalist interest, the resultant initial resistance movements of the tribal people, the ultimate achievement of success of the colonial masters to introduce their capitalist interest by way of cash payment of the *posa,* gradual monetization of tribal economy and establishment of politico-economic dominance in certain areas of the hill region, etc., within the purview of a paper is wellnigh impossible. Further, diverse opinions prevail among the scholars regarding the origin and nature of the system itself. An humble attempt has, therefore, been made in this paper to discuss only some important aspects of the system in a way of understanding the history of Arunachal Pradesh in the medieval and colonial period based mostly on secondary and some primary sources.

The Background

In order to understand the origin and introduction of the *posa* system in the history of the medieval North East we are to know something about the Ahoms who introduced the system. It would also be necessary to know about the geographical and topographical location of the tribes of the present day Arunachal Pradesh for some of whom the system was introduced.

Medieval Assam witnessed the inception of a very important historical event bearing consequences of immense importance for the subsequent history of the region, and that was the coming of Sukapha to Assam with his band of several thousand Tai-Ahom migrants in the first part of the 13th century (1228 AD) with a view to permanently settle here. These carriers of Tai culture to Assam had long left their pre-literate stage behind and had prior taste of some kind of a political society already before they quit Mogaung, an important Tai (Shan) principality of Upper Burma and Yunnan. With this kind of a 'political society', it is generally held by the scholars that the Ahoms brought with them several such politico-economic concepts, such as, the *khel* system, the *posa* system (some kind of feudal concept), the policy of assimilation, the knowledge of wet-rice cultivation, ploughing with buffaloes, etc. The process of assimilation was a special characteristic of the Tai-Ahoms, which has been confirmed by E.R.Leach in these words, "The Valley Shans have every where, for centuries past been assimilating their hill-neighbours".[1]

Further, for their own strategic and economic needs the Ahoms in Assam adopted a policy of absorption and assimilation of the autochthons.[2] This they did by pursuing a policy of 'give and take' and 'conciliation and coercion'. The Ahoms first conquered and assimilated there Naga, Moran and the Barahi neighbours and then the Kacharis, the *Bara* Bhuyans and the Chutias in the north of the Brahmaputra. Infact after occupation of the Chutia kingdom in the 3rd decade of the 16th century (1523 AD) by Suhungmung Dihingia Raja, the Ahoms came into contact with most of the hill tribes of the north of the Brahmaputra.

By Arunachal and Arunachalee in this paper we mean the landmass and its people evolved through historical process, over a time and space, as a political unit of this vast country. Arunachal Pradesh, the erstwhile North East Frontier Agency (NEFA), comprises of mountainuous territory on the Southern slopes of the Eastern Himalayas with spurs coming down from north to south from the crest of the main range to the valley of the Brahmaputra in the State of Assam, except in the district of Tirap where the Territory consists of the northeastern slopes and spurs of the Patkai range, the crest which divides India nd Burma (Myanmar). Geography also influenced the cultural development of the area to a great extent. The northern region had little contact with the lower region, particularly the Brahmaputra valley and has been greatly influence by the Indo-Tibetan culture. The middle zone remained comparatively backward and both Tibetan and Assamese influences are visible here. But the southern zone of the foot hills had intimate contact with the plains of Assam from time immemorial in various aspects of life.[3]

The economic life of the region has been largely conditioned by its physical and topographical features. This made the economy of the hills mostly jhum-oriented, which was supplemented by hunting and fishing. Though almost all the tribes grew more or less all that were necessary for their simple daily life, for shortfall of many consumer and non-consumer goods the tribes had to depend on the plains below. Thus the Eastern Himalayan Region including the present day Aruanchal Pradesh had an integrated economy with the plains. There used to be no hill-plain dichotomy and movements across the hills and plains were normal activities owing to the complementary nature of economic relationship of the plains of the Brahmaputra valley and the hills around. Thus the flow of resources and use of resource base in this frontier region inhabited by various tribes greatly depended upon the interactions of the tribes with the political systems of the Brahmaputra valley and the highlands of Tibet and Burma.[4]

Origin of the Posa system

The Ahom *Buranjis* (Chronicles), both in Tai and Assamese languages of medieval period, throw considerable light on the relationship of the Ahoms including that of *posa* with various frontier tribes. The history of the *posa*, therefore, begins in the North Eastern region with the history of the Ahoms. It is told by some old administrators that the word *posa* originates from the Assamese word *punha* (to rear or domesticate) that gradually corrupted to *pucha* and then to *posa*. The word *posa* later on literally meant a collection or subscription. When this term is used to explain the payments made to the hill people, it represents the subscription which was collected by the villagers concerned in order to meet the customary demands granted by the Ahom rulers to the hill tribes.[5] It has been argued that in order to conciliate the hill-tribes and to prevent them from committing raids in the plains which were primarily to meet up their deficiencies in the hills, the Ahom rulers introduced the *posa* system which infact provided the main basis of the superstructure of the Ahom-tribal relations.

From the survey of medieval historical literature it becomes apparent that with the gradual expansion of the Ahom kingdom its administration became more heavy and complex. Further, in the 15-16 centuries the Ahoms had to continuously faced the brunt of the Muslim aggressions from the west, thus adding a new dimension of problem to the Ahom regime. In order to keep intact their entire strength for successfully combating the Muslim aggressions, the Ahoms rulers thought it expedient to bring to an end the occasional tribal raids and consequent disturbance in the hill frontiers. This was also necessary to secure the people of the Ahom kingdom in the foothills plains from the raids of the hills-tribes and assure thereby a healthy economic pursuit by the people. Moreover some kind of understanding with the study and conrageous hill people would pave the path for their enrolment in the Ahom military might to meet the new challenge of the Muslims. Further, it was practically impossible to deploy forces on the extensive border of the Ahom kingdom with the hill tribes (which got reflected in the failure of numerous punitive expeditions) to prevent the raids on the plains.

Considering all the factors mentioned above the Ahoms initiated the diplomatic alternative means of the *posa* system, with which, it was told earlier, the Tai-Ahoms were familiar with, to conciliate the hill-tribes to maintain law and order in the frontier region on certain specific conditions. King Pratap Singha (1603-41 AD), therefore, was the first Ahom monarch to introduce the *posa* system with various tribes of the frontier like a section of the Bhutias (present day Monpas and Sherdukpens), Akas (Hrussos), Nyishis and the Hill-Miris.

The Chief of the tribe with whom *posa* was granted had to come down once in a year and render his submission (*Palseva)* to the Ahom ruler. Further, the chief while coming for *Pal Seva* had to bring with him from his own area certain articles as present to the king. The Monpas and the Sherdukpens (Bhutias) paid the tribute in terms of horses, yak-tails, gold-dust, musk and blankets.[6] Hill-Miris and Galo-Adis paid *mithuns,* dear-hunting dogs, wreath of jewels, *mirijins* (a course cotton quiit) and *daos* as tribute.[7] The Noctes presented *mithuns, bulua chhag* (possibly *Nilgai,* a kind of antelope), red-hair, red cane strips, salt and other articles produced in their area.[8] Similarly other tribes getting *posa* right had to pay the products of their own region to the Ahom kings.

The Ahom kings, on their part, made settlement of a class of Assamese *paiks* called *bahatias*[9] in the foot-hill areas, who were obliged to give their services to the respective hill-tribes. Each hill-tribe enjoying the privilege was allowed to receive certain articles in the form of *posa* from the *bahatias* assigned to them. It has been found that the Akas (Hrussos) were entitled to receive from each house of their allotted *khel* one portion of a female dress, one bundle of cotton thread and one cotton *gamocha* (a kind of handkerchief).[10] The Nyishis of *Charduar* were entitled to receive from every ten houses of their allotted *khel* are *khamia* (double cloth), one *cheleng* (single cloth), one *gamocha,* one *dao,* ten hormed cattles and four *seers* of salt.[11] The Nyishis of *Naoduar* received 20 *seers* of paddy and 20 *cowries* from each family in the *duar* areas.[12] About the Nyishis of *Chaiduar*, the Hill-Miris of Bordoloi and the Galo Adis of Sissi-Dhemaji areas it is reported that they received from the *ryots* in cloth of their own manufacture (possibly *Miri-Jim),* rice, pigs, fowls, dogs, *daos,* etc. and they resided for months in the plains.[13] The Noctes received the *Khats* (assignment of lands) for paddy cultivation, *beels* (water logged areas for fishing) along with serfs to cultivate the land.[14] On the other hand we find that the Monpas and the Sherdukpens were granted as *posa* the right of usufruct in the *Naoduar* and *Charduar* areas perspectively.[15]

In return for their services to the hill-masters, the Ahom Government granted a concessional rate of assessment to the *bahatias.* Each *got* of *bahatias* (unit of 3 *paiks*)[16] paid to the government an amount of Rs. 3 instead of the usual Rs. 9.[17]

Nature of Posa: Was it a Blackmail?

Scholars widely differ in their opinions on the nature of the *posa* itself. S.K.Bhuyan states, "on the extremity of the plains of the two banks of the rivers lie the snowy hill ranges inhabited by people who have still retained their primitive ways of living and whose alliance with the government at Gargaon was procured by a system of blackmail, and long-standing agreement of friendship".[18] H.K.Barpujari, however, opines "The conciliatory policy of granting right might be a 'mutual compromise between conscious weakness and barbarian cunning' and the levying of the *posa* differed little from the Maratha Chauth or payment of the denegeld."[19] Following this most of the European writers who came to the Brahmaputra valley in the beginning of the second quarter of the nineteenth century denominated '*posa*' as Black Mail.[20] Even as late as 1994 one prominent scholar wrote, "As the main objective of the system was to purchase immunity of the weak peasants of the rich plains from the plundering raids of the hillmen, it amounted to blackmail".[21]

From a critical and closer examination of the details of the *posa* system, it would be difficult to accept the views given by scholars like Bhuyan and Barpujari. During the Ahom rule it was neither a black-mail nor had any resemblance with the *Chauth* of the Marathas. Infact the *posa* system was based on certain well-defined principles.[22] They were:

1. The Chief of the tribe to whom *posa* was acceded had to come down once and render his *pal seva* to the Ahom ruler;
2. The Chief, while coming for *pal Seva,* was to bring with him from his locality certain articles as present to be offered to the Ahom king as a sign of his submission; and
3. The Ahom ruler in return for this granted the right over an area adjancent to the particular *duar* (pass) *as posa* and allotted some people in that area known as the *bahatias* to the chief to collect the fixed and prescribed articles necessary for him and his tribe.

From the above mentioned conditions it becomes apparent that the grant was usufructuary one and presumably at the pleasure of the Ahom ruler. So the right was not permanent and the tribal chiefs in lieu of the feudal rights granted to them over particular areas had to pay obeisance and tribute in kind. Both the parties – the tribal chiefs and the Ahom rulers – were obliged equally and responsible to execute the terms and conditions of the deal to maintain peace and order in the frontier. So during the Ahom rule specially during the hay-days of the regime when the rulers were more powerful, the *posa* system was never a black-mail or it had any resemblance to the Maratha *Chauth* system. The hill-people then were allowed to visit and collect *posa* between the months of November to May, because in this period the harvesting season in the plains was over, the roads became passable after the rainy season and the plains men could weave cloths after the harvesting season to make it ready along with other items of the *posa* to hand over to the *posa* holders.

A scrutiny of the Ahom policy towards the hill-tribes further indicate that the Ahom rulers introduced the *posa* to some of the tribes and granted some other tribes cultivated lands and fishing areas along with *paiks* in the plains like to the Adis, the Nagas, etc. Those tribes who were greatly dependent for their livelihood on trading activities with the plains like the Monpas, the Sherdukpens, the Khamtis, the Singphos and the Mishmis, the Ahom rulers offered them trading facilities with the plains on condition of good behaviour and payment of annual tribute. There were numerous passes known as *duars* along the Himalayan foothills and it was through these *duars* that the people of the present day Arunacahl Pradesh mostly interacted with the plains people since time immemorial. There were as many as nineteen *duars* or passes from the trijunction of Bhutan, Assam and Arunachal Pradesh known popularly as *Naoduar*, *Chaiduar* and *Charduar*. Further Ahom king Pratap Singha is also said to have established a number of trading centres in *duar* areas to encourage trading activities between the plains and the hills with officials like *Datiyalia Bishayas* and *Duaria Baruas* to look after the trade. It also should be noted that the trading activities in general were localized and the hillmen in general exchanged goods with the goods of the plains of Assam in such a manner that the deficit in one area was met by the surplus of the other.

Then the question comes why most of the British officials and writers termed the *posa* as black-mail. The answer to this question can be traced in the following historical development. During the decaying days of the Ahom regime, the different tribes of the North East Frontier region began to come down and establish themselves on the plains down below their hills. From the second half of the 18th century, the Ahom kingdom started suffering from internal disturbance like the Moamaria rebellions and intrigues and conspiracy among the Ahom officials, which paved the path for rapid decline of the kingdom. The decaying and weak authority of the Ahom kingdom failed to control the border areas as was done earlier and this encouraged many hill-tribes to overthrow the Ahom allegiance. Many of them, taking advantage of the political situation had encroached the foothill areas granted to them by the Ahom rulers to collect their necessary articles under the *posa* system.

They further started considering these areas as their sole preserve and claimed the prescribed articles on the basis of earlier right over the *bahatiyas,* of course, without offering *Pal Seva* to the leigehords *i.e.,* the Ahom monarchs. According to Mackenzie "Many of them advanced claims to rights more or less definite over lands lying in the plains; others claimed tributary payment from the villages below their hills, or the services of *paiks* said to have been assigned to them by the Assam Authority".[23] The *bahatiyas* had no alternative but to purchase forbearance of these hillmen either by payment of *posa* or to desert the village. They, however, according to R.B. Pemberton "preferred submitting to this tax rather than incur the resentment of these ....neighbours".[24] J.B.Ganguly has echoed more or less a similar view:[25]

The third source of surplus was the forcible collection of agricultural products, cattle, cloth, slaves, etc., from the Assamese villages in the foothill areas. During the later days of Ahom rule the government was unable to stop the tribal people from exacting the things they needed from the villages by force. The tribes claimed these plains as their own territory and hence they had the right to collect a share of the produce of the villages in the plains. The recognition of the right of the tribes to collect the produce from their respective 'mahals came to be known as *posa*. In economic terminology income from *posa*, if the cost of collection is ignored, was a surplus.

Naturally the Europeans who came to the Brahmaputra valley in the beginning of the 3rd decade of the 19th century were acquainted with only this situation which perhaps made them remark on the levying of the *posa* as "Black-mail" or like "differ little from the Maratha *Chauth*". Capt. Welsh while reporting on the relations of the Ahom rulers with the tribal chiefs mentions, " Suddia, Miree, Duffala, Bhutan, Naga, Kapachor, Jaintia and the Garows paid tribute to the monarchs of Assam".[26] But only after about thrity years later David Scott, appointed as Agent to the Governor-General for the North Eastern Frontier in November 1823 and who continued in this post till his death in 1831 wrote in a Note like this, "The Duplas, Bhooteeyas and Ankas pay a nominal tribute, and in return levy black-mail to a very oppressive and continually increasing extent in the districts both of the river...".[27] After David Scott's using of this terminology for *posa*, almost all European writers began using so. R.B. Pemberton[28] in 1835, M'cosh[29] in 1839, Robinson[30] in 1841 while mentioning about the tribes and *posa* have invariably used the term 'Black-mail' Capt. J.T. Gordon, Asstt. Agent to the Governor-General, Durrang, on the other hand, has mentioned like this, "the share or revenue which the hill-tribes allowed to collect, entitled "black-mail" or "*posa*" which appears to have been conceded to them through the weakness of former rulers under the Assam Government, resembling the *Chauth* of the Marathas..."[31]

These comments referred above made in a changed political situation mentioned earlier that has brought a change in the nature of the *posa* infact created the confusions in interpreting *posa* as the black-mail or its comparison with the *Chauth* of the Marathas.

We may sum up the discussion on this aspect of the *posa* like this that the system of *posa* during the Ahom rule was quite different in its nature from that of this on the eve of coming of the Europeans to the Brahmaputra valley. *Posa* thus was a deal or settlement between the Ahom rulers and the tribal chiefs on the basis of some well-defined principles, as has been mentioned earlier, to be observed by both the parties. It was not a levy of black-mail during the Ahom regime atleast upto the end of the 18th century. The weak Ahom rulers of the early 19th century could not retain their power over the tribal chiefs as well as in the areas granted to them on some kind of feudal terms. The tribal chiefs continued their claim over the assigned areas and the assignees *i.e.,* the *bahatia-paiks.* The word *posa* continued to be used on the articles and the service of the *bahatias* to the assigned tribes. The demand of the tribes on the people living in the foothills infact gradually increased. Now it became one sided leaving thus no difference between levying *posa* and levying black-mail. The Europeans coming at that moment of time were acquinted only with this situation and so they believed and worte that the *posa* was nothing but black-mail imposed by the tribes.[32]

Posa System During the Colonial Period

After the annexation of Assam to the British dominion, the British found the valley surrounded on the north, east and south by numerous hill tribes who, as has been mentioned earlier, from the early part of the 19th century, advanced claims to rights, more or less definite, over lands lying on the plains; some claimed tributary payments from the villages below their hills or the services of the *paiks* of those villages. The British came to Assam during the Anglo-Burmese war of 1824-26 and occupied it as a conquered territory. The Treaty of Yandaboo (1826) did not define the boundary of Assam; it only stipulated that the Burmese would not interfere in Assam and its dependencies. The British thus who stepped into the shoes of the Ahom kings, who ruled for near about 600 years from 1228 onwards, had now to face the tribes of the surrounding hills including those of the present day Arunachal Pradesh.

The tribes living to the sub-montane belt and the contiguous hills of the Brahmaputra valley came into contact of the plainsmen due to, as has been mentioned, complementary nature of economy. Their relations varied between peaceful trade and violent confrontations, but symbiotic nature of the economy of the two contiguous regions used to bring about normalcy very soon. The Ahom rulers formalized the relations between the hills and the plains people, as we have seen, by regulation of *posa* and also by adoption of measures of furtherance of trade between the Brahmaputra valley on the one hand and the frontier and transfrontier regions on the other. Such process definitely took times to bear fruits and hence, sometimes the policy of economic blockade and occasional punitive expeditions were also resorted to by the Ahom rulers. But the Ahom rulers never tried to annex the tribal territories and kept themselves satisfied with the tribute, allegiance, submission and friendship offered by the hill tribes of the area.

On the other hand the British economic and commercial as well as strategic and political interests in this hilly region shaped the trend and pattern of colonial intervention. The cause of colonial intervention culminating into the establishment of British paramountcy over the hillmen of the region and their gradual incorporation into the colonial cobweb was, seemingly, determined by the colonial interests in the Brahmaputra valley and the commercial and strategico-political interests beyond the frontier.[33] The growing colonial prospective economy in the Brahmaputra valley in the form of Tea, Petroleum, Coal, Rubber, and increased revenue from improved agriculture on the foothills of the border area greatly depended upon the capacity of the colonial administration to maintain law and order in the border areas.

The British authorities, therefore, after much debate on continuation, abolition and modification, adopted the policy of the Ahom rulers towards *posa*, system to suit the colonial priorities. These changes did not take place all at once and were spread over a long time span. To make a long story short, measures were adopted either to pay the commuted amount of respective shares of *posa* collected by different chiefs through the local revenue collectors or their equivalent amount in cash from the government treasuries. But in course of time in no case the *posa* holders from the hills were allowed to collect their respective *posa* from the individual *paiks* (now British *ryots)* as was so long the practice during the Ahom period. Considering the limitation of a paper only the briefest mention has been made of the commutation of *posa* from kind to cash made by the Britishers with the different tribes.[34]

Posa to the Hrusso (Aka) Chiefs

David Scott succeeded in concluding an agreement with the Hrussos (Akas) by which they agreed to forego their right of direct collection of *posa* from individual riots for an annual payment of Rs.175/- by the British government.[35] An agreement was made with Taghi *Raja* wherein he agreed not to attack the *ryots* in the plains for a monthly pension of Rs.20. Suitable stipends amouting Rs.360/- per annum were also granted to other leaders of the Akas[36] with further extension of six more pensions in 1848 to another six leaders. Capt. J.T.Gordon concluded agreements with Hrussos (Aka) chiefs in Febtury 1844 for commutation of their *posa* to cash on prevailing market prices of goods. Monetory payments to the Aka chiefs were finally fixed at Rs.668/- in aggregate in 1848.[37] It seems that the relations of the British with the tribe began to improve after the grant of *posa* in cash to the chiefs. Though later on the chiefs tried for enhancement of the amount and casused some truble, the stipend was withdrawn, the chiefs finally surrended in 1888 and their *posa* was restored from 1890 and the practice of payment of *posa* is extent even at present.[38]

Posa to the Nyishi Chiefs

In 17th April 1836 after much persuation eight Nyishi chiefs of Charduars entered into an engagement with the British by which even though they refused to accept cash instead of articles but agreed to resign the right of collection from individual ryots. They agreed to receive the *posa* articles in future from the *Malgoozari* (local revenue officer) who would collect the articles from the *ryots* of their respective villages as per revised rates.[39] In accordance with the direction from the Governor General-in-Council, that appreciated Capt. Methie's agreement with the eight Nyishi chiefs, his successor Lt. Vetch, carried on negotiations with the remaining five Nyishi chiefs of *Charduar* who made similar agreements on April 5, 1837.[40] The Nyishis of *Naoduar* also agreed to receive the *posa* through the village revenue officer by 1938-39.[41] Captain Gordon's letter No.3 of 1844 dated 13 February 1844 states that Rs.2494-0-1 was annually paid to the Nyishi chiefs of *Charduar* and *Naoduar* commuting their rights to raise *posa* in the *Duars*.[42]

The presence of petty clans, independent of each other, suggest that inter-tribal sub-divisions existed in the Nyishi society. There were 30 to 40 chiefs in the same clan or village representing an oligarchical from of government.[43] The chiefs were called *Gams*. Dalton, therefore, noted that 238 Nyishi *gams* of chiefs were in receipt of Rs.2543/- as *posa*. In 1853, the total amount of *posa* to the Nyishi chiefs was Rs.4129-15-0 with 24 *maunds* of salt to the Nyishis of Bankotta in lieu of certain *hat* (weekly market) dues.[44] M.L.Bose, however, has mentiond on the basis of a file of 1884, "But in 1853-54, the total amount of *posa* reched Rs.4129-15-0; besides 234 *maunds* of salt in lieu of *hat* (weekly market) dues and right of fishing and gold washing, a diet allowance of Rs. 5 and 26 bottles of rum were also paid.[45]

It is evident from the official records that it was only by 1852 that the *posa* paid to the Nyishis along with other tribes like the Sherdukpens, Akas, etc, were finally commuted for money payments.[46] After about a year of the commutation of *posa* into money payments, Gordon has mentioned like this, "No adverse effects on peace has been felt due to commutation of *posa* to money payments 'as stipends to the chiefs'. Great numbers of these clans have left the hills and settled in the plains since the commutation was effected."[47]

Posa to the Sherdukpen Chiefs

In 28 February, 1836 Captain Mathie entered into an agreement with the *Sat Rajas* of the Sherdukpens commuting the *posa* to an amount of Rs.2526-7-0 annually.[48] The *Sat Rajas* received this amount regularly upto 1839, when their payment was stopped inconsequence of their having allegedly murdered Madhu Saikia, the Revenue Officer of Orung in Panbari village.[49] In 1884, however, the Sherdukpens came to terms and on recommendation of Capt. J.T.Gordon the payment of *posa* was resumed. The amount of *posa,* however, was reduced to Rs.1740 annually. Since then the Sherdukpens seemed to be reconciled to the change and behaved peacefully in general.

Posa to the Monpa Chiefs

In early 1844, Capt. Gordon entered into an agreement with the Sat Rajas of the Kuriapara *Duar* along with the *Gelong* of

Talung *Dzong Gompa* and *Nyetsang* as the representative of the *Tawang Deo*, binding the chiefs formally to relinquish all their claims to the lands of the Kuriapara *Duar* in consideration of an annual payment of Rs.5000/-.[50] The relation of the British with these *Sat Rajas* remained peaceful till 1852 when a misunderstanding developed because of interception of the amount of *posa* by one of the *Gelongs* who had supervisory authority over the Chiefs. But the peace was restored through a treaty signed on 28th Janyary 1853 at Kuriapara[51] by three representatives of the *Tawang Deo* ratifying the earlier agreements of commutation of *posa* to cash amounting to Rs. 5000.

Posa to the Monpa chiefs of Thembang

The Monpa chiefs of Thembang collected *posa* from the Mazbat area in Charduar. In 1844, they were allowed an annual a sum of Rs.145-13-6 as commutation of their *posa* to cash.[52]

Posa to the Hill Miris

From the *Report on the province of Assam* of Mills in 1853 it is known that Hill Miris were also allowed by the British to draw *posa* in cash and kind annually.[53] The Hill Miris got Rs.851-3-9 and 12 *maunds* of salt annually. From a resolution of the Chief Commissioner of Assam of 1884 it seems that the different clans of the Hill Miris were in receipt of annual *posa* of Rs.281-7-5, Rs.930-4-9 and Rs.25/- in lieu of their rights of collection in the Sisi, Dhemaji and Bordoloni *Mouzas*[54] of the present Dhemaji district of Assam.

Posa to the Adis

While discussing about the *posa* in case of the Adis Mackenzie writes, "so far as can be gathered, the Abors, though much more powerful than any of these tribes, had no such rights. This was owing no doubt to their comparatively remote situation, cut off as they were by the great river Dihang from the cultivated country along the Brahmaputra valley".[55] But some *Burajjis* written in the 19th and 20th centuries mention that *posa* to the Adis had been granted along with the *paiks* of some villages. These *paiks* cultivated paddy for their Lords and fishermen of their allotted *khels* supplied them with fish.[56] These cultivators and fishermen allotted to the Adis were exempted from paying revenue to the Ahom government. According to Lakshmi Devi this arrangement was probably the recognition given by the Ahom government of the claim of the Abors (Adis) over the Miris (Mishings) and the chronicles had probably mistaken it to be the introduction of *posa* system that was arranged with the other neighbouring tribes.[57]

Initially the different sections of the Adis were paid *posa* in kinds such as, iron hoes, salt, rum, abkaree opium and tobacco. But the *posa* payment was commuted to annual payment of allowances in cash and also in terms of salt and rum as early as 1854. In case of Padam-Miniyong section of the Adis the *posa* payments in kind were commuted to cash payment in 1877 and began to be paid from 1878. It is noteworthy to mention here that the right to *posa* as police payments to maintain law and order in the border had been extended to the Padam-Miniyong Adis through different agreements between the years 1862 and 1866. After that, we see that annual monetary payment to different tribal chiefs and *gams* continued till the end of the British rule in India except for the Padam-Miniyong section of the Adis, whose payments were stopped in 1894 and was never resumed.[58] The amount granted to the different clans/villages of the Adis was Rs. 3312/- per annum and was distributed as follows:59

Bor Adis (Padams)	—	Rs. 1096-0-0
Adis of Mebo	—	Rs. 562-0-0
Adis of Padu	—	Rs. 264-0-0
Adis of Duku and Silli	—	Rs. 425-0-0
Pasi-Miniyong Adis	—	Rs. 465-0-0
Adis of Kebang	—	Rs. 393-0-0
Adis of Mankong	—	Rs. 55-8-0
Adis of Retung	—	Rs. 51-8-0

Posa to the Noctes

A brief description of *posa* arrangement with the Noctes will be in fitness of things. The Noctes were granted land and retainers like ordinary Assamese nobles and in lieu of that they paid tributes to the Ahom rulers.[60] According to *Assam Buranji* under the *posa* arrangement the *khats* (land grants) were granted to the Noctes along with the retainers to enable them to procure paddy and other articles which were not available in their hills.[61] Even after the occupation of Assam by the British the Nocte Chiefs continued to retain their *khats* managed by their respective *kotokies.* The British decided to continue the system and in 1841-42 Captain Brodie entered into agreements with these chiefs by which they were allowed to use those *khats* in lieu of payment of a trifling tribute. In addition to that he abolished tools and cesses collected from the Noctes on brine springs held in their possessions. In 1873-74, the government resumed some of the *khats* of the Namsangia and Borduria Nocte Chiefs, which had already been concented into tea gardens, for annual payments in cash.[62] By 1920-21, however, all their *khats* were resumed by the government and annual payments in cash were allowed to the concerned chiefs.[63]

Conclusion

While concluding our discussion on the *posa* system we like to mention certain changes that took place in the soio-economic life of the people of both plains and hills as a result of changes that was affected in the nature of the *posa* system of the Ahom Age by the colonial masters in the British period.

- It is to be noted here that the terms stipends, allowances and pensions were used by the British Authority for 'Commutation of *posa*' indiscriminately. S.N. Mishra, therefore, remarks, "The shell of *Posa* remained but the meat had been taken out of it. ... The Shadow of an over bearing State power ... finally fell on the tribes and the tribes lost their virtual independence which they had enjoyed since times immorial.[64]
- During the Ahom period the relationship among the State (Ahom State), *posa* holders (tribal chiefs and people) and the allotted paiks (*Bahatias*) were interwoven in a system. But after the annexation of Assam by the British the *paik* factor was eliminated from the *posa* system. Now it became on agreement between two contracting parties *i.e.,* the Colonial State and the *Posa* holders in which the State took the responsibility initially in kind and subsequently in cash to pay them. Also no remissiion was made in the revenue to be taken from the earstwhile *paiks.*[65]

- It has further been observed that through innovation in the *posa* system by the colonial rulers, the old ties between the *posa* holders and their *paiks* came to an end. Thus here appeared a cleavage in the old socio-economic ties of two important sections of the society in the border areas. The *bahatia-paiks*, who so long served their masters and practically adopted the culture, language, food habits of their respective masters (tribes), after this clevage either assimilated themselves completely in the societies of their masters or shifted further to the plains to have a livelihoods and social existence like the other Assamese people of the plains. For, now-a-days only an insignificant remnant of the *Bahatia-paiks* is traceable, which requires an indepth study of this socio-economic transformation.
- The commuted *posa* payment in cash to the *posa* holders were made either in the district town in a *posa durbar* organized for the purpose or in annual trade fairs of the foothills at Udalguri and Sadiya. In both the cases the receipants could get ample scope of spending the amount received in buying things of their needs and liking and that they used to do. J.B.Ganguly has rightly remarked, "Annual system of payments of sums of money in lieu of *posa* also injected money into the tribal economy".[66] Further easily available foreign manufactured cheap goods of the colonial masters paved the path for rapid decline of whatever cottage and handloom industries existed in the tribal societies.
- During the Ahom period the annual amount of *posa* was based upon the use value of the things and services obtained and hence, there was no question of depreciation over a time span. But during the Birtish period the respective amount of posa in cash in most of the cases remained throughout the same or in some cases even reduced subsequently. Since it was based upon the exchange value, the force of market mechanism was operating in this age also. So the value of cash paid as *posa* depreciated over the years and here the loosers were the innocent tribals.[67]

- Lastly, during the Ahom period *posa* was paid to the chiefs or the community as a whole. Under the British rule these were paid either to the chiefs or to the representatives of the community. In no case the community as a functional unit was allowed to collect its *posa*, which brought some kind of cleavage in such community having the right to collect *posa*.[68] Further such inflow of resources into individual hands (mostly chiefs and *gams)* from outside as cash payments of *posa* set in motion the process of growing inequalities in income and wealth in the tribal villages.[69]

We have tried to discuss the *posa* system in its multi-faceted dimensions that serve as a very important source to know about the colourful history of Arunachal Pradesh. It infact provides a lot of scope for micro-level studies on the various left out aspects of the *posa* system.

References

1. Amalendu Guha, "The Ahom Political System', E.R. Leach (cf) *Tribal Politics and State System,* pp. 152 f.
2. The original Tai Ahom Population that came with Sukapha could not cope up with the demand of manpower in an ever-expanding Ahom Kingdom.
3. M.L. Bose, *History of Arunachal Pradesh,* New Delhi, 1997, p. 16.
4. B.N. Jha, *British Colonial Intervention and Tribal Responses in the North East Frontier of Assam (1825-1947),* Ph.D. thesis (unpublished) Department of History of Arunachal University, 2002, p. 16.
5. L.N. Chakravorty, "A Short Note on Posa", *Resarun,* Vol. 3, Shillong, July 1977, pp. 1-10.
6. L. Devi, *Ahom-Tribal Relations,* Gauhati, 1968, p.258.
7. *Ibid.,* p. 202.
8. *Ibid.,* p. 37.
9. S.K.Bhuyan, *Anglo-Assamese Relations,* Gauhati, 1949, 2nd edition, 1974, p. 37 (wherein he mentions that the *bahatias* allotted to the Daflas (Nyishis) were generally culprits convicted on various offences).
10. Bengal Political Proceedings, 1825, 5th February.

11. Bengal Revenue Proceedings, 1834, 11th August, No. 5; Alexamder Mackenzie, *The North East Frontier of Bengal,* 1st Published 1884, reprint Delhi, 1979, p. 27; Devi, *op. cit.,* p. 173.
12. L. Devi, *op. cit.,* p. 227.
13. Assam Secretariat Records, File No. 181J of 1882, p. 8; E.T. Dalton's letter No. 162 of 19th May, 1852.
14. Harakanta Barua, *Assam Buranji* p. 41, quoted in L. Devi, *op. cit.,* p. 37.
15. Mackenzie, *op. cit.,* p. 10; L. Devi, *op. cit.,* p. 262.
16. King Rajeswar Singha reduced the Strength of a *Got* from four to three.
17. L. Devi, *op. cit.,* p. 174.
18. S.K. Bhuyan, *Lachit Barphukan and his times,* Gauhati, 1947, p. 4.
19. H.K. Barpujari, *Problems of the Hill Tribes: North East Frontier,* 1822-42, Vol. I, Gauhati 1970, p. 17.
20. I.S. Mumtaza, "Posa: was it a Black-mail", S. Dutta (ed) *Studies in the History, Economy and Culture of Arunacahl Pradesh,* Delhi, 1998, p. 237.
21. J.N. Sarkar, "The Land System and Revenue Administration", H.K. Barpujari (ed.) *The Comprehensive History of Assam,* Vol. 11; Gauhati, 1994, p. 99.
22. Kashinath Tamuli Phukan, *Assam Buranji* (1844), 1906, p. 26, Harakanta Barua, *Assam Buranji,* (ed.) S.K. Bhuyan, Gauhati, 1962, p. 33; *Assam Buranji Sar,* (ed.), P.C. Chaudhury, Gauhati, 1964, p. 23.
23. Mackenzie, *op. cit.,* p. 297.
24. R.B. Pemberton, *Report on the Eastern Frontier of British India,* 1835, Reprint Gauhati, 1975, p. 7.
25. J.B. Ganguly, Presidential Address, Seventh Session of North East India History Association, 1986 cf S. Dutta (ed.) *op. cit.,* p. 260.
26. Capt. Welsh's Report on Assam to Secretary Govt. of India, dated 6th February, 1794. This has also been cited in Mackenzie, *op. cit.,* p. 383.
27. *Ibid.*

28. Pemberton, *op. cit.,* (1955) Gauhati, 1966, p. 80.
29. John M'Cosh, *Topography of Assam* (1837), Delhi 1975, p. 181.
30. William Robinson, *A Descriptive Account of Assam,* (1811), Delhi, 1975, p. 297.
31. A.J. Moffatt Mills, *Report on the Province of Assam,* 2nd edition, Gauhati, 1984, pp. 1969 ff.
32. I.S. Mumtaza, *op. cit.,* pp. 238 f.
33. M.L. Bose, *op. cit.,* p. 53; Mackenzie, *op. cit.,* p. 6.
34. For details please see M.L. Bose, *op. cit.,* B.N. Jha, *op. cit.,* Mackenzie, *op. cit.,* AU Aitchison, *A Collection of Treaties, Engagements and Sanads,* part III, Calcutta, 1909.
35. Assam Foreign Proceedings, March 1885, No. 40; Mackenzie; *op. cit.,* p. 22.
36. Aitchison, Vol. XII, (1931), 1983, pp. 149-50.
37. A.J. M. Mills, *Report on the Province of Assam* (1853), Gauhati, 1984, Appendix-'M', Letter No. 40 of 29th June, 1853.
38. B.N. Jha, "Politics of Posa: A case study of Pre and Post-independence Scenario in Arunachal Pradesh and Assam". *Proceeding of Indian History Congress,* 57th Session, pp. 446-58.
39. Indian Foreign Political Proceedings, 18th July, 1836, No. 77.
40. Bengal Political Proceedings, 1837, 8 May, No. 62.
41. Bengal Political Proceedings, 1839, 13th May, Nos. 10-11.
42. A.J.M. Mills, *op. cit.,* Appendix-'M'; Indian Foreign Political Proceedings, 1844, 20th April, No. 127.
43. Joram Rina, "The Nyishis and the Posa", J. Begi (ed.) *Itanagar: A Profile,* Itanagar, 2003, p. 65.
44. A.J.M. Mills, *op. cit.,* p. 214.
45. Lakhimpur Deputy Commissioner's Collection, No. XII, File 7 of 1884 of M.L. Bose, *op. cit.,* p. 62.
46. Bengal Judicial Proceedings, 1852, 8th April, No. 171.
47. A.J.M. Mills, *op. cit.,* pp. 159-182.
48. Letter from Gordon to Jenkins dated 13th February, 1847 in A.J.M. Mills, *op. cit.,* p. 17.
49. Assam Foreign Proceedings, March, 1885, No. 40; A.J.M. Mills, *op. cit.,* p. 172.

50. Letter from Gordon to Jenkins, 13th February, 1844 in A.J.M. Mills, *op. cit.,* Appendix-; 'M'.
51. Bengal Political Proceedings, October, 1853, No. 64; Aitchison, *op. cit.,* p. 154.
52. Indian Foreign Political Proceedings, 1884, 20 April, No. 127.
53. A.J.M. Mills, *op. cit.,* p. 53.
54. Lakhimpur Deputy Commissioner's Collection, No. XII, File 7, 1884, quoted in M.L.Bose, *op. cit.,* p. 66.
55. Arunachal Pradesh State Archives, File No. 39 J. of 1885.
56. *Ibid.*
57. L. Devi, *op. cit.,* p. 200.
58. Indian Foreign Political Proceedings (External 'A') June 1908, Nos. 33-38.
59. L.N. Chakravorty, *Glimpses of the Early History of Arunachal,* Itanagar, 1973, p. 38.
60. S.K. Bhuyan, *op. cit.,* p. 42.
61. Harakanta Barua, *Assam Buranji,* (ed.) S.K. Bhuyan, Gauhati, 1930, pp. 11-12.
62. Assam Political Proceednigs, August 1874, No. 18.
63. B.N. Jha, *op. cit.,* p. 131.
64. S.N. Mishra, "Arunachal's Tribal Economic Formations and their Dissolution", *The Economic and Political Weekly,* Vol. XVIII, No. 43.
65. B.N. Jha, *op. cit.,* p. 137.
66. J.B. Ganguly, *op. cit.,* p. 260 ff.
67. B.N. Jha, *op. cit.,* p. 133.
68. *Ibid.*
69. J.B. Ganguly, *op. cit.,* p. 268.

17

Theravada Buddhist Sources of Arunachal Pradesh

Byomakesh Tripathy

Introduction

Considered to be an ethnographical paradise for the study of tribal history and culture, the North Eastern Frontier State of Arunachal Pradesh, is a meeting ground of various ethnic groups, having diverse cultural heritage. The heritage of the state is reflected in pre-historic and megalithic remains, Brahmanical monuments, forts and fortifications, Buddhist antiquities in the form of monasteries and *stupas*, colourful dances, religious festivals, and rituals, traditional Arts and Crafts, oral traditions, indigenous faiths and belief system etc. The state is the abode of 26 major tribes and a number of sub-tribes. The tribes traditionally are believers of their indigenous faiths or Buddhist creed; a few, however, are influenced by Neo-Vaishnavism as propounded by the great socio-religious reformer of Assam, Sankardeva in 16th century. Among the tribes, the Monpas, the Sherdukpens, the Nahs, the Membas, the Khambas, the Meyors, the Khamptis, the Singphos and the Tikhak Tangsas (a sub-tribe of the Tangsas) follow Buddhism as their religious faith. It may be mentioned here that the Monpas, the Sherdukpens, the Nahs, the Membas, the Khambas, the Meyors, etc., settled in western and northern frontier of the state[1] bordering Bhutan and autonomous region of Tibet (China), professing *Mahayana* Buddhism considering the prefered influence of Buddhism from Tibet,which can be termed as Tibetan form of Buddhism. The tribes like the Khamtis, the Singphos and the Tikhak Tangsas, are however, believer of *Theravada* form of Buddhism.[2] As per the census of 2001, in Arunachal Pradesh, the total number of Buddhist population are 1,43,028, which is 13.03% approximately of the total population of the state *i.e.,* 10,97,968 as per census, 2001.[3] These Buddhist tribes have contributed immensely to the art and culture of the state and their socio-cultural-religious life, monuments etc. are an important component of Arunachal Culture.

Theravada Buddhist Tribes: A Profile

As we have seen the Khamptis, the Singphos and the Tikhak Tangsas are three *Theravada* Buddhist tribes of Arunachal Pradesh. In the adjoining state of Assam, one can locate a few more *Theravada* Buddhist tribes like the Aitons, the Khamptis, the Khamyangs, the Phakes and the Turungs. Even in Tripura and Meghalaya, *Theravada* tribes such as the mags, mons and the Chakmas are settled.

The Buddhist tribe of the state are settled in the eastern frontier – particularly in district Lohit and Changlang, on the Indo-Burma (Myanmar) border. The Khamtis are mainly settled in district Lohit, in Namsai and Chowkham circle. Major Khampti villages of the state are Chowkham, Kherem, Namsai, Empong, Ningro, Manmow, Lathow, Jonapather, Momong etc. Though the Khamptis are one of the tribes of the state, but any outsider having the idea of tribals of other parts of India will be surprised to see the Khamptis in their original settings. T.T.Cooper in 1873 says "To speak of the Khamptis as a tribe is to do little justice, for there is that about the word tribe which conveys the idea of wildness and want of culture, very far from forming a characteristic of the Khamtis, for from some of their social laws even civilized nations might take a lesson".[4] The Khamptis belong to the great Tai group and said to have immigrated to this part of India from Mung Khamti or Borkhamti area of upper Burma,[5] the mountainous region which interposes between the extremity of Assam and the valley of Irrawady. It is told that they migrated to their present settlements in Arunachal, and some parts of Assam, when the Shan empire of Pong, which once touched Tipperh, Yunnan and Siam was finally broken up by Alomphra, king of Burma about the middle of 18th century.[6] The Ahom Buranjis of medieval period the *Tungkhungia Buranji* and *Ahomar sesh Yugar Buranji* mention that about the middle of 18th century, stray parties of Khampti emigrants, appeared on the borders of

Sadiya.[7] The Khamtis made their first settlements in Arunachal on Tengapani river, with the permission of the then ruling Ahoms. However, during the reign of the Ahom king Gourinathasimha, the Khamtis were successful in ousting the Ahom warden of the Sadiya outpost known as *Sadiya Khowa* Gohain and the Khampti chief became the *Sadiyakhowa Gohain* in 1794 AD having absolute authority in the area.[8]

The Singphos, once considered as one of the most powerful tribes of the Indo-Burmese border, have played an important role in the history and culture of northeast frontier.[9] Colonel Hanney[10] considers the Singphos to be identical in race with the *Kakhyens* of Burma, whose chief habitat was on the great western branch of the Irrawadi river. As per their oral tradition, regarding migration, we are told that originally a hill people from Burma and unable to resist the superior might of the Burmese, the Singphos, left their original home, crossed the Patkai ranges of hills on Indo-Burmese border and entered Assam in late 18th century AD.[11] The *Tungkhungia Buranji* and the *Ahomar Sesh Yugar Buranji* refer, in certain terms to their migration to eastern frontier of Arunachal Pradesh sometimes in 1793 AD.[12] As per their history, the Singphos are said to have first made their appearance on the eastern tip of Assam during the days of the famous Moamaria rebellion in the reign period of Ahom king Gaurinath Simha and came across the Khamptis, whom they successfully ousted from their settlement east of Sadiya and gradually occupied the whole tract of the country watered by the Buri Dihing, the Nao Dihing and the Tengapani rivers.[13] The Singphos are at present settled in Miao and Bordumsa sub-division of district Changlang and Chowkham circle of district Lohit. The prominent Singpho villages are Bordumsa, Kherem Bisa, Dirak Pathar, Gidding, Wakhetna, Ningrang, Saimuy, Piyong, Wagun, etc.

The Tikhak Tangsas, a sub-tribe of the Tangsas, originally belonged to Burma (Myanmar) and as per their tradition and oral literature, the Tikhaks were the first among the Tangsas to migrate and settle in eastern frontier of Assam. According to Shri Yan Tikhak, the Tikhak Tangsas originally belonged to south-western China and subsequently, they established a Kingdom in the Northern Myanmar known as Mok-Le-Longiam, a part of the Mungri-Mungrang, the Kingdom of the Taishan, who later on came to Northeast Frontier of India and established the Ahom kingdom.[14] It is told that after the Ahoms, the Tikhaks have migrated to eastern part of Assam in 13th century; however, the *Buranjis* do not provide a clear cut idea regarding their migration.[15] The Tikhakas, we are told, said to have migrated to their present settlement in a as many as five batches under different tribal leaders.[16] At present the Tikhaks are mainly concentrated at Jairampur, Nampong, Miao, Kharsang and Bordumsa circles of district Changlang.

History of Theravada Buddhism

The Khamptis profess a pure variety of Buddhism after the Burmese school, designated as *Theravada*. As early as 1842, William Robinson noted that "their customs appear precisely the same as those of Ava".[17] John Butler in 1847, while referring to the Khamtis pointed out the prevalence of Buddhism in their society and believed that it seemed to have imbibed them with few prejudices debarring them from the unrestrained indulgences of their natural inclinations.[18] E.T. Dalton in 1872 referred to the Khamptis as Buddhist, and pointed to their regular establishment of priests, who were well versed in the recondite mysteries of their religion.[19] T.T. Cooper (1873)[20] made an interesting observation by mentioning that though in religion, the Khamptis were the followers of Burmese Buddhism, excepting among the priests, their religion was little more than polytheism under a thin veil of Buddhist pantheism and the beauty of Gautama's teachings being utterly unknown among them. The census report of 1881 echoed the sentiment of Cooper, when it states; "The doctrines of their (Khamtis) religion are contained in sacred books written in Khampti character, but believed in some cases to be of the Pali language. They have not, however, any definite notion of the religion they profess".[21] Writings of Michel (1883), Mackenzie (1884), J. Errol Gray (1893), Gurdon (1895), Shakespear (1904)[22] and a few report of British political officer of Sadiya Frontier Zone,[23] have categorically mentioned about the prevalence of Buddhism and Buddhist establishments among the Khamptis in 19th and early part of 20th century. It seems that at the end of 19th century, Buddhism among the Khamtis was a mixture of Theravada Buddhism with those of indigenous faith and belief.

That the Singphos are followers of *Theravada* Buddhism is known from the writings of British Scholars of 19th century. J.B. Neufville in 1828 mentions regarding the worship of Gautama among the Singphos, whose temples and priests were found in all their principal villages and further stated that the Singphos borrowed this concept from the Shans and the Khamptis.[24] Butler writing in 1847echoes the same sentiment as stated by Neufville.[25] E.T. Dalton (1872) while mentioning the religious life of the Singphos, observed that there was no regular priesthood amongst the Singphos but they used to pay great deference to Pungyes or Priest of the Buddhist Shans.[26] A scrutiny of literature of 19th and early 20th centuries reveals that the form of Buddhism among the people is not pure as those of the neighbouring tribe Khamptis. Buddhism, says Verrier Elwin,[27] retains its hold on the Khamptis, but the religion of the Singphos, has been considerably modified by a belief in witchcraft and sorcery and by the importation of local gods into its pantheon.

A few oral traditions of the Singphos throw light on their religious life.[28] As per one tradition, the Singphos vaguely imagine *Chau-ci-giya*, a Buddhist god as the maker of all things. Another Buddhist deity locally called *Chau-khung-Chang* is adopted in their pantheon. A Singpho legend refers to one spirit, *Sori Mittiya* or *Ari Mittia*, who is said to have destroyed the earth by causing violent rains which washed away all the cinders and ashes and made the earth refreshed and re-fertilized. In another legend, the *Ari Mittia* is described as one who brought everything into being and is identified with sun. It may be mentioned here that this name *Ari Mittia* is derived from the Khampti theology, which mentions *Ari Mittia* as one of the past incarnations of Lord Buddha. Ari Mittia is no other than *Arya Maitreya* – a *Bodhisattva* of the Buddhist Pantheon.[29] It is to be mentioned here that the *Maitreya* is the only *Bodhisattva* known to *Theravada* Buddhism and statues of Him are found in Ceylon, Burma and Siam, usually in company with Gautama Buddha.[30]

Some of the Singphos were Buddhists before settlement. Late Umbondwee and Umbontang are considered as the first Singpho Buddhists who migrated to Assam during the middle of 18th century AD. It is told that they carried a wooden Buddha image while coming from Burma and this historical Buddha statue is still kept at Kumsai Buddhist Temple, Lekhapani in Assam.[31] It is also known that one Pienduin Chow Siradow, a Burmese Buddhist scholar, popularised Buddhism among the Singpho community with a missionary zeal.[32] On 5th July 1882 Siradow left Burma (Myanmar) and came to the eastern frontier of Assam for propagation of Buddhism among the Khamptis and Singphos. He is said to have arrived at first at Khumming village (modern Vijoynagar in district Changlang) and stayed there for eight days. Then he reached Khagam village, where a Singphos chief Late Kumku Nong embraced Buddhism. Chiradow travelled extensively in all the Singpho villages in Miao areas, where he converted many Singphos into Buddhism. He also said to have visited Singpho villages Khagam, Ningru, Mohong in Lohit and Bordumsa and Bisa villages in Changlang area. In 1890, he proceeded towards Lazum, Tazi Umbon, Koli and then went back to Chowkham, Shengchap, Sunpura, Kharem and Sadiya. In 1892, he constructed two ordination temples, one at Chowkham and another at Borphakey village of Assam. Siradow credited to have popularised the concept of having at least a monastery in every village of the area, and advised the people to give up their traditional sacrificial ritual, practise non-violence, love, kindness and the teachings of Buddha. He introduced the procedures of *Sangkham* (ordination of monk) and many Buddhist festivals among the Singphos.

It is generally believed that the Tikhaks, like the Khamptis and Singphos, while migrating to Arunachal Pradesh, were under the influence of *Theravada* Buddhism. One Buddhist monk venerable Narendra Mahabhikshu popularised Buddhism among the Tikhaks sometimes in last part of 18th century AD.[33] However, at the end of the 19th and early 20th century, Buddhist monks visited different parts of Tikhak land and gradually converted many Tikhakhs, who were following their animistic religion. According to Sri Venerable Narendra Bhikkhu, chief priest of Buddhist temple at Miao, the Tikhak village Kamba near Lekhapani was the first to adopt Buddhism among the Tikhaks in late 19th century AD, when a Buddhist temple was constructed in the village under the guidance of Venerable Sri Tiringda Bhikhu[34] near Margherita town of upper Assam. He is of the opinion that due to the association of the Singphos, another Buddhist tribe, who lives in their vicinity, the Tikhaks got converted into Buddhism. Among the Tikhaks, people of Longchung village of Nampong circle are said to have accepted Buddhism in early 20th century AD and subsequently, most of the Tikahak Tangsa villages have adopted *Theravada* Buddhism and at present, except 2-3 villages in Miao and Jairampur circles, people in almost all the Tikhak villages are following the *Theravada* Buddhism.[35]

Buddhist Monuments: Prerequisits

The Buddhist monuments in the form of monasteries, and *stupas*, are noticed in the length and breadth of Khamti, Singpho and Tikhak Tangsa area. All the three *Theravada* Buddhist tribes, refer the monastery (*vihara*) as *kyong, chang* or *bapuchang*. Sometimes the proper temple is called *kyong*. To be a full-fledged Buddhist monastery, some of the most essential structural requisites within a monastery compound are temple (*kyuaung* or *kyong*), living quarters (*kuti*) for monks (*bhikkhu*), novices (*samanera*), and temple boys (*mong-yang*), number of rest houses (*sarap*) for male and female devotees (*upasaka* and *upasika*), *chedi* or *chedi kong-mu* (*chaitya* or *stupa*), *Bodhi* tree (*tun-pothi*), boundary stone (*sima* or *simaghar*) a flower garden (*chun bok-ja*) a boat like structure (*hang-lin*) makeshift temple (*chongfra or kyangfra*) etc.

Almost all the Buddhist temples are built in eastern part of the villages, mostly situated on the bank of rivers or streams. One can not think of a *Theravada* Buddhist village, which has no *Vihara* and *Bhikkhu*. The Khampti monastic compound is, if anything, more impressive. The spacious and airy monastery is usually located in the midst of a campus like garden surrounded by rows of trees. The village monasteries consist of a single building inhabited by its chief monk, several other monks and a small number of postulants and novice. The compound may at times have a small hut inhabited by a pious layman who has retired to the monastery and looks after the needs of the society.

The most attractive feature in Buddhist villages is the sacred Buddhist *Viharas* with its unique architectural design very different from the villagers' houses. The land of the monastery officially belongs to the *Sangha*[36] and once it is used for the temple the land can not be used for any other purpose but for paddy cultivation, similar custom is said to have followed among the Tai of Thailand. Villagers built their houses in the immediate vicinity of the monastery so that monks could receive required hospitalities from the householders.[37] In this aspect, Robinson (1842), writes, "their (Khamptis) priests every morning hurry through the village or town, preceded by a boy with a little bell, each priest holding a lacquered box, in which he collects the offerings of the people, presented generally by the women, who stand waiting at their respective doors with a portion of their ready cooked meal".[38] Instances from Thailand indicates to this aspect, when it is told that the Buddhist monasteries has to be built at a distance of at least 1.25 miles from the next so that there would be sufficient households in the vicinity of the monastery to assure that the monks would receive enough food on their daily alms round.

The *Bapu-chang*, like the houses of the richer Khamptis are of timber and thatch but they are carved elaborately. Dalton in 1872 noted the temple and priest quarters of the Khamtis were made of timber and thatch and mentioned that the temples were elaborately carved and great neatness and taste were evinced in the arrangement of the internal fittings.[39] In the outward form of the *Bapuchang*, there is an attempt at the appearance of a Burmese *pagoda*. The temple compound is fenced round so as to keep it as sacred place from any of the structure of the monastery. The respective temples are used for prayer hall, as they do not have separate hall of meditation and to conduct religious services. Noticeable thing inside the prayer halls, are those of statues of Lord Buddha, of different shapes and sizes, made of marble stone, bronze, silver, brass, wood and ivory. These statues are the donations of the laity to the monastery and mostly brought from Burma, showing the Almighty in touching the earth, protecting the people, and spreading the message of Buddhism. V.Elwin has aptly mentioned the fine skill of the Khamptis in carvings of images of Lord Buddha and some of these hidden in small temples in out of the way villagers, according to him, are of singular grace and beauty.[40] Even Buddha images of amber and glassware were kept in the Khampti monastery. P.R.Gurdon in 1895 noticed holy books as well as brass and stone images of Buddha, kept in the prayer halls of some Khampti monasteries and further observed that, women were not allowed to enter the *Bapughar.*[41] The altar, where the statues are kept called *plang* of about three to four feet of the height from the level of the floor and the images are kept facing to the east, as it is believed to be the right direction in which Gautama received enlightenment under a Bodhi tree. J. Errol Gray in his Diary of a journey to the Borkhamti in 1892-93 country provides a very picturesque note of the numbers of temples and *pagodas* in the Khamtilong and mentions that some of their temples are of great size. One of the temples mentioned by him stood in a forest covered island in the Nam Kiu river and was in regular Burmese style, 95 feet high and 125 feet in circumference at the base; four flight guarded by giganatic figures of fabulous beings and having at each face of the compass on the plinth are four marble images of Buddha of excellent workmanship.[42] This account provides an eyewitness to the Buddhist architecture of the Khamti of the later part of the 19th century.

Within the monastery, the next attraction is the group of shaven headed monk in saffron robed garments. They are known as *Bhikkhu* or *Bhikkhus*, who always follow the Buddhistic principle as contained in the vinaya texts. These priests received their office from Buddhistic institutions in Burma, which is attested by T.T.Cooper (1873), who noted that the *Bapus* received their appointment from the Buddhist church of Burma, [43] but the office was not hereditary. The priests have shaven heads, put on amber coloured garments and carry rosaries. Dalton (1872) also refers to the regular establishment of Khamti priests, well versed in principles of Buddhism. Villagers address the *Bhikkhus* as bhante, *chao-mun* and *mahathera* as *chaosara.*

Among other structures of the monasteries, mention can be made of *chedikangmu* (*Stupas*), *bhikkhu's kuti*, which served the purpose of an educational centre and a boat like structure used in *Sankyen* festival for setting up a temporary temple for images with an indigenous mechanism for spraying out from a boat (*hang-lin*), which are invariably associated with the *Theravada* monasteries of the area.

Monasteries of the Khamtis

Khamti monasteries are noticed in the length and breadth of Lohit area. One of oldest and biggest *Theravada* monasteries is noticed at Chowkham. As per the history of the Khamtis,[44] a Khamti ruler of Sadiya, named Chaucha who happened to be a direct descendant of the Nomsoom clan constructed a Buddhist temple and a religious institution called "*cham-muk-thang*" for Buddhist *monks* at Chaukham about one and a half centuries ago, sometimes before 1850's. Towards the later part of his life, there broke out a heavy fire in Chaukham, which most probably affected the monastery. Another Khamti Raja, Chaufartak, said to have donated valuable Buddhist scriptures and images of Lord Buddha to various Buddhist temples including that of Chowkham in late 19th century AD. At the beginning of 20th Century, Chaufa-kanan, rebuilt the Buddhist temple at Chowkham. This beautiful monastery was locally called as *Chongkhamp* (*Chong-monastery; Khamp-gold*) meaning the monastery decorated with gold. However, the monastery does no longer exist today and in place of it, one can notice a new monastery, which was inaugurated by Vishnu Sahay, the Governor of Assam and Nagaland on 21.01.1968. The present structure is beautifully and strongly built of timber and is covered with corrugated iron sheets. The architecture of the monastery does not tally with the other monasteries of the area, as it does not belong to the Chang type of architecture in true sense. Rather the structure is of a single storey, modest in nature and can be approached through a courtyard. The temple has a long hall. Behind the hall, one can locate the library. On the pedestal at the centre is a number of icons of Buddha made of stone and bronze, which are specimens of Burmese and South East Asian sculpture. The typical dress, ornaments, and physical traits indicate its affiliation to Burmese art. A few clay icons of goddess *Vasundhari i.e.,* the Naga goddess is shown standing besides the Buddha images on the altar, who it is believed, witness *dana* and offerings to Buddha. On both the walls of temple, a number of *thankas* or printed paintings, the series depicting the tales of *Jatakas* like those of *Vessantara* and *Bhuridatta* with legends in Thai language are particularly attracting one's attention. Just behind the alter, a small hall, used as library, where hundreds of *Theravada* Buddhist scriptures particularly the *Tripitakas* written in cloth and Pali language along with musical instruments and other articles associated with day to day activities of monastery are preserved. As many as half a dozen of votive *stupas* are noticed inside the boundary of the monastery, of varying length and sizes and it contains beautiful votive images of Buddha in their niches. Besides, as one enters the monastery, on the right side a big Buddha image of along with goddess *Vasundhari*, made of clay of recent time can be seen and near it a boat like structure, where the god is washed and worshipped during *Sankyen* festival. Other structures like two store rooms, rooms of *Sramanas* and *Bhikkhu* can be located. At present the monastery has one monk of Burmese origin, 20 *Sramanas* and two ordinary laity without robe. At a distance of 100 yards from the monastery stands a big peace pagoda constructed by a laity recently.

One of the oldest *Theravada* temple is noticed at the village Momong and locally called *Momong Vihara,*[45] at a distance of 22 km from Namsai. The monastery was constructed in 1881 AD. This monastery contains one of the earliest bronze images of Buddha of the area brought from Burma, sometimes in late part of 19th century. The temple consists of a big and spacious prayer hall with an altar. On the left wall of the altar, mural paintings depicting stories from Buddhist *Jatakas* can be identified. The monastery has at present 2 *bhikhus*, 7 *sramanas* and 7 lay disciples. Just outside the boundary of the *Viharas,* a small *Kuti* can be noticed, where lives four nuns, of them three are married and have left their home to stay here and become nun and the other is an unmarried one. These nuns are not typical *Bhikhuni,* like that of Burma, Thailand and Srilanka and are called *Yasi or Sadhuma* and follows *astashila.* The Lathow Buddhist *Vihara*, at a distance of 12 km from Namsai is said to be another Buddhist structure, constructed in early part of 20th century.[46] The monastery is said to be constructed in 1942, after the establishment of the village in the present size, in 1939. However, the recent renovated structure was constructed in 1962. The monastery consists of a wooden temple and just behind it, another structures, specially used for monastery school where 24 students are imparted education which includes general education, Buddhist studies, and Pali and Khamti literature. The school has a small library, where Buddhist texts of 18th – 19th century written in Tai language are preserved in good numbers. The Vihara has one *Bhikkhu,* and 24 *Sramanas* at present. The Sulungtoo Buddhist temple,[47] 11 km from Namsai, originally constructed in later part of 19th century but renovated after 1950's, is another old temple of the area. The spacious monastery has one temple, *Kuti* for the *Bhikkhu* and a few *stupas*. Except Buddha and goddess *Vasundhari*, no other gods and goddesses are worshiped. Besides one *Bhikkshu*, 5 *Sramanas* and one novice (without robe) are found in this monastery. The monastery at Empong, 38 km from Namsai flourished sometimes in early part of 20th century and as per the tour diary of political officer in 1932, this established Khampti village had a Buddhist school and a monastery. The structure got renovated after 1950's. This monastery is considered very sacred for the lay Khamtis, and here various Buddhist rituals are perfomed and *dana* and *dakshinas* are given to the people. One *Bhikkhu* and one *sramana* live here. The *Vihara* is the store house of hundreds of old Tai Khamti manuscripts and those who do not read the *pothi* here, goes to hell, believe the devotees. Another temple, of early 19th century is of Kherem, known as Kherem Buddhist temple and was renovated in 1965. One Burmese *Bhikkhu*, two *Sramanas* and five general laity are attached to the temple. Another monastery, noticed at a distance of 7 km from Namsai, called Sengsap monastery though originally built in early 20th century it got destroyed by fire and recently only the modern monastery has come up. Another modern monastery is the Nalung Buddha *Vihara*, constructed in 1993, where 2 *bhikkshus* and 12 *sramanas* are living.

One of the biggest and the finest monastery of the area is located at Namsai, known as *Namsai* Paryati or Buddhist *Sasana* built in 1974-75.[48] In the compound, we can notice a main *stupa* of colour resembling that of golden polish, and a typical specimen of Burmese/Thai *stupa* architecture. The commanding *stupa* is one of the finest specimen of *Theravada* monuments of the area. A Buddhist temple having a standing colossal image of Buddha with typical Burmese *Sikhara*, one double storied meditation hall, one community kitchen, one building for staying of *sramamnas* and novices, and another one for the head monk, are the other notable structures of the monastery. The standing Buddha image of the temple, seated Buddha of the meditation hall and another seated Buddha of clay holding a bowl are the finest specimens of modern Buddhist art. Besides one *bhikkhu*, 46 *sramanas* and 17 novices reside in the monastery. Another temple is seen at Piyum village called

Dhamma Rakhita Buddhist temple, at a distance of 12 km from Namsai in the Diyun road. Originally started in 1964, the monastery was completely renovated recently in 1991. Four *bhikkhus*, five *sramanas* and two ordinary laity are staying here. At Nampong, also, thee is a monastery constructed sometimes in 1970's, besides one meditation hall, where lives two *bhikkhus* and one *sramana*. The most auspicious and revered *Vihara* among the Khamtis is the Phaneng monastery, 14 km. from Namsai in the Diyan road. No *Sramana* or laity is seen here because three is no village to maintain and look after them and the monastery, except the family of *Gaonburah* (village headman). Though this is a sacred site, the recent Buddhist temple is constructed only in 1970's. It is believed that river Dihing used to create havoc among the people of the area but after the construction of the monastery, the Dihing river has stopped eroding the area. By praying here, wishes are fulfilled, believe the Khamtis. This *Vihara* is associated with the oldest *pothi* of the area, called *Dhamma Sangani* and if one looks at it, blood comes out through the nose, as believed by the local people.[49]

Buddhist Stupas

Archaeological explorations and excavations have yielded a few Buddhist *stupas* of Arunachal, both belonging to *Hinayana* and *Vajrayana* sects. However, is has to be mentioned here that the natural hazards like nature of the soil, frequent landslides, heavy rains and floods have considerably damaged most of the archaeological sites. These sites though few in number provide an idea of origin and development of Buddhist architecture of the area concerned.

As far as *stupas* of *Hinayana* sect is concerned, the most notable one is that noticed at a place called Vijayanagar in district Changlang, near the Indo-Burmese border.[50] During exploration in 1970, only two sides of the platform of the *stupa* were partially visible, which prompted the scholar to excavate the site in 1971. The monument is noticed on the right bank of the river Noa Dihing. The excavated structure is heavily damaged one. The plan of the *stupa* indicates its octagonal shape. An imaginative reconstruction make the excavator to believe that originally the *stupa* must have been a massive pile composed for a conical structure, super-imposed on an octagonal base. The *stupa* had probably two main divisions, the octagonal base with relief designs and the central tumulus built over it. The octagonal platform, about 2.13 m high, is horizontally divided into three zones, the lowest one, broadest at the bottom (2.44 m) rise in on five diminishing tiny terraces. Over the lower terrace one can notice the slender most middle portion (1.62 m wide) while the upper zones is said to have widened out in two extending tiers. On the frontal portions of the octagonal platform, rosette marks have been introduced in base-relief. Further up, on each of the eight corners of the platform, seated on semi circular bases are small solid domes and in between these corner members, can be seen similar domes placed on v shaped seats. Thus most probably, there were sixteen miniature domes in the original *stupa* as a whole. The central tumulus of the *stupa*, which is completely lost at present, was probably a solid conical super structure, which was crowned by a tapering finial ending either in a multi-formed umbrella or a pointed one. According to the excavator originally the *stupa* would have been 8m high. The whole edifice is a brick structure with an external plaster in lime concrete.

The excavation has also yielded few flat metal images of Buddha, made of quartz, amber, steatite, clay besides of small metal images of alloy numbering fifty, which are very significant findings. These images, which are now preserved at Jawaharlal Nehru State Museum, Itanagar can be categorized into two groups – the larger ones have a replica of the *stupa* on the reverse and the smaller bear a pointed vertical column at the back. One interesting point to observe in these images is that all of them have the curious hornlike protuberance on the crown of the head, tapering to a point, which is typical of the images from Burma and Siam. Besides the images, a few potsherds and an octagonal Ahom Silver coin of King Gaurinath Singha (1780-1794) are being reported from the site.

As a whole, the structure lacks uniformity and the execution reflects imperfect in many respects. The whole edifice is a modest work of architecture. This *stupa* is of *uddesika* type and stylistically may be compared with the medieval *stupas* such as that of Hmawza and Pagan of Burma and adjoining Thailand area.[51] It is believed that while Khamtis migrated from Burma, to their present settlement in Lohit area, they settled at

Vijayanagar for some time in late 18th century and to cater their religious need, they built this modest but very important *stupa*. The finding of the Ahom silver coin from the excavation do indicate that when the Ahom currency was in use, the Buddhist *stupa* site at Vijayanagar was a living centre and the pilgrims from Assam used to visit the sacred site. Taking all the above things into consideration, the *stupa* may be assigned a date of late 18th century AD.

Two brick built *stupas*, one each at Chowkham and Lathaow of 19th century in Lohit district, were noticed earlier, which have been completely washed way by the Bareng and Tengapani rivers respectively. Unfortunately now, we know nothing about the remains of these *stupas*. Another brick built *stupa* can be found near Namsai of district Lohit, which is of modest type and built after the independence. Another small *stupa* is noticed at Lathaow, known as Lathaow Buddhist stupa situated 2 km from Namsai and built in 1939 AD. Among modern *stupas*, a big *stupa* has been constructed on 10th March, 1990 by Sri Chowkham Gohain. Another new but colossal magnificent *stupa* can be seen at Namsai Paryati Buddhist *sasana*, which was built in 1997, and the architecture reflects those of the Burmese and Thai Buddhist *stupa*. Besides, many Buddhist monasteries of the area, found at Chowkham, Sulongtoo, Empong and at other places in district Lohit invariably have votive *stupa* associated with the monastery complex. Though these modern *stupas* are not much of importance from archaeological point of view, still they reflect the living tradition of Buddhist *stupas* in this part of the country and part and parcel of the cultural heritage of the *Hinayana* Buddhists of the area.

Buddhist monuments of the Singphos

In every Singpho village, one can notice a monastery, which they call *chang* or *kyang*[52] generally in the eastern part of the village. Most of the older *changes* are built of timber and thatch which is attested by Dalton's writings,[53] though we do have examples of concrete *changs* nowadays. A full fledged Singpho monastery has a Buddhist temple proper (*chang*), living quarters (*Kuti*) for monks, (*Bhikkhus*) novices and temple boys, *stupa* (*Chedi or Chedi Kangmu*), *Bodhi* tree, boundary stone (*Sima* or *Simaghar*), rest houses (*Sarap)* for *Upasaka* and *upasika*, a boat like structure (*hanglin*) and so on. In Bordumsa and Miao circle of district Changlang, a number of Singpho monasteries are noticed in villages like Guju, Bordumsa, Wakhet, Nalung, Kiding, Dirakbasti, Mohong, Mogando, Kherembisa, Balijan, Wakhetna, Dirakpathar, Gidding, Lalung, etc.

One of the oldest monasteries of the area is noticed near the village Bordumsa. The Venuban Buddhist monastery is said to have been constructed in 1870 by the Villagers and as per the *Bhikkhu* of the *Vihara*,[54] the monastery has undergone renovation three times since its inception. The structure measuring 35x25x15 ft is of single storey and consists of one prayer cum meditation hall, two big rooms for preservation of religious texts, besides the monks' hostel. About 400 religious texts of Tai script are preserved here. The Buddha idols of stone and bronze kept on the altar are said to have been brought from Burma in late 19th century AD. The village Guju, hardly 3 kms from Bordumsa, has preserved two Buddhist monasteries, one of the earlier period and the other one of recent times.[55] The older *chang*, constructed sometimes in the 1980, consists of a big prayer hall, monk's *kuti* and three rooms for preservation of manuscripts. Known as Buddha Pradipa *Vihara*, it measures 45×35×18 ft and near it, a few vitive stupas are found. The other monastery, originally constructed in 1957-58, but has undergone renovation in 1992-93. This monastery consists of a magnificent Buddhist temple of 71 ft where can be noticed a standing Buddha image of 12 feet. A few votive *stupas*, *Kyang-fra* and a magnificent gate have been added to the structure, where one would clearly glean the touch of Burmese Buddhist architecture.

The Kherem Bisa Buddha monastery dates back to 1890, measures 40x20x21ft and consists of a prayer hall, Bhikkhu's kuti and two rooms for preservation of religious literature. Almost all the Buddhist festivals of the Singphos are celebrated in the monastery.[56] The village Dirakpathar (1984), Lalung (1972), Wakhetna (1983), Gidding (1983), Balijan (1984) and many other villages of the Singpho area have a monastery each in the years specified. Most of the Singpho monasteries noticed at present are constructed after 1950s or have renovated completely as most of the older monasteries were built of bamboo and other perishable materials. Monasteries are being constructed now-a-days in various parts of Singpho areas and people of the respective localities take care of the monastery.

Monuments of the Tikhak Tangsas

The earliest Buddhist temple of Tikhak areas was established near Lekhapani in late 19th century. Later on another Buddhist temple was constructed in the Long Chong village in Nampong circle of district Changlang. During 1960's, the Govt. of India sanctioned Rs.30,000/- for the construction of Buddha temples in the Miao area and as a result Buddha temples were established in Miadkhachang, Phap and Ningrang villages.[57] In Kovin a Buddha temple was constructed in 1967 and after 1970's, a number of temples are being constructed in most of the villages inhabited by the Tikhak Tangsas.

A survey of the Tikhak areas reveal that Buddhist temples are noticed at villages like Khachang (of pre independence period), motongsa, kovin, Rima, old chimpo and in other villages.[58] Infact most of these earlier temples are being renovated and now instead of using bamboo and thatch, concrete structures are coming in the form of temples in the Tikhak area. Architecturally, the Tikhak temples are similar to those of the Khampti, but in comparison, they are not so grand and spacious as of the Khamti's monasteries.

In retrospect, the Theravafda Buddhist monuments of the area provide insights to the socio-cultural-religious life of the people. The Theravada Buddhist art and architecture reflect the artistic skill of the people. Besides, various Buddhist festivals, rituals, traditional arts and crafts, etc. also can be utilized as source of the history of Theravada Buddhism in Arunachal Pradesh.

References

1. Niranjan Sarkar, Buddhism among the Monpas and Sherdukpens, Shillong, 1980.
2. Kondinya, Monastic Buddhism among the Khamtis of Arunachal Pradesh, New Delhi, 1985.
3. Information collected from Director of Census Operations, Arunachal Pradesh and Meghalaya by personal communication.

4. T.T. Cooper, New Routes for Commerce: The Mishmi Hills, London, 1872, pp. 144-46.
5. Ney Ellias, Introductory Sketch of the History of the Shans in upper Burma and western Yunnan, 1876, p. 40.
6. L.W. Shakespear, History of upper Assam, upper Burma and North Eastern Frontier, London, 1914, p. 26.
7. U.N.Gohain, Assam under the Ahoms, Jorhat, 1942, pp. 7-8.
8. Edward Gait, A History of Assam, Calcutta, 1926, p. 10.
9. E.T. Dalton, A Descriptive Ethnology of Bengal, Calcutta, 1872, pp. 5-11.
10. A Mackenzie, History of the Relations of the Government with the Hill Tribes of the North East Frontier of Bengal, Calcutta, 1884, p. 61.
11. *Ibid.*, p. 62.
12. Lakshmi Devi, Ahom Tribal Relations (A Political Study), Guwahati, 1968, pp. 246-48.
13. Edward Gait, *op. cit.,* pp. 307-308.
14. Yan Tikhak, The Genesis of Tikhak, Miao, 1999, p. 1-3.
15. N.S. Rao, The Tikhak Tangsas of East Arunachal Pradesh in J.B.Bhattacharjee *et. al.*, (ed.) Proceedings of North East India History Association, Shillong, 2004, pp. 133-146.
16. *Ibid.*
17. William Robinson, A Descriptive Account of Assam, Delhi, 1975, (reprint), p. 80.
18. John Butler, A Sketch of Assam, 1847, inserted in Lila Gogoi (compiled), The Tai Khamtis of North East India, Chowkham, 1971, p. 183.
19. E.T. Dalton, *op. cit.*, p. 5.
20. T.T. Cooper, *op. cit.*, p. 145.
21. Lila Gogoi (compiled), *op. cit.*
22. *Ibid.*
23. Political Proceeding of Lohit Frontier Area of Arunachal from 1910-1935 occasionally refers to Buddhist villages and monasteries of the Khamptis.
24. V. Elwin (ed), India's North East Frontier in the 19th century, Shillong, 1962, pp. 398-399.

25. *Ibid.*, pp. 400-401.
26. E.T. Dalton, *op. cit.*, pp. 9-10.
27. V. Elwin, A Philosophy for NEFA, Shillong, 1964, p. 24.
28. T.K.M. Baruah, The Singphos and their religion Shillong, 1977, pp. 92-93.
29. Alice Getty, The Gods of Northern Buddhism, New Delhi, 1978, pp. 21-24.
30. *Ibid.*
31. Ven Mahathero Narendra, The Wheel of Dharma, Arunachal Pradesh, Bhikkhu Sangha, Tinsukhia, 2001, p. 15.
32. Bhikkhu Bornachar, Pieuduin Chow Siradaw, Margherita, 1980.
33. N.S. Rao, Theravada Buddhism among the Tikhak-Tangsas of Arunachal Pradesh, paper read in the seminar (Buddhism in North East India, held at Arunachal University, Itanagar on December 2-3, 2002).
34. Vide interview with Tringda Bhikkhu, A Tikhak-Tangsa Monk on May 15, 2003 at Miao.
35. N.S. Rao, *op. cit.*
36. Lulang Suriyabongs, Buddhism in Modern Thailand, Bangkok, 1954, p. 84.
37. Ruth Inge Heinze, The Role of the Sangha in Modern Thailand, Taipei, 1976, p. 16.
38. William Robinson, *op. cit.*, pp. 77-82.
39. E.T. Danton, *op. cit.*, pp. 5-6.
40. Verrier Elwin, The Art of the North East Frontier of India (Shillong, 1959), pp. 84-85.
41. Lila Gogoi (compiled), *op. cit.*
42. *Ibid.*
43. T.T.Cooper, *op. cit.*
44. Lila Gogoi, *op. cit.*, pp. 31-36.
45. Interview with Bhikkhu Vimalananda at Momong on 13.06.2002.
46. Interview with Venerable Rajinder Bhikkhu, Lathow, on 10.06.02.

47. Interview with Gyanananda Bhikkhu on 11.06.2002.
48. Interview with the head monk (Mahathera) Agadhamma of the Namsai Buddhist Vihar on 14.06.2002.
49. It is stated by Bhikkhu Usera Mere, who is originally from Tripura vide interview on 13.06.2002.
50. Y.A. Raiker, *Vijoynagar: The Forgotten Khomong* (a small brochure), published by Research Department, Govt. of Arunachal Pradesh, Shillong, 1974.
51. For Buddhist Stupa in Siam, please see, Rajanushab Damrong, *History of the Buddhist Stupas of Siam,* Bangkok, 1926 and also see, Upendra Thakur's "*The Stupa in Thailand*" in B. Chatterjee (ed), *History and Archaeology,* New Delhi, 1986, pp. 222-230.
52. S.Dutta Choudhury, *Arunachal Pradesh District Gazetteers,* Lohit district, Shillong, 1978, pp. 68-72.
53. E.T. Dalton, *op. cit.,* pp. 5-6.
54. Vide interview with Ven. Gyanodaya Bhikkhu Monk of Venuban Monastery on 28.05.2002.
55. The History of the Monastery is provided by Ven. Waradhamma Bhikkhu, a monk of Srilanka Origin at Buddha Pradip Vihar, Goju on 7.6.2003.
56. Vide interview with Sumedhu Bhikkhu, headmonk of Kherem Bisa Buddha Vihar on 12.6.03.
57. Narinda Mahathero (ed), The wheel of Dharma, Souvenir, Diyun, 2002.
58. The information is collected by the authors during his fieldwork in the area in May, 2003.

18

Mahayana Buddhist Sources of Arunachal Pradesh

Byomakesh Tripathy

Arunachal Pradesh, the abode of various colourful tribes is notable for its tribal history and cultural heritage. The heritage of the people is reflected in their socio-cultural-religious institutions. The prehistoric remains, ruins of temples, forts, Buddhist monuments, traditional arts and crafts provide fine examples of Indian cultural relics. Here one can notice belief in *Donyi-Polo* (worship of Sun-Moon) animism, nature worship, worship of Vishnu as well as Buddha. Interestingly out of about twenty five major tribes, more than half a dozen of tribes profess living Buddhism- both *Theravada* and *Mahayana* forms. While tribes like the Khamtis, the singhphos, the Tikhak Tangsas are believers of *Theravada* Buddhism, the Monpas, the Sherdukpens, the Naths, the Membas, the Khambas and the Meyors are following the tenets of *Mahayana* Buddhism.

The *Mahayana* tribes are mainly noticed in the Indo-Tibetan border area of Arunachal. The Monpas and the Sherdukpens live in Kameng frontier (Tawang and West kameng area), the Nahs in Upper subansiri, the Membas and the Khambas in Upper siang and the Meyors inhabit the Lohit frontier[1]. These *Mahayana* Buddhist tribes are said to have migrated to their present settlement from Tibet sometimes in the past. Credit goes to *Guru Padmasambhava* or locally called *Lopon Rimpoche,* who planted the seed of Buddhism in Monpa-Sherdukpen area sometimes in 8th Century A.D. As per the legends, various places in Kameng area are associated with the visit of

Padmasambhava. In the Monpa area, places like Taktsang. Jiktaksang, Bagajang, Kimnash, Terma Bumgan, Bigha and Komefuk were said to have been visited by the great Guru. The Sherdukpens also cherish nine places like Jambring, Khang Gisih, Flujima, machula, Chupt, Jakhung, Pemaloso, Urgyan Pemagom, (Chaksung) and Shra-ha-noma, hallowed by association with the Master [3]. Tradition has it that it was *Padmasambhava* who predicted the construction of three oldest Buddhist temples in this area and as if to fulfill it, a *Nyingmapa Lama* from Bhutan, Sherbum by name, built the three oldest *Nyingmapa* temples of Urgyeling, Sangeling and Tsorgeing [4] sometimes in 11th-12th century AD. These three oldest monasteries are situated near the town of Tawang.

However, the history of *Gelugpa* sect in this region starts with Thangston Gyalpo, a Lama from Tibet (1385-1462), an architect and propagator of *Gelugpa* sect of Buddhism. Later on Tanpei Dronme and his brother Lopsang Khecham, who were contemporary of second Dalai Lama Gedun Gyatso (1475)-1543), after their training in Tibet built a number of Gelugpa monasteries in Kameng area. They are credited to have established a number of monasteries, such as, the Brakar *Gompa*, Arikadun *Gompa*, Lhangten *Gompa*, Sanglamphe, Tadung *Gompas*, Taidung *Gompa*, surchung *Gompa*, Lalung *gompa*. "The *Gelugpa* sect thus introduced by Tanpei Dronme, was sustained, consolidated and extended in these areas by a series of his incarnations. The fourth incarnation of Tanpei Dronme was Lord Gyatso; also known as Mera Lama, who gave a new direction to *Gelugpa* sect by establishing the celebrated Tawang monastery sometimes in 17th century AD. However, the arrival of Buddhism among the Monpas of Dirang area in Central Kameng was comparatively late. It is believed that one Lama of *Karmapa* sect Droang Rimpoche popularized Buddhism among the Monpas of Dirang sometimes after the construction of the Tawang monastery in early part of 18th century, when the Rupa *gompa* was constructed in West Kameng in 1742 AD.[7] It is also told that one Meme Gyapten, whom the Sherdukpens honour as their ancestor, came to the Sherdukpen area as a lay associate of Tanpei Dronme sometime between 1475 and 1543. But credit goes to Khechang Doyen Tanjing, the sixth incarnation of Tanpei Dronme, for establishing Buddhism among them sometime around 1742 AD. Here it may be mentioned that the *Karamapa* sect of Buddhism in Tawang area could be established by one Rangchong Dorjee who established the *Karmapa* temple of Kimnash, constructed in 13th century AD, as per an inscription found there.[8]

The other *Mahayana* tribes have their own history regarding the adoption of Buddhism. The oral traditions of the Monpas point to the fact that they were converted into Buddhism from the faith of various categories of spirits and necromancy in Tibet. They are said to have migrated to their present area by the Lama Cheeji Longbo, who belonged to *Ningmapa* sect of *Mahayana* Buddhism and for which the Monpas still practise *Nyingmapa* sect of Buddhism". The Nahs, the Meyors and the Zhakrings, who have come to their present area in early part of 20th century are said to have brought Buddhism with them from Tibet.

Monastery is the most important component of Buddhist architecture since early historical period. In Sanskrit, a monastery in called a *'Sangharama'* or *'Vihara'*. However, the *Mahayana* monastery in Arunachal is called *Gompa*.[10] These *Gompas* are constructed at some distance from villages and on the face of a cliff or spur of a hill. The track to the monastery is the temple, known as *Kakaling*, made of wood and the ceilings and top of the side walls are decorated with Buddhist paintings. The chief building in the monastery is the temple, known as *lha-khan* (God's house) having a courtyard in its front. The temples are generally single-storied and sometimes double-storied. The temple consists of an entrance room (*Gokhang*) and a prayer hall, locally called *Dukhang*. The walls are profusely decorated with Buddhist themes. One or more minor buildings for Lamas and caretakers, storerooms and the like are also noticed. Various minor structures are also noticed in or around the *Gompa*. Prayer flags or *Phans* are seen everywhere. Varieties of flags like *darsingh, hungtow, chephan*, etc, are noticed. Among other structure, *hung-piung* or *laptse*, are noticed on the summits of all passes. These are pile of stones with an upright stick in it. Passers by worship it to propitiate the local spirit. Another structure called *Sangbum*, made of stone and about 6 feet high is noticed in front of temples and houses and juniper twigs are burnt in it as incense during ritual performance.

In Tawang area, various places associated with the legend of *Padmasambhava* have a *Gompa* each. These are the Taktsang *gompa* Sarong *gompa*, Baggajang *gompa*, Kimnash *gompa*, Komefuk gompa, etc. It is believed that all these Gompas were constructed at least two or three centuries before construction of Tawang monastery. Here it may be mentioned that in Tawang and West kameng area, *Gompas* of *Nyingmapa*, *Gelugpa* and *Karampa* sect are noticed.

The *Nyingmapa* monasteries were very popular in Tawang area. Three early *Nyingmapa* gompas are noticed at Tawang. These are Urgyelling, Sangelling and Tsorgelling gompas. These monuments were built by one Lama Sherbum sometimes in 11th-12th century AD. However, later on, one Mongol prince Gussri Khan[11] said to have destroyed these three early *Gompas* to establish the supremacy of the *Gelugpas* over the *Nyingmapas*. Subsequently *Nyingmapas* could rebuild the *Gompa* at Urgyelling and Sangeyelling but Tsorgelling laid in ruins. The *Gompa* at urgyelling is a gem of Buddhist art and architecture.[12] The double-storied structure, in its second floor, has preserved various icons and fine mural paintings. On the altar, one can see Buddhist deities *Jeyapchesum*. *Nache*-the God of wealth, image of Lama *Kechopchen*, Lama *Sherbum*, the fifth Dalai Lama and the sixth Dalai Lama. Clay icons of *Drema Wanmo*, *Paldan Atisha, Chenreji*- the *Avalokitesvara* etc. are of considerable interest. On walls of second floor paintings of *Lopon Rimpoche*, paintings of father of sixth Dalai Lama, *Tashi Tenzin*, mother of sixth Dalai lama, *Tsowang Lama*, *Lama Urgen Tsangpo*, *Palden Lhamo Tsongkhappa* founder of *Gelupga* sect, Mera Lama-founder of Tawang monastery, Deshi Sangey *Gyastso, Ningme Chan*-guardian deity of Tawang, etc. are fine specimens of mural paintings. The ground floor contains as many as nine *stupas*. The *Gompa* is said to be associated with the birth of sixth Dalai Lama. The Sangeyling *Gompa* is at a distance of 8 kms from Tawang town. The single-storey building consists of two rooms- the entrance room (*Gokhang*) and the Prayer hall (*Dukhang*). The Dukhang has preserved clay sculptures of Guru *Padmasambhava* in eight forms and those of other Buddhist deities like *Avalokitesvara* and *Arya Maitreya*.

The *Nyingmapa Gompas* are also noticed in Tawang, Dirang and Kalaktang area. In Dirang and kalaktang area (in West Kameng district), a number of *Gompas* like the Lhagyala *Gompa* at Morshing, the Zangdo Peri *Gompa* of Kalaktang, the Rupa *Gompa*, Rupa, the Zengba *Gompa*, Shergaon, the Jangcho choiling *Gompa* and the Namthung *Gompa* of Dirang, the Duntsi *Gompa*, Sengedzong, the Boha *Gompa*, Boha, the Gompatse monastery and Guru Rimpoche *gompa* of Bomdila, the Talklung *gompa*, Sanglem, the Gyoti tantric monastery, Tenzingaon, the Zhim and Norbuling *gompa* at Nyokmadung, the Namshu *gompa*, Namshu, the Gonthung *gompa* of Thembang, the Lagam chenrezig *gompa* at Lagam, Buddhist *gompas* of Angkaling village etc. are noticed. The Lhagyala *gompa* at Morshing is notable for the repository of hundred Buddhist icons. It is one of the oldest and largest *gompas* situated in the Indo-Bhutan border land in the Kalaktang administrative circle of the West Kameng district. It was established before the Tawang monastery and is considered as of the second position in religious status in the area. The hundreds of scrolls of deities are being hanged up on the walls of the *gompa*. The walls of *gompa* are decorated with mural paintings of the moral teaching of the great masters of the lineage. Hundreds of large and small idols made of clay, brass and sliver, and even of gold-wash are available in the *gompa*.

Mahayana gompas are also noticed in Upper Siang region. In this aspect, the monastery at Gelling, Tuting, Mankhota with their Buddhist art, architecture and mural painting of late medieval period are of much importance, to understand Buddhism among the Membas and Khambas. The Pema Tsoling *Gompa* of Rupa is the most important *Gompa* of Rupa area. This Gompa of the Sherdukpens was constructed in 1742 AD. The structure is three-storied and the ground floor consists of the *Dukhang*, where images of *Witbma*, *Chendrezi*, *Guru Padmasambhava* and the local deity *Shawang* are worshipped; on the second floor, also noticed a number of Buddhist deities like *Avalokitesvara, Tara* etc. Interestingly an image of Vishnu with Laxmi and Sarasvati on his both sides are worshipped. A few votive *stupas* are noticed near the monastery.

The Tawang monastery is the heart and soul of the *Mahayana* Buddhist people of the area. It is one of the largest monasteries of the world. The full name of this monastery is *Tawang Gadden Namgyal Lhatse*. It was constructed by one Mera Lama, sometimes in 1681-82 AD.[13] There are as many as twelve subordinate *gompas* of Tawang and Monks from Tawang *Gompa* are required to work as caretakers for these monasteries under the control of Tawang monastery. These are Kyipney *gompa*, Brakar *Gompa*, Ayidung *Gompa*, Thongmein *gompa*, Khromten *Gompa*, Sharmang *Gompa* and Urgyelling *Gompa*, Located at an altitude of little over 3,050 meteres above the sea level; the monastery looks like a fort on its hill side from a distance.

The monastery is a large complex resembling a castle. Enclosed by a 610 meteres long wall, it extends over an area of 135 square metres. The monastery can be approached from the North along a ridge. Before one reaches the monastery, one can see a double-storied building *Dungjur* and a *Chikhang* (water-building) from where water is supplied to the monastery. At a distance of nearly 75 feet, to the South of *Chikhang* is noticed the *Kakaling* (ornamental gate), which is full of mural paintings. The paintings of *Buddha*, *Maitreya*, *Jambhala*, *Tara*, *Avalokitesvara* and many other Indian Buddhist Pandits are fine specimen of Budhist art. The drawing of *Ningmechan*, who according to *Bonpo* religion, is the guardian deity of Tawang area, is also noticed and who has been incorporated in the local Budhist pantheon and being worshipped in the Buddhist style and without animal sacrifice. The paved path then passes through a big open gate, and above this gate is a double-storied building used as monks' quarter. The eastern boundary wall starts from the open outer gate and encloses the eastern side of the monastery. There is another gate near the southern end of the wall, fitted with a huge door. A narrow path runs all along the outside of the eastern wall connecting the gate with the *Kakaling*. The entire eastern half of the monastery is covered with sixty dormitory buildings called *Shak* for housing the resident Lamas, which has a capacity for housing 500 to 800 monks. At present about 370 monks are residing here.

A building locally called *Shingda Ahpa-Bumpa* stands to the west of the main path in the area between main gate and outer gate. The single-storey structure preserved an image of Lama *Tanpei Dronme Drolma, Thangston Gyalpo*, the famous Lama builder, two small *Chortens* and a few fine specimens of mural painting. The paved path runs from the main gate towards the rear of the monastery, leading to a cobbled court, where religious dances and out door ceremonies are organized. A three-storied building stands on the western side of the court, known as *Par-khang* (Library). But the actual library is housed in a big square hall, covering the entire first floor. The library contains two printed sets of Tanjur, three sets of *Kanjur* and five volumes of *Changea Sungbum.* The set consists of more than hundred volumes. In the ground floor of the library, the wooden blocks with the pages of scriptures cut out on them used to be preserved, but all these were damaged by insects. To the north of the library, there is a small building called *Dugjur mane.* A part of the building is used as store for the provisions of the Lamas. The other part is occupied by the *dratsanguk* (estate manager) and his entourage. A single-storey building on the eastern side of the court is used for cooking the food offerings for the rituals as well as refreshment for the Lamas on ritual days. The kitchen attached to the temple is locally called *Hrum-khang.*

The most important building of the monastery is the assembly hall, known as *dukhang.* It is a three-storey building and stands on the north side of the court and houses the temple and the *Labrang* (establishment of the abbot). The entrance to the temple is by a wide vestibule, the walls of which are decorated with coloured murals, showing the Budhist guardian deities, the wheel of life and the daily life of the Buddhist Lamas. On entering, one can find a large hall measuring about eighty eight feet by seventy five feet with 36 wooden pillars arranged in six rows at equal distance from each other. The upper gallery of the first floor is supported by 32 pillars. The four other pillars, higher than the rest, go up to support the ceiling of the first floor. The eastern, southern and western walls are profusely painted in bright colours. Here mention can be made of paintings of *Ningmechan,* Buddhas known as *Maneha Deshegke*, thirty-five confessional Budhas. The altar occupies the entire northern wall of the hall, where a seated image of Buddha of 26 feet high can be seen. A big wooden case near the altar has preserved a number of Buddhist images. Behind the altar, there is a door, leading to a chamber in the rear hall, where images in standing posture of eight celestial *Bodhisattvas* collectively called New *Shechinge*, images of fearsome deities like of *Jigje, Gompo* (*Maha-Kala*), *Chorge, Paldan Lhamo,* Namshe and *Chamsing,* who are considered as the defenders of Buddhist doctrine against the demons and other enemies are noticed. A stone staircase, outside the assembly hall takes to the first floor, where lives the *Abbot.* Another chamber in the first floor contains murals of twenty renowned Buddhist Pandits, five from India and other from Tibet. The second floor consists of a big room, where are placed a drum and two conches calling the resident lamas to assemble in the *dukhang* during the regular functions. The roof is surmounted by three-gilt copper spires-one in the middle and the other two on either end of the ridge. On the back of the assembly hall is the *nga-khang* (Defenders Room). In the double-storied structure, the image of *Gompo, Akshobhya Tsepame* and others Buddhist icons are preserved.

A few nunneries of *Gelugpa* sect are noticed in or around Tawang locally known as *Ane gompas.* These are the *Gaing-Gong* Ane *Gompa* and *Brahmadung Chong* near Tawang tow Nuwang Ane *Gompa* at Shekpret village in Lumla circle, and the Sing-sor *Gompa* at village Lhau, all in district Tawang. Here mention may be made of the two Ane Gompas, located at a short distance of Tawang monastery.[14] The history of the Gainggong Ane *Gompa* goes back to the late 17th century AD, when Tawang monastery was being constructed by Mera Lama. Mera Lama had a sister, who wanted to be a nun. As no woman could reside in the Tawang monastery, subsequently Mera Lama provided financial support to construct a nunnery for his sister and thus the said Nunnery was established on a hillock at a distance of about four miles north of the Tawang *Gompa.* The Gainggong Ane *Gompa* in the present shape is a double-storied structure and is affiliated to the Tawang monastery. Measuring 16.70m.

12.50 m and 7.60m in length, breadth and height respectively, the *Gompa* has a small portico, the prayer hall (*Dukhang* or the assembly hall) is the biggest room of the *Gompa* with small residential buildings for the nuns around it. One can notice a number of clay and metallic sculptures in *Dukhang* and *Shamjong.* The clay images of *Je Lama*, locally known as *Lobsang Drakpa*, founder of the *Gelugpa* sect, *God Che-de-se* (*Avalokitesivara*), *Jigchen Drema*, *Thowangku* image of Budha, three images of god *Je Yebse sum*, one icon of *Lopon Rimpoche* (*Guru Padmasambhava*) and others are quite attractive. A mural painting depicting the goddess *Paldan Lhamo*, the tutelary deity, can be identified in the *Dukhang.* Now there are 35 nuns living in this Nunnery. A date of 17th century is attributed to the monument.

The other Nunnery is the one known as *Bramadung Chong*, at a distance of 8 km north of Tawang monastery. As the oral tradition goes, the nunnery was established due to the initiative of one nun Yeshi Khand Drama and liberal donation from Lopsang Thapkey. The south facing Nunnery is of double-storey. Consisting of a small portico, common kitchen, *Dukhang* has preserved a number of clay and metallic icons. The icons of Buddhist goddess *Drema Nishi Chakchai,* god *Sungma Damchin*, Buddha, god *Avalokitesvara, Je Lama, Tsongpa, Paden Atisha, Chepamay, Jog* and others are priceless heritage of the Buddhist art of this *Gompa.* Adjacent to the monument, one *Chhikhang* (water building), a few *Manes* and Nun's quarters are noticed. 37 nuns are staying in this nunnery at present. As this Nunnery is not affiliated to the Tawang monastery, the nuns are to depend upon voluntary charity of the people and each nun earns her livelihood by undertaking various ritual services in the villages. The adjacent villagers used to provide food grains liberally for the sustenance of the nuns. This Nunnery is said to be constructed in early part of 19th century.

In the *Mahayana* area of Arunachal, one can notice a number of stupas locally called as *Chorten*, meaning 'the receptacle of relics'. Exoterically, different parts of a *Chorten* collectively represent a combination of five elements-Earth,

Water, Fire, Air and Ether. The *Stupa*, satisfies both a physical and metaphysical indigence and has three functions as a reliquary containing the Buddha ashes or some other symbol of His *Dharma*; as a memorial marking the location of an event in the Buddha's life; and as a votive offering. In Arunachal, the *Mahayana* tribes have their own nomenclature regarding various forms of *chorten* or *Chosten.* When erected as a cenotaph, enshrining the earthly remains of the departed, the *stupa* is called *Kudung*: on the other hand the *chorten* containing personal possessions of the departed is known as *dungten.* As far as their architecture is concerned, the *Kudung* consists of a hemispherical dome enclosing the relics and rests upon several plinths, while the dome is surmounted by a square capital with a spire consisting of thirteen steps like segments which in turn is topped by one or more umbrellas, the sides of the capital sometimes bear a pair of eyes. In the other but more common form of *Dungten*, a solid square dome rests on a five-tier platform, set on a square base and the dome is surmounted by a thirteen ring spire, topped by a solar disc set on a lunar crescent; a circular device being rests on the solar disc. These cenotaphs were being set up with the hope that the departed soul may get a good rebirth. But most of the *Chortens* contain only sacred images and religious texts and erected by the laity to ensure communal welfare. Miniature *Chortens* of metal or clay are also placed as offering on the temple altar and sometimes the niche of a *mane* wall of *stupa.*

Among the *Mahayana stupas* of the state, the *Chorten* of Gorcham is the biggest one.[15] Gorcham is a place near Zemithang in the Lumla sub-division of Tawang district, near the Indo-Tibetan border. Built in stone and mud plaster, the cenotaph has a base of 120 feet square and a height of about 100 feet. The hemispherical dome rests upon three terraced plinths. Four miniature stupas are constructed on the four corners of the lowermost terrace of the plinth. The base is square with each side about 175 feet in length with a niche running all along its whole length and as many as 120 manes (Prayer wheels) are set in frames of wood in the niche of each side of the base. A paved path goes all around for the pilgrims to follow in respectful circumbulation 'keeping the chorten on their right, turning the manes and chanting *"Om mani peme hum".* Small clay *Chortens* and miniature clay base reliefs of *Tsepame* (*Amitayus*), the Buddha of infinite life along with the *manes* can be located, which are the offerings of the pilgrims. The dome is surmounted by a square capital with a spire of thirteen steps like segments topped by an umbrella. An illustration of this stupa can be noticed in the book, *My Land and My People: The Autobigoraphy of His Holiness.* The Dalai Lama, 1962, (plate No.13),[16] where it is mentioned as Gonsum *Chorten.* In this illustration, two sides of the capital are visible and the side facing the track from Zemithang bears an enormous pair of the all seeing eyes of the supreme Buddha. Now also we can notice this feature. Just behind the *chorten*, stands the double-storied Gorcham *Gompa* made of clay and wood, containing a few traces of mural paintings, which are difficult to identify due to lack of preservations.

The *Chorten* was constructed by one Lama Pradar, a Monpa Lama of the nearby village Kharmin. This *stupa* is said to have been modeled after the Bodhnath *stupa* of Nepal.[17] The *stupa* said to have contained three sets of copper images of Buddha of three different sixes, each set consiting of 108 models, sets of *Kanjur*, each containing 108 volumes and three sets of copper model of a *chorten.* The local Monpas call it as Beyu *Chorten.* Infact the Gorcham *Chorten* reflects the engineering scheme of the Monpas at its best. During the fifteenth and thirteenth days of the first lunar month according to Monpa calendar, devotees from all over the area visit Gorcham *stupa* for worship. A small booklet published by Buddhist Cultural Preservation society, Bomdila mentions that the *Chroten* is about 700 years old. However, on the basis of the architecture and circumstantial evidence, the stupa can not be dated to prior to the date of Tawang monastery. Besides, one can notice a number of *stupas* of small and medium in size, throughout the region of Arunachal, inhabited by the *Mahayana* tribes, particularly in Monpa-sherdukpen areas. The *stupa* culture is still in vogue and are being constructed as the people believe that the building of a *stupa* is a meritorious act and is a means of propagating and reaffirming the *Dharma.*

The *Mahayana* Buddhist tribes of Arunachal observe a number of festivals and ceremonies through out the year.

Besides the daily services, the monastic community observes seasonal rites and festivals. The ceremonies like *Losar* and *Monlam Chenmoh* (first Monpa month), *Gyalwa Kalzang Gyatso Lomchoh* (second month), *Sangdui* (fourth month), a ceremony for *Nilok* (fifth month), *Drukpa Chisi* (sixth month), *Jigje Drumche* (seventh month), *Yanglin* and *Lhabap Duichen* (ninth month), *Gadndan* Gamchut (tenth month), a ceremony for *Nilok* and the *Torgya* festival (eleventh month) are the most important ones and are celebrated in Tawang monastery regularly.[18] Infact, there is hardly any major ceremony in the third, eight and twelfth months of the Monpa calendar.

The *Losar*; the New Year festival is the most important festival of the *Mahayana* Buddhists. It is celebrated during January-Febrary and continues for five to fifteen days. The first day of the Buddhist New Year is called as Lama *Losar*: as on this day the junior monks call on Lamas to pay respect to them. All wear new clothes, and celebrate it by eating, drinking and entertainments Lamas are called in every house to perform ceremonies for a happy new year for the family, The second day of the festival is called *cyano losar* or king's losar, for in the old days the kings used to visit each other on this day and in commemoration of the day, friends meet each other to wish happy losar and sports meet are held. On the third day known as *yuitha losar*, religious flags are hoisted on house tops and the people pray to god for health prosperity. The concluding day of the festival is marked by prayers in the village *Gompas* for blessings of the compassionate for the New Year. Horse-racing is an attractive feature of the day, besides a lot of fun and frolic.

Another important festival is the *Torgya* festival, basically a dance festival held in Tawang monastery in January – February every year. Here dances are performed by Lamas in the huge courtyard of the monastery before a large gathering. In this festival, a pyramidal structure of about one metre high and made of millet flour is prepared, known as *torgya* to serve as a ritual offering. The Lamas in full warrior dress carry the *Torgya* in a procession in the afternoon of the last day of the festival to a place outside the monastery where the abbot consigns it to fire. A variant of dances including devil dance,

dance of the good spirits and others are presented. This festival continues for three days. Every third year, this festival is called *Dungjur*, when it is performed on a grander scale.

Choikor or *chosker* is another ceremony observed by the people in the seventh month of the *Mahayana* Buddhists. In this ceremony, religious scriptures are recited by the Lamas and carried in ritual circumbulation. It is basically an agricultural ceremony performed for the protection of crops. On the last day of the ceremony, the Lamas and laity go round village cultivation fields in a procession led by a senior Lama with sacred texts on their back and in front of the procession, two young men in wooden monkey masks and wooden replica of the phallus go on dancing and it is believed that their dress, mask and movements would frighten away the evil spirits so that the villagers could secure better harvest and prosperity[19].

The *Mahayana* tribes also perform pantomimes of different varieties on the occasion of festivals[20]. The *Thu totdam Pha-cham* (Boar dance), *Jam cham, Ara Kachocham, Grei Cham, Lo cham, Ja Phomo, Dam-Chin, Chhoige, Geyehin-Namsekor. Gelong Cham, Cham-Chin, Ajilhamy, Yak Cham* are fine examples of pantomimes noticed in the region. Various dances, songs, traditional arts & crafts like making of masks, scroll printing, wooden crafts and paintings are other cultural heritage of the tribes.

Conclusion

The Buddhist monuments of the area are rich repositories of Buddhist art, architecture, sculptural and mural paintings. Every *gompa* has hundreds of Buddhist manuscripts, which contain a lot of information on Buddhist religion, philosophy, logic and other secular aspects also. The Buddhist sculptures betray the influence of medieval Tibetan sculptures. The nicely executed paintings reveal the socio-cultural life of the people and development of Buddhism in this part of the country. The dances, festivals, rituals are very much importance, for the study of *Mahayana* Buddhism of the area. The socio-cultural life of the people also indicates to various aspects of *Mahayana* Buddhism of the area.

References

1. The Monpas, the Sherdukpens, the Nahs, the Membas, the Khampas, the Meyors, the Zhakirngs and a few Tibetans living in some parts of Western and Northern frontier of the State of Arunachal Pradesh along the Indo-Tibetan border, are the followers of Mahayana Buddhism or so called Tibetan form of Buddhism.
2. For the legendary history of Padmasambhava, please see, A. Waddell. The Buddhism of Tibet or Lamaism, Cambridge, 1959, pp. 380-382.
3. Niranjan Sarkar, Buddhism among the Monpas and Sherdukpens, shillong, 1980, pp. 1-3.
4. G.N. Mehra, Bhutan, Land of the Peaceful Dragon, Delhi, 1974, pp. 70-71.
5. D. Snellgrove and H.Richardson, A Cultural History of Tibet, London, 1968, p. 42.
6. For a detailed history of Tanpei Dronme and his religious work in Monpa and Sherdukpen areas, please see, Souvenir, Tawang Monastery, and Tawang.2000. (Published on the occasion of two day workshop on Traditional system and functioning of Tawang monastery). PP. 1-5.
7. Niranjan Sarkar, *op. cit.,* p. 13.
8. Information colleted form Chenzi Lama Phuntso. Lama Tashi Dorjee and Daktse rimpoche of Tawang Monastery during 10th 12th May, 2002.
9. D.K. Dutta, 'An Ethnographic Notes on the Membas of Arunachal', Resarun. Itanagar, 2000, pp. 45-64.
10. For local terminology of Mahayana Buddhist architecture, please see, Niranjan Sarkar, *op.cit.,* pp. 17-23.
11. This Mongol Prince is said to have invaded Tibet in circa 1641 at the request of the fifth Dalai Lama and established the Supremacy of the Gelugpa over the other sects there. Please see. T.W.D. Shakbpa, Tibet: A Political History, London, 1967, p. 112. Here it may be mentioned that the Tawang Lamas are of the opinion that one Sokpo Jomkhar, the Commander of the Mongol forces, was responsible for destroying the three old Nyingmapa monasteries of Tawang and interestingly, a mural of Sokpo Jomkhar is adorning the eastern wall of the assembly hall of the Tawang monastery.
12. T.K. Bhattacharjee, 'Tsangya Gyatso' The sixth Dalai Lama and Urgeylling Gompa'. Resarm, Vol. IX, No. 7, (Spring and summer Issue), Shillong, 1983, pp. 1-7.

13. Scholars have divergent opinions regarding the year of construction of the Tawang monastery. Ram Rahul provides a date of 1680 AD. (Vide Modern Bhutan, Delhi, 1971, p. 29), while Niranjan Sarkar ascribes a date sometime between 1643 and 1647 AD as the year of construction of the monastery. However, The Souvenir (2000) of Tawang monastery makes it clear that its foundation was laid on the sixth day of the seventh month of Iron male monkey year (*i.e.* 1680 AD), 2225 year after the death of Buddha Sakyamuni and completed in the8 month of Iron Bird year (*i.e.* 1681 AD).
14. S. Dutta & B. Tripathy, 'Anne Gompas of Tawang', Proceedings of Indian History Congress, 63rd Session, Kolkata, 2003, p. 1343.
15. A small booklet entitled Mystic Land of Monyul is published by Budhist Cultural Preservation society, Bomdila, 1997, which describes Gorcham chorten in brief.
16. David Haworth (ed), My Land and My people: the Autobiography of His Holiness the Dalai Lama, New Delhi, 1962, pp. 129-129.
17. D.L. Snellgrove, Buddhist Himalaya, Oxford, 1957, Plate 14(a)
18. Niranjan Sarkar, *op. cit.,* pp. 83-87.
19. S. Dutta Choudhury, Arunachal Pradesh District Gazetteers (East Kameng, West Kameng and Tawang Districts), Shillong, 1996, pp. 76-78.
20. For variety of Mahayana Dances in Arunachal, please see, Niranjan Sarkar, Dances of Arunachal Pradesh, Shillong, 1974 and Tashi Lama, the Monpas of Tawang: A Profile, New Delhi, 1999.

19

Reconstruction of Surface Comunication System in Arunachal Pradesh: An Archaeological Probe

Amrendra Kumar Thakur

Introduction

Archaeologists in India have extensively worked on the early periods of human activities mainly of the heartland or economic, political, and cultural centers of India; and by and large neglected these aspects of less important areas specially archaeology of the tribal dominated areas in their studies. The present paper is an attempt to bridge this gap. It is a study on the aspects of surface communication system in pre-colonial and colonial period of Arunachal Pradesh and is based upon the works of archaeologists, historians, military reports, diaries, memoirs etc. of the administrators and personal contact with the land and people and the field studies of Tawang, West Kameng and East Kameng districts of Arunachal Pradesh.[1] It is also intended through the presentation to stimulate experts to encourage researches of neglected regions and people, bring into focus some important features of archaeological panorama of Arunachal Pradesh and to utilize archaeological evidences of Arunachal Pradesh and neighbouring areas for the reconstruction of the history of pre-colonial Arunachal Pradesh in particular and Northeast India in general. For the same, the paper has been divided into three parts. The first part analyses the aspects of the surface communication; the second part deals with tribal village fortification and forts and the third is in the form of a conclusion besides an introduction.

At the outset it is important to point out that archaeological evidences along with other movers of social transition have been discussed by the writer at length elsewhere, towards the study of states in Arunachal Pradesh.[2] The aspects of pre-colonial trade and displacement of natives in trade have also been discussed by me on some other occasions.[3] So far studied in space and time, a continuous dominance of traditional tribal chiefs has been observed. The traditional chieftains emerged as the slave owners, feudal landowners and later as political and economic elite of the society in successive periods of history. The process explains that in the custom exchange and gift in the early phases might have been an insignificant proportion of total production in a subsistence economy, but these small amounts had become significant in later differentiation in the society. It can also be suggested here, that with loss of their traditional professions and the enclosure of the commons land on which they lived, during the British period and after, the general people are in fact, left with no other alternative. However, what is too easily left out and forgotten is that the people of Arunachal Pradesh were traders and suppliers of grain and other forest produces in various areas of Aruanchal Pradesh, Assam, Tibet and Burma from their remote past. The colonial intervention into the Northeast India completely changed the situation. The popularization of trade fairs in Assam, promotion of sale of finished goods from plains into the hills of Aruanchal Pradesh, the payment of *Posa* in cash, the exchange of gifts during the fairs, the participation of the British, Bengali and Marwari traders and Nepale coollies etc. displaced them from trade and contributed towards the drain of wealth from Aruanchal Pradesh. Due to the British forest policies, the natives of Aruanchal Pradesh no longer remained the sole masters of the forest resources. The misery of the people of Aruanchal Pradesh further aggravated due to the changed exchange rate of the Tibetan *tanka.* It is reported, "The Tibetans have raised the exchange value of their *tanka* in terms of the Indian rupee since last year. Previously the ratio was 8 *tankas* to 1 rupee, but now it is 4 *tankas* to a rupee".[4] The new situation adversely affected the interest of the people of Aruanchal Pradesh in trade and it seems that it completely ruined their already diminishing economic prospects, which heavily depended upon the trans-border trade in the past.[5] The people of eastern part of Aruanchal Pradesh lost the monopoly over preparation and trade of salt and encroachment of their land for colonial and plantation works adversely affected their socio-economic and political interests. The growing pauperization of the natives of Aruanchal Pradesh and ceased participation in trade provided the colonial and post-colonial scholars ample scope to analyse the socio-economic life of the natives as primitive, static etc. and the people themselves as the cultural isolates.[6] The impacts of these writings were such that the researches of even recent decades were not interested towards the life and condition of the people of pre-colonial period of Arunachal Pradesh. The archaeological studies also suffered the same way. The studies concerning the fortification of village, fortresses inside the hills, agrarian and industrial technologies, water and windmills, etc. never caught the attention of trained and professional archaeologists. In this paper my tool is the both, text-aided archaeology and the archaeology-aided text.

I

Formulation of Problems

Since time immemorial the communication system has played a very significant role in the gowth and development of human society. Hardly any society can survive in isolation. Interaction with the sorrounding environments and the socio-economic conditions and its responses to the consequential changes are some of the basics to the survival of human society. It may, however, be appreciated that these acts are scarcely possible without having means of communication in general and surface communication in parciluar. As in the society of the proto-historic and historical periods, the existence of some form of communication system is quite likely in the prehistoric society as well. The theme, in its broader perspective, is known to have drawn the attention of the researchers for quite long. To this end, some studies are available also for the prehistoric period. However, the emphasis on these studies was, perhaps, mainly on trade and/or trade routes. It was confined broadly to the question of exchange of goods, both luxurious and essential.[7]

The problem we attempt to investigate is thematically, perhaps, quite different from those of the trade & trade routes. Our central theme concerns with some specific aspects, other than important function of the communication, system also forms an aspects of this investigation, however, it is hardly the central theme we propose specifically with the structural, functional and the planning aspects of the system on regional level. In this endeavour we seek to identify the various components of the above aspects. The structural components may broadly constitute of such physical features as are basic to the formation of surface communication systems. Obviously, such features vary in different terrians with varying topography.

The examples of such features bring in the terrain of our study – areas are the passes, pack-tracks, forts, etc. The functional components concern with the various functions for which the means of communication was used; for examples, acquisition of food, exchange of product, supply of raw material from long distance, collection of taxes and tributes, etc. For the investigation of the problems as formulated above, the study area is extremely suitable. Besides the geo-archaeology information available for the area, the physiography of the same is also high compatible with the situation. These probably function as approaches to the valleys from Arunachal Pradesh and *vice-versa.* Besides the two main rivers, the area is marked with some perennial tributatries. The presence of forts at places on these water channels is an interesting feature of the surface communication system in Aruanchal Pradesh.

The possibility of water communication is completely ruled out. Obviously the mechanism of interaction was though the surface. In view of physiographic features of the area the implementation of the mechanism was not an easy task. Among the areas of contact, there are high mountain passes (Sela and Bomdila) and also a thick forest through out. These had to be considered as the most vital feature of the structure of the prehistoric communication system in this physiographical situation. The pack-track association with the pass is another important general, suggests that they normally adopt the shortest and most convenient route to the desired destination. The tracks, as formed out of animal movements, might have served as an excellent guide to prehistoric man for selecting appropriate tracks. The passes and associate tracks in the area are being used even today, both by man and animal. Hardly about three decades back, the passes and the associated tracks were the principle means of surface communication among the people of this area. Many of the passes and the present pack-tracks are very likely the reminiscent of the old mechanism of interaction. It may be assumed that they represent the reminiscent of the basic structural features of the pre-colonial surface communication system of the area. Archaeologically, the availability of the remains of the sites of the relevant periods and the information in the area provide some dependable basis for the spatial stratification and tracks identified thereon.

The physiographic setting of the area is highly suitable for the study of the structural features of the surface communication system. For example, mention may be made of the presence of the passes, pack-tracks, forts etc. Similarly, for the sources of the ethnographic information the area is equally suitable. As regards the question of the genesis of the tracks, it appears that it is basically a contribution of the animal kingdom. Animals, long before the prehistoric man might have used some of the tracks associated with the passes. It may reasonably be expected that the animals, inhabiting the area, had perhaps regular interaction between the two landforms for food and water. The animal behaviour suggests that they normally adopt the shortest and most convenient route to the desired destination. Pre-colonial man in the course of time adopted some of the tracks so formed by animal movement.

Discussion

To begin with the discussion on the surface communication system in Aruanchal Pradesh it is important to mention that we have the evidences of planned destruction of centuries old archaeological features of defence technology of various tribes of Aruanachal Pradesh. The British officially planned the destruction because the fortification was regarded as the symbol of resistance to colonialism. The destruction combined with the tendency to shift village from one place to another also provided the scholars a scope, to neglect the aspect of surface communication system in pre-colonial Arunachal Pradesh. The defence technology in Aruanchal Pradesh had some sort of advancement during the ages. During the periods of internal feuds the technological advancement of both the sides was practically the same. But, during the period of aggressions of outsiders necessities made the indigenous techniques more effective in respect of defence technology; it was also so because of exposure to the neighbouring world and consequently the response. Here, it is important to mention that Arunacahal Pradesh, bounded by Tibet and China in the north, Assam in the sourth, Myanmar in the east and Bhutan in the west; provides today the best example of a cultural continuity that has survived a long and diversified history in which changes have occurred, old images of life have been altered and new elements and influences have been absorbed and amalgamated, enriching and variegating the cultural strands, without, however, mutilating them; because it lies at the tri-junction of the Indo-Chinese, Indo-Myanmar and the Indian sub-regions.

The selection of site for establishing a village was an important aspect of the defence technique of most of the tribes of Aruanchal Pradesh. The approaches to the villages were often up through tortuous narrow coverd ways or lanes, with high banks on either sides, sometimes through a steep ravine and the bed of an old torrent. It has been rightly stated that they selected, very inaccessible places for their villages. Surrounded with bamboo palisads or protected by a stockade of tree trunks, with all approaches carefully 'panjeed' and flanked by 'chutes' the village present very formidable position to an attacking party".[8] The unpublished archival materials for the reconstruction of the archaeological past of the pre-colonial Arunachal Pradesh. It has reported that the initial British operations against the Singphos (1824-26) were invariably against fortified villages and entrenched position.[9] More detailed account of the Singpho technological base of stockades, warfare etc. have also been reported subsequently. It mentions, "The Singphos like to have their villages on bank of a running stream... a number of their villages are stockaded..."[10] Further, F. Jenkins writes in details to formulate a policy regarding the Singphos. He writes "The Singphos country is eminently unfavourable to the operation of regular troops, owing to the closeness of the country, its mountainous character... on these grounds unless absolutely necessary, I think war should be avoided – the more so that a little experience must teach the Singphos how to take advantage of the natural defence of their country, and recent evidence show that they improving in this respect".[11]

The Khampti villages were also strongly fortified. Not only during those troubled years but even half a century later. The military report clearly shows that village fortifications were not a thing of past, "All the big villages are stockaded: the stockades are very strong and high 16 to 20, the stockades are double and up to a height of 4 from the ground the space between area filled with earth and stone; the tops of stockades are pointed; a sharp pointed *panjees* are ingenuously placed to prevent men from scaling up the sides. Within the stockades which surround the village is often an inner one, in which is built the house inhabited by the Raja".[12]

The control over iron by the Khamptis in their hills and the technology evolved by them for the *Daos* and other war weapons and the settled agriculture in the Dihing river valleys [13] must have positively contributed to the beginning of the communication system in the easten Arunachal Pradesh.[14] The permanent place of Khampti chief in the "Great Council" of Ahoms is also indicative of the power and privileges enjoyed by them. Even the British continued their privilege after the occupation of Assam [15] and were proposing to procure the Khampti *Daos* for the British soldiers stationed in the area.[16]

Though among the Adis there did not evolve the chiefdom like that of the Singphos and the Khamptis, in the pre-colonial polity formation among them, [17] the defence technology of a village clearly indicating the surface communication system is very important. The defence technology of the Adis had some sorts of advancements during the period of British aggressions of the area. The response and necessities made the indigenous techniques more effective like that of the Singphos [18] and other tribes. The advancement is in form of rapid strategic changes and advancement in stockades techniques. The system of double row of stockades with earth and stone in between is a late innovation and was the result of the introduction of firearms by the British. Another technological development is in the placing of the stockades. Earlier it was a defence perimeter" of village, later on for the safety of the villages, minimum loss of the defenders of the village as well as the villagers and making the evacuation of the village more safe and easy, the stockades were even "two miles" away from the village.[19]

A brief discussion of the three British aggressions in the Adi area will make my formulations clear. It has been reported [20] that in the expedition of 1858-59 "...in three cases it was necessary to use the howitzers to open a way for the assault", and the British were able to defeat the natives. But the victory was not so easy during the second campaign (1893-94). It has been mentioned 'The Abors (Adis) fought well standing to their defences and keeping up showers of arrows on the attackers who have to back away the Chevaux de fries of bamboo stakes and long 'panjis' which prevented the stockades being reached. At last the Abors gave way and the defences were carried, many dead were found inside, maxwell's casualities being 25. Success occurred, however, too late in the evening to allow of any further move on the village, which next moring was found deserted".

Further advancement in the defence technology is witnessed during the third and final expedition in the year 1911-12. It has been reported, "Here it was found the large stockades believed to have been at the village was two miles south of it, defending the crossing of Egar river from the top of a steep spur. As the advance guard neared it the Abors cut loose a number of 'rock shoots' sending down an avalanche of boulders, narrowly missing the General, who was close up, and knocking one of his staff down the *'Khud'.* And Abors then opened fire with arrows and muskets, one of the former (fortunately for the attackers was non-poisoned) hitting the G.O.C. slightly in hand. Two companies climbing high up while the defences were held in front out-flanked the stockade which was the then rushed but found to have been evacuated".

The features of defence technology during this expedition can be seen as the combined use of stockades, stone-shoots and fire from the arrows and muskets. As a consequence the possibility of heavy and tactical casualties on the aggressor became quite real and the defences of the local population became more effective. The defence techniques of the Adis, on the one hand, demonstrate the gradual advancement and on the other it also demonstrates state of defence arrangements according to the status of the village. As reported [21] (during the expedition of 1911-12), "This brings us to the next occasion on which the British encountered with the Abors..... To punish the tribes and also to explore and survey this country, for owing to China's moves in Tibet and along its south-eastern boarders a real interest was at last being stirred in this long stretch of unknown border lands... From Rohtang reconnoitering parties of Goorkhas and Militace/Police located very large stockades some 3 miles up the Dihang Valley at Kakyar Monying....Unlike other such defences, this one could be seen built down to the water's edge, which beyond it was a large Abor encampment, and here it was hoped to inflict a severe blow before the chief village was reached" (Kebang village).

In the discussion on the surface communication system of pre-colonial Arunachal Pradesh the analysis of the remains of the forts, fortress are also very important. Here, it is important to mention that after independence much of the energy and Resources of the Department of research, Government of Arunachal Pradesh was utilized in the ethnographic studies of different tribes and on the studies of Itafort and the forts of Bhishmaknagar and Rukmininagar.[22] The remains of forts/ fortress of Bhalukpong and Thembang could not catch the attention of earlier scholars practically. Though forts of Arunchal Pradesh cannot be compared with the Muslim, Maratha and Rajput forts of India in their structural technology, the forts of Arunachal Pradesh would have been best suited to the nature of terrain and to the warfare of those days and are a significant pointer towards the surface communication system in Arunachal Pradesh.

The Itafort [23] (built between 1350 and 1450) is within the new capital of Arunachal Pradesh, Itanagar. The fort could be identified with Mayapur, of a local king Ramchandra alias Mayamatta and his son Arimatta. The fort is actually a fortified area of an irregular shape enclosed with natural ridges and brick ramparts. There are two brick walls and three gates. The walls cross over uneven terrain and deep *nallahs,* where remains of culverts, steps etc. exist. The area thus fortified is more than a sq. km., is slopping from south to north and has a number of *nallahs* and gorges providing ample water as well a escape routes. The bricks are of varied sizes. Even decorative bricks are also available. Most likely, their production was carried at the site itself. The sand stone seems to have been brought from nearby hills. Thus, the entire complex is, indeed, a meticulously planned work. It is a monumental task based on intimate knowledge of the terrain and involving immense resources, human as well as materials.

The forts of Bhiskmaknagar and Rukmininagar actually represent the first Aryansied kingdom of the easternmost India that extended in the plains between the Dibang and Lohit rivers. The tradition of Rukmini, the daughter of Bhishmaka, the king of Vidarbha (Berar) who was kidnapped by Lord Krishna, can be associated with this area. The forts existed as early as in the 10th century and in the 13th century came under the Chutiyas and passed on to the Ahoms in the 16th century. The excavated evidence is clearly indicative of their know-how. Besides, classical fort architecture they also knew wheel-turned pottery, terracotta art and advanced metallurgy.[24]

The fort of Bhishmaknagar, [25] is built on a flat piece of land, jutted out towards the south, from the northern hills. In the mountain wall provides natural defence and three other sides an eastern rampart runs about 5 kms in length, though broken in between. The fort has an elongated semicircle shape, extending over area of about 10 sq. kms. After the excavation of the area "...it became quite clear that it was a well-planned and well-protected city inhabited by the people who reached a high degree of culture and civilization.[26]

Regarding the study of Bhalukpong fort, very pathetic scene emerges on account of non-existence of remains today. It is shocking to see that a road (connecting three districts of Arunachal Pradesh with Assam) passes through the fort complex and its bricks were used for construction purposes. And, the entire area was levelled mainly for the construction of the government buildings and also for the private purposes. However, recent archaeological find [27] of 248 silver coins of mainly two types (small and big) of Muslim rules of Bengal encourages us to look afresh on the aspects of the fort and the surface communication system in Arunachal Pradesh and neighbouring areas. As reported,[28] and can be observed from the remains, the fort was situated on a hillock about 300 ft. high at the debouch point of the Kameng or Bhareli river. Three sides were surrounded by a brick-wall and on the fourth the fortifications carried across to an adjoining hillock that sloped gradually to the plain. Hewn stones remain of plinths within the ramparts and a steep pathway paved with stones leading to the eastern face of the hills also existed.

As the outcome of field studies of the fort area, the writer came across of a treasury of the king which was in the northwestern side of the complex. A very thick (3 to 4 fts.) boundary wall, almost touching the treasury was constructed over a rivulet (50-60 ft deep) perhaps for the protection of the fort in general and treasury in particular. Alternative source of water was obtained in the fort complex by digging two wells – one in the southest and the other in the southwest parts of the complex. The whole complex of about three sq. kms. provides ample scope for archaeological excavations and studies by experts.

An Aka legend initially reported by R.S.Kennedy and confirmed during my field studies is a significant pointer towards the Bhalukpong fort. It mentions, [29] "Long long age, all men descended from heaven to earth by means of ladder. The Assamese and Akas of the royal blood came down by a golden ladder, the remaining Akas had a silver ladder; the Tibetans and Monpas were given a ladeder of iron; the Daflas and Abors had to be satisfied with the bamboo ladder; whilst the Cacharis and Khoas shared a plantain ladder. All these men came to earth on the Longkapur Hills in the Lohit Valley, when they scattered in search of land… The Akas spent so much time in resting and drinking bear that the others got the best land and they had to accept what was left… They first settled near Bhalukpong… built their respective capitals…" In a slightly different way it has also been reported, [30] "At Bhalukpong in the gorge of the Bhareli… are the ruins of a fort, which is said to have been the capital of Bana's grandson, Bhaluka, from whom the Akas trace their descent". The Akas were able to establish a pre-colonial state with its tax bases in Aruancahl Pradesh and Assam. Some passes were also under their control during the pre-colonial period.

The fort (*Durga*) and treasury (*Kosa*), which are the important elements of state described by Kautilya, are also significant in case of Aruanchal Pradesh.[31] The forts lie along the foothills, connected with rivers and were constructed actually on stragegic spots, intelligently fortified for defence purposes. A position of geographic ventage, water supply, sufficient land to support the population inside, secret routes for escape, the expected direction of enemy's attack, and communication with Brahmaputra Valley have been the major considerations in building in the foothills and sufficient land to support the population inside is another important factor in constructing fort in Aruanchal Pradesh, which provides great potentials to be discussed in our studies on the surface communication system of Aruancahl Pradesh. A brief description of the findings of my field study of this fort, not yet studied by any scholar so far, of this area is worth mentioning in this regard.

The fort, fortifying the village Tembang, under the Dirang circle of West Kameng District, Bomdila as the headquarters, is yet to be fully connected with pitch road. The Buddhists inhabit Thembang and the villages have separate identity as "Thembang Monpa", [32] The village was fortified after shifting the village from the plain land to the slope of a hill mainly because of persistent pressure from Rupa, Rurang and Sangti villages of the area. The fortified area is about 400 mts east-west and 200 mts north-south of the village surrounded the compact houses of the kings (*Bapus*) and their dependents (*Gilas*). In the eastern and western sides of the village two heavily built gates were constructed of stone pieces of irregular sizes of the provision to close them during night. Though the gates exist, the 8 to 10 feet high boundary wall of the village (as reported by the villagers) is almost non-existing presently.

The fortification was possible mainly with the manual labour of the villagers of Khoina, Boot (now Jirigaon), Khoitam and Rahung as well as the *Gilas.* Their services were also utilized for seed sowing (*ungyangben*), plantation of tree (*ungashing cheewn*), carrying goods (rongbanghen), construction of houses (*phijangben*), and the most important here is construction of fortification wall (*jangri*), adopting the method of *tchikpen* (putting the stone pieces one above the other) etc. They also had to help the *Bapus* while they were attack. The villagers of Khoitam beheaded the military commander of Rupa village while he was returning from an attack from Thembang. They sent the head of the commander to their kings (*Bapus*) and body to Rupa (the Shertukpen *rajas, Thongs)*. From the incident the people of Rupa area call the villagers of Khoitam the *songa-sha-benkenba* (divider of human flesh). The forts provided the kings of Thembang (better known as the Thebengia Bhutias in the Britsh Records) upper hand in the area and to some extent also upon their neighbouring counterpars. The Tibetan gun/rifle under the possession of the *Bapus* was another advantage, which the others lacked.[33] These two elements combined with high agricultural production and fairly a large tax base extending up to modern Assam, significantly contributed not only to the establishment of their authority in the area but also successfully resisted the expansion of the Monastic Order in their areas.[34] All these provide us a good scope to study the aspects of surface communication system in pre-colonial Aruanchal Pradesh.

The Monastic Order of Tibet established its initial control in Tawang area of Aruancahl Pradesh and for administrative reasons divided the area into a number of terrirorial units (*Tsosum*): (a) the Pangchen-Ding-Drug (whole of Zimithang area), (b) the Dakpo-tso-gye (below Zimithang ara), (c) the Shar-ngima-tso-sum (proper Tawang and nearby area up to Sela Pass), (d) Drangnang-chu-gye (below Sela Pass, *i.e.,* present Dirang Circle, Bomdila) and (e) Hrongnang-toe-me (present Kalaktang Circle, Bomdila). And a surface communication network was established connecting Tibet to the one end and Assam at the other, in between about 300 kms. of Arunachal Pradesh. However, even before the establishment of the Order, the social formation had already taken place in this area and the Tawang area was already divided into three territorial units: (a) the ara from Tawang to Kitpi as Shar-tso, (b) the Lhou area as Lhou-tso and (c) the Jung area ss Sher-tso (also known as Jung-tso).[35] Our field studies provide us clues to suggest that the control over the area provided the initial material base for establishment and subsequent expansion of the order in Arunachal Pradesh. The structural organization of the Government of Lhasa in Arunachal Pradesh was quite elaborate. The whole area under Tawang *Deo Raja* or *Deo Abott* was divided into three *dzonas:* the Tawang, Dirang and Kalaktang, each under a *dzonas.* However, the Gelong (an officer under *dzonas*) was responsible for the collection of taxes and tributes and performing religious rituals in the area. The Lamas at village provided it with the necessary condition to achieve this. The existence of a common script (the Tibetan Bhoti) must have helped the process. An attempt at bringing about homogeneity is reflected at the ideational level in the form of the policy of Lamaism and construction of the Gompas all over the area of influence. It was sought to be a vehicle of persuasive assimilation, not the military confrontation, in which conforming to the broad ethical ideas of Lhamaism was central. The three to four storied buildings of the *dZong* at Gyangher (near Tawang) and Dirang sometimes also served the purpose of jails to punish the defiants of the Order.[36]

For the success of the ideological state, the mining and forging of iron (Leh Cheme Rong) near Tawang Monastery for building a bridge, connecting Kitpi and Mukto with Tawang also contributed significantly to better surface communication system for effective control. The Monastery controlled over the iron mines and the same was also utilized for weapons etc. Subsequently it became the symbol of power and control in the area. Among the weapons spear (*Dung*) and sword (*Podung*) are most common and the gun from Tibet a rare one. Iron remained under the exclusive control of the Monastery and its use in the plough was never promoted.

III

Thus, it can be suggested that like many unfolded aspects of the life and conditions of the people of Aruanchal Pradesh of pre-colonial period, the aspects of the surface communication system too need more careful and serious studies. And certainly archaeology is going to provide the most important clue in this regard. However, literary sources and field studies of the area will be also be important towards the studies.

References

1. I am grateful to the ICHR, New Delhi, for providing financial assistance to my research project *Archaeology of Aruanchal Pradesh.* The grant helped me to carry out archival and library researches and field studies.
2. For details see, A.K.Thakur, "Peasantisation and State Formation in Early Arunachal Pradesh", *Proceedings of Indian History Congress,* (hereafter PIHC), 58th Session, Bangalor,

1997, pp. 303-12; idem, "Social Transition in Pre-colonial Arunachal Pradesh: Servitude as a Prime Mover" *PIHC,* 60th Session, Calicut, 1999, pp. 391-403; idem, "Evolution of Social Stratification in Aruanchal Pradesh", Journal of *North East India Council for Social science Research,* 22, 1 April 1998; idem, "State Formation in aruancahl Pradesh", *NEHU, Journal of Social Science and Humanities* (new series), I, 1, 1998, pp. 73-87, (revised version of earlier paper, 'Archaeological Remains and Socio-Political Complexitis in Aruancahl Pradesh: A Probe into their Correlation).

3. For details see, "Pre-colonial Trade in Aruanchal Pradesh: A Reconstruction of Economic History", *Resarun* vol.XXVII, Journal of the Directorate of Research, Govt. of Aruanchal Pradesh, Itanagar; idem, "Pre-colonial and Colonial Trade in Arunachal Pradesh" The Monpas in Perspective", *Journal of Historical research,* Vol. XII, 2002, Department of History, Dibrugarh University, Dibrugarh, Assam; idem, "Arunachal Pradesh and Tibet" A Study of Trade Relation and its Impact" for the book being edited by S. Dutta, Aruanachal University, on Displacement of Natives of Arunachal Pradesh; idem, "Pattern of Pre-colonial Trade and Polity Formations in Aruanchal Pradesh: A Study of their Relationship" in the *Proceedings of the North East India History Association,* Imphal Session, 2000, pp. 299-318.

4. Governor's Secretariat Assam, Tribal — 'A', Nos. 1-41, March, 1941.

5. The Discovery (fortunate but totally unplanned) of about 250 coins of different sizes and denominations belonging most probably to the rulers of the Shah dynasty of Bengal (official report yet to be published) from a ruined fort complex at Bhalukpong, the gateway of Bomdila and Tawang can also be an important pointer in this regard. Most likely it served as the central place of contact between traders of Bengal and Assam at the one hand and Aruanachal Pradesh and Tibet on the other. For details see the Letter No.BPG/DEV/B/10/98, datd, 248.98 from the EAC, Bhalukpong to the Director of Research, Itanagar.

6. For details see, Sudatta Sikdar, "Tribalism versus Colonialism: British Capitalist Intervention and the Transforamtion of Primitive Economy of Aruanchal Pradesh in the Nineteenth Century", *Social Scientist,* No. 115, December, 1982; and for other details see, A.K.Thakur, "Social transition in Pre-Colonial Aruanchal Pradesh", *op. cit.*

7. For details see, D. Mandal, "The Prehistoric Surface Comminication System in the North East Vindhyas", *Presidentail Address Section V (Archaeology)* Indian History Congress, 62nd Session, Bhopal, 2001. I am greatly benefited by this address.
8. A. Hamilton, *In Abor Jungles of North, East India,* (Indian Reprint), Delhi, 1984, p. 22.
9. Military Consultations, 16 Dec. 1828, Nos. 28-29. Even as late as December 1828, Capt. J.B. Neuville was asking for light mountain howitzers and rockets against these fortification. For details of the village forticication in North East India see the article of Imdad Hussain, "Village Fortification in Tribal North East India: A Preliminary Note" in J.P. Singh and G. Sengupta (eds), *Archaeology in North Eastern India,* New Delhi, 1991.
10. Foreign Dept. Political Br. 12 June, 1837, No. 64.
11. Letter from F. Jenkins to H.T. Prinsep, Esq. in Foreign Dept. Political Branch, 18 April, 1838, Nos. 56-57.
12. For details see, C.R. Mac Gregor, *Military Report on Khampti – Singpho,* Calcutta, 1887.
13. For details see, Muhammad Kazim, *Alamgir Nama (ed.)* Khadim Husain and Abdul Hai, Calcutta, 1863-73, in Shireen Moosvi's *Man and Nature in Mughal Era,* (Indian history Congress, Thematic Symposium), Delhi, 1993.
14. For details of the areas of the possessions, military force maintained by the chiefs, populations etc. see Foreign Dept. Political Branch, K.W. File, 7 Jan. 1833, No. 82. This file is not only important for the pre-colonial chiefs of Arunachal Pradesh but also for most other chiefs of north east India.
15. For details see, letter from J. Brodie to F. Jenkins, Foreign Dept. Political Branch, 1 March, 1840, Nos. 176-77.
16. *Ibid.*, No. 169.
17. For details see, A.C. Talukdar, "Political Evolution of Arunachal Pradesh", *op. cit.*
18. From F. Jenkins to H.T. Prinsep, *op. cit.*
19. For details of the Adi expeditions see, *Frontier and Overseas Expedition from India,* Vol. III, Official Account of Abor (Adi) Expedition, Delhi, 1984, pp. 31-58 and 219-23 and L.W.Shakespeare, History of Assam Rifles, (Indian reprint) Gauhati, 1980, pp. 42-43 and 118-39 (passim).
20. *Ibid.*

21. L.W. Shakespeare, *op. cit.,* pp. 125-26 and 129-30.
22. For details see, Y.A. Raiker, *Itafort,* Itanagar, 1990 (1976); L.N. Chakravarty, *op. cit.,* pp. 93-121; Y.A. Raiker and S. Chatterjee, *Archaeology in Aruanchal Pradesh,* Itanagar, 1980, pp. 24-34 and A.K. Thakur, "Defence Mechanism in Arunachal: A Study of Fortification and Forts", 3rd World Archaeological Congress, New Delhi, 1994 (under the theme papers *State City and Society).*
23. For details see, Y.A. Raiker, *Itafort, op. cit.;* D.N. Das, "Ruins of Mayapur", *The Journal of the Assam Research Soceity,* Vol. VIII, No. 2, 1941, pp. 43-49 and L.N. Chakravarty, *op. cit.*
24. Y.A. Raikar and S. Chatterjee, *op. cit.,* p. 28 and L.N. Chakravarry, *op. cit.,* pp. 119-20.
25. Y.A. Raiker and S. chatterjee, *op. cit.,* pp. 28-29 and L.N. Chakravarty, *op. cit.,* pp. 117-21 (passim).
26. L.N. Chakravarty, *op. cit.,* p. 117.
27. The coins were sent to the Director, Dept. of Research, Govt. of Aruanchal Pradesh, vide letter No.BPG/DEV/B/10/98 dated, 24.8.98. This was unearthed while making a toilet pit for the residential quarters in the fort complex, presently a complex of the GREF.
28. Though good number of Government records provide information regarding the fort, they are mostly in slipshod manner. For some other details of the fort see, the relevant parts in B.C. Allen, *Assam District Gazetteers,* Vol.V, Darrang, Allahabad, 1905, B.C. Allen *et. at., Gazetteer of Bengal and North East India,* Delhi, 1979 (first reprint).
29. For details see, A.K. Thakur, "Peasantisation and State Formation", "State Formation", and R.S. Kennedy, *Ethnological Report on the Akas, Khoas and Mijis and Membas of Tawang,* 1914.
30. B.C. Allen, *et. al., op. cit.,* p. 549.
31. For details see, A.K. Thakur, "State Formation".
32. The Buddhists of Western Arunachal Pradesh are of the two socio-cultural groups *viz.* the Shertukpens, and the Monpas (the Thembang — Namsu Monpa, the dirang Monpa, the Kalaktang Monpa, the Tawang Monpa, etc.)
33. The gun/rifle is preserved in the *Chhorten* of the Thembang Gompa and is not open to any researchers to exactly determine its features.

34. For details see, A.K. Thakur, "State Formation" and "Peasantisation and State Formation".
35. The book by N. Sarkar, *Tawang Monsatery,* Shillong, 1981, though discusses some aspects of the monastic order in the area, was unable to analyse the role of iron, communication network, role of surplus accumulation, etc. For a comprehensive picture see the forthcoming book of A.K. Thakur and B.N. Jha on Pre-colonial States of Aruanchal Pradesh.
36. Here it is worth-mentioning that the Monpas have resented the exaction of tributes and forced labour by the Tibetan Government to the British. The extension of the British rule in the ares of Buddhist influence was smooth unlike the other areas of Arunachal Pradesh because people had in their minds that the British rule would not be so harsh and exploitative in nature as of the Tibetans. For the same reasons the Tibetans are called Zakpas in Dirang area meaning the plunderers. For some more details see,Robert Reid, *Hisotry of the Frontier Areas bordeing on Assam,* Shillong, 1942, pp. 288-89; N.N. Chaudhury, *Arunachal Through the Ages,* Shillong, 1982. For the Tibetan oppression in Sikkim and Bhutan see, J. Ware Edgar, *Report on a Visit to Sikkim and the Tibetan Frontier in October; November, and December,* 1873, Calcutta, 1874, pp. 23-24.

20

Some Light on the Lesser Explored Sources of the History of Arunachal Pradesh

Dipankar Banerjee

On the question of definition of history E.H.Carr, in his pioneering work, *What is History*, has observed that essentially "History is a kind of research or Inquiring". Young scholars of historical studies of North East India have a very common complaint – the paucity of data in relation of historical research and to undertake rational enquiry. For the students of modern history of the North East India, archival materials remain to be the Primary sources, as materials from other sources of the british period are few and fare between. However, the callous attitude of the authority has resulted in absolute mismanagement of the Secretariat files, reports and other records of the government archives. That is definitely a handicap in relation to scientific analysis of the archival data.

For Arunachal Pradesh, which got the status of a state relatively later the problem is compounded by the fact that the files related to former NEFA are scattered in different archives and in most cases, those are not properly listed. However there still remains a good number of records, reports and books relating to North East Frontier of the yeaster years (now Arunachal Pradesh), authored by British writers, planters civil servants and other officials stationed in India during the colonial period. Some of those materials have been preserved quite systematically at the India Office Library and Records (IOLR) at London and the Cambridge South Asia Archives (CSAA). While some of those works like that of Elwin Verrier, A. Mackenzie, Lt. R. Wilcox, R.B. Pemberton, A.J.M. Mills, l.W.

Shakespeare, A. Hamilton, B.C. Allen, F. younghusband, E.T.Dalton, Edward Gait and W.W.Hunter have been reprinted and widely used by the research scholars of the region today, there remains a lot of other reports, books, travelogues, records, reminiscences and other works in relation to Arunachal Pradesh, which this author feels, have neither been utilized nor have been sufficiently explored.

This small essay, which is essentially a sweeping survey of some early printed works on Arunachal Pradesh that the author has come across while consulting the records at the IOLR and CSSA, would try to throw some light on these lesser explored Sources of the History of Arunachal Pradesh. The first edition of the books/records/reports listed herewith are available at the above mentioned British archives. This list *excludes* the works of a dozen of writers whose names have been mentioned above, as scholars engaged in historical research are acquainted with their works as those still remain invaluable documents of research in relation to North Eastern region.

List of Books/Records/Reports. Travelogues

- G.W. Beresford; *Notes on the North Eastern Frontier of Assam.* This note was published from Shillong, Assam, twice: once in 1886 and again in 1906 with some updates.
- F.M. Bailey: *Report on the exploration on the North East Frontier of Assam, 1913,* (Simla, 1913). A book titled *No Passport to Tibet* was published by Bailey later in 1957, which by the author's own admission is "an abridged version of his 1914 Report". The report contains interesting accounts of the Mishmis and Monpas. This author has another publication titled *China-Tibet-Assam* which was published from London in 1945.
- C.U. Aitcheson: *A collection of Treaties, Engagements and Sanads Relating to India and neighbouring Countries,* (Calcutta 1902). Published in two volumes.
- B. Duff: *Reports on the Miri country and the operations of the Miri missions.* (Simla, 1912).
- R.N. Cust: *A sketch of the Modern Language of the East Indies.* (London, 1872).

- John Butler: *A sketch of Assam, with some accounts of the Hill Tribes.* (This is one of the earliest books written on the region and was published from London in 1847. Butler had a fourteen year stay in Assam and on his retirement from service of the East India Company wrote a travelogue titled "*Travels and adventures in the Province of Assam during a residence of 14 years*" which was published from London in 1855).
- T.T. Cooper: *New Routes for Commerce: The Mishmi Hills,* (London, 1873). This British Civil Servant was the first to suggest the possibility of a new trade route from Assam to Burma and China through the Mishmi Hills.
- Capt. John F. Michell; *The North East Frontier of India: A Topographical, Political and Military Report* (London, 1883).
- J.P. Needham: *Report of a trip into Abor Hills.* 1884. (Needham also submitted a report on his visit to two Abor (Adi) villages — Padu and Kumku in 1885).
- W. Griffith: *Journal of Travel in Assam, Burma, Bootan, Afganistan and the Neighbouring Countries.* (Calcutta, 1847). (In This work the author refers to the life of the people and depicts the geographic features of NEFA).
- C. Von Furer Haimendorf: *Himalayan Barbary,* (London, 1955). [The book is an interesting narrative of different Himalayan tribes which includes much information about different facts of the life of the people in NEFA with specific focus on Apa Tanis and Daflas (Nyishi) and the author's travels in the Subansiri areas. Earlier in 1947, Haimendorf also published *Exploration in the Eastern Himalayas,* which is essentially reflection of his experience of his travels in the Subansiri tract during the period].
- G.W. Dunne: *Preliminary Notes on Miris, (Mishings)* (Simla, 1896).
- Kaulback Ronald: *Tibetan Trek.* [Published in 1934 from London, this is a small booklet on the author's first hand experience with the Mishmis and Adis].

- W.B. Hore: *Report on the Abor Country*, (Simla, 1913).
- J.S.S. Moir: *Report on the Khampti Long Mission, 1912-13*. (Simla, 1912-13).
- G.A. Grierson: *Linguistic Survey of India*, (Calcutta, 1909). [This survey was published in several volumes. Volume III, Part-I is relevant to the present Arunachal Pradesh].
- C.E. Buckland: *Dictionary of Indian Biography*. (London, 1906).
- Geoffrey Toyson: *Forgotten Frontier*, (Calcutta, 1945). [This is a very interesting book which depicts the plight of the British officials in the Burma Frontier during the Second World War. There are several references in the book about the assistance and cooperation extended to the British officials particularly, to the Indian Tea Association, by the Singphos, Mising, Adi and other tribes in assisting and evacuating people from different border areas and Burma during the World War].
- Walter Hamilton: *Report on the Dophlas*, (Calcutta, 1820). [This small booklet contains the correspondence of Boora Gohain of Assam with the Bengal Presidency who attributed the desolation of a considerable portion of the incursions of this tribe].
- H.S. Bevar: *An Agreement between the British Government and eight Communities of Meyong Abors*. [This small booklet contains the provisions of agreement between the Meyong Abors and the British Government signed on 5th November at Lalee Mukh camp by which the Meyong Abors recognized all persons residing at the plains in the vicinity of the Meyong Hills as British subjects. The agreement, signed in English had fifteen provisions was drafted by Major Bivar who was the Deputy Commissioner; First Class, Likhmpure, Upper Assam and Agent to the Governor General, NE Frontier].
- G.L.S.Ward: *Assam Adventure*, (London, 1842) [This is one of the earliest accounts of Assam written on the personal experience of author's visit in the area, who was stationed in Assam from 1826-37].

- R.S. Kennedy: *Ethnological Report on the Akas, Khoas and Mijis and the Monpas of Tawang*, (Shillong, 1914).
- S.F. Hannay: *Sketch of the Singphos, or the Kakheyens of Burma; the position of the Tribes as regards Bhauno and the Inland Trade of the Irrawaddy with yunan, followed by an account of the Shans,* (Calcutta, 1947).
- J.H. Lorain: *Dictionary of the Abor Miri Language*, (Calcutta, 1910).
- F. Hamilton: *An Account of Assam* [This was possibly the first book which contains references of the tribes of the North East Frontier. It was first compiled in 1807. This very book was later edited by S.K.Bhuyan and published from Guwahati in 1940].
- L.W. Shakespeare: *History of Upper Assam, Upper Burma and North Eastern Frontier,* (London, 1914).
- Richard Clarke: *Digest on Consolidated arrangements of the Regulations and Acts of the Bengal Government, 1793-184.* (London, 1955).
- Major V.C.P. Hudson: *List of the Officers of the Bengal Army (1758-1834).* (London, 1928). [This list gives an account of the posting of different officers in the East India company's army in the Eastern India].
- W.R. Little: *Report on the Abor Expedition, 1894,* (Simla, 1895).
- G. Llylo and J.H. Hutton: *Report on the Census of Assam, 1921.* [This census report contains, comparatively detailed notes (compared to earlier census reports) on North East Frontier tribes like Adis, Mishings, Akas, Apatanis, Singphos, Nyishis and Mishmis].
- W. Robinson: *A descriptive account of Assam,* (London, 1841).
- R. Reid: *History of the Frontier areas Bordering Assam from 1883-1941.* (Shillong, 1942).
- Alastair Lamb: India China Border: *The origins of Disputed boundaries.* (London, 1964).
- A.M. Crowe: *Mr. Crowe's Account of a journey to Apa Tanang Country,* (Shillong, 1890).

- *A Report upon the Subject of Slavery,* A report published by the Indian Law commission, (Calcutta, 1841). [An important report in relation to slavery. It also refers cases where the Assamese inhabitants of the area were made slaves].
- *H. Vetch: Report of a visit by Captain Vetch to the Singpho and Naga Frontier in 1842.* (Calcutta, 1873). [This report consists of selected papers in relation to the Hill tracts and route between India and Burma and Upper Brahmaputra basin].
- W.F. Badgley: *Report on the Treacherous Attack made by the Nagas: Report on the Topographical Surveys of India for the session 1874-75.* (Calcutta, 1876). [The report consists vivid description of massacre of members of a government survey party by the Wangcho tribe of Nino].
- J. Beames: *Outlines of Indian Philology,* (Calcutta, 1967). [This book possibly contains the first prints of Nyishi numerical].
- Elanor Bor: *Adventures of a Botanist's wife,* (London, 1952). [Contains interesting account of the Sherdukpens, Adis and Nyishi, as observed by the wife of a dedicated botanist who spent a decade of his in search of flora and fauna in Assam].
- R.A. Way: *Report on Assam-Burma Connection, Railway Survey,* (Calcutta, 1896). [Incorporates an interesting episode of establishing railway links between Dibrugarh in Upper Assam and Myitkina in Burma through Patkai and Mougong in 1878].
- In addition to the above, India Office Library and Records (IOLR) contain a good number of Survey maps of North East Frontier and the entire region. The Library also has a good collection of different articles and research papers on North East Frontier and the hill tribes of the region which were published in different journals. These journals included *Antrhropos Journal of the Asiatic Society of Bengal, Journal of the royal Asiatic Society of Great Britain and Ireland, Man in India,*

Journal of the Royal Anthropological Institute, Journal of the Royal Society of Arts, Asiatic researcher, Geographical Magazine, Journal of the Geological Survey of India and some more. There remain a good collection of private papers related to Arunachal Pradesh *i.e.,* formerly NEFA both at IOLR, London and Cambridge South Asia Archive (CSAA) which still remain to be explored.

The collections at IOLR and CSAA are important for a few other reasons as well. Firstly, this author has reasons to believe that there may not be any other archive elsewhere where so much of original manuscript and books on NEFA is stored. Secondly all these books mentioned above are essentially the first edition of the books. Even all the first editions of the works of the celebrated historians – Elwin Verrier, A. Mackenzie, Lt. R. Wilcox, R.B.Pemberton, A.J.M. Mills, L.W. Shakespeare, A. Hamilton, B.C.Allen, F.Younghusband, E.T. Dalton, Edward Gait and W.W.Hunter are housed in these libraries. These first edtion books have some additional historical value as many a times the subsequent editions or reprints of the books are edited by the concerned editors. Thirdly, many of these books have been donated by the authors themselves from their personal libraries to LOLR or CSAA. In some cases these libraries collected/ purchased the manuscripts, diaries and books from the authors or their descendents. Many of the files and manuscripts in the collection of LOLR and CSAA have personal observations, comments of the writers on the body of the manuscripts or books. Scrutiny of those comments may throw light on new interpretation of the earlier views of the author himself on the subject. Finally, though these reports and books are printed, and printed materials are many times considered as secondary sources – that should not be valid in relation to these early written sources of history of a state like Arunachal Pradesh. These writings of the British officers, army men, botanists, civil servants stationed at the North East Frontier of India are undoubtedly the first written documents in relation to the history of Arunachal Pradesh and hence those are essentially primary sources, written on the basis of their first hand experiences. It applies to their biographical writing as well, some of which have been referred to above.

While exploring these sources, a researcher has to keep in mind that these materials have to be handled with an open mind as almost all these works mentioned above have been pioneering works in relation to a secluded and hitherto unexplored part of our planet earth. Naturally, traditional historical methodology has been followed by most of the authors. One of the most important characteristics of traditional method is that these are in many cases, not systematic and consistent. Thus they reflect a kind of *methodical adhocism* and are characterized by dominance of subjective perception. But that does not undermine their value in any way as that is quite natural in such pioneering works in respect of the History of Arunachal Pradesh. History in actuality means all that has been felt, thought, imagined, said and written in relation to another and in it is this context, these works are extremely important.

21

Observations on Verrier Elwin's India's North East Frontier in the Nineteenth Century as a Source Book of the History of Arunachal Pradesh

S.D. Goswami

Many decades prior to independence the present state of Arunachal Pradesh, then called NEFA, was visited by a number of European explorers, administrators and missionaries who left behind them vivid accounts of the land they traversed and the rich and varied culture of the people inhabiting the region. These accounts were written on the basis of their personal experience, what they had seen with their own eyes and what they had heard about the tribes. Many of such notes were published in contemporary journals like the *Asiatic researches, Journal of the Asiatic Society of Bengal, Geographical Journal Man in Indian* etc., whereas some others, submitted to Government in the form of official reports, are still available in the achieves of India and England. Unfortunately, many of these highly valuable articles and accounts are today not easily accessible to the administrators, policy makers and academics and for which a proper assessment of the tribal life in those days has become all the more difficult. Verrier Elwin, a distinguished anthropologists and ethnographer, who acted as Advisor for Tribal Affairs to the North East Frontier Agency (NEFA) administration for many years, took the trouble of digging out from old records extracts of several articles and publishing them along with his full length introductory note under the title *India's North East Frontier in the Nineteenth Century* (Madras, 1959). The articles included in this work have a bearing on the history, people and problems of the present state of Arunachal Pradesh and are of immense value to everybody.

The compiler of this volume Verrier Elwin was infact 'a visionary and a romantic personality'. He had very good knowledge of the tribal people and was always regarded as 'a friend of the tribal folk'. As one who had lived and worked with them for a long time, Elwin was asked by Nehru's government to evolve a theoretical framework of independent India's policy towards the north eastern tribes. Like Elwin, Nehru had great concern for these people,[1] for their fast eroding social and cultural values following the attempts made by the outsiders to foist their own culture on them. Thus their mutual admiration for each other and their common concern for the tribal people eventually led to the formulation in 1958 of the famous *Pancha Sheela* or the five principles of tribal development. In reality Nehru was profoundly influenced by the voluminous writings of Elwin and also by his 'evangelical mission' of drawing attention to and improving their quality of life. Already in 1957, in his *Philosophy for NEFA,* Elwin had underlined his views on tribal development and advocated a policy of bringing them into the same footing of equality and development with their more 'advanced' neighbours in the plains not by imposing other's way of living on them but by letting them live freely, free from all kinds of interference in their social and cultural life. It is important to note that Elwin's ideas on tribal development were broadly in conformity with Nehru's own ideas. In the fitness of things Nehru wrote the foreword to the second edition of Elwin's *Philosophy for NEFA* published in 1958 where he said: "My liking for them (tribes of NEFA) grew and with it came respect. I had no sensation of superiority over them".[2]

As mentioned already the book *India's North East Frontier in the Nineteenth Century*is, a collection of extracts from 'forgotten literature' about the colourful people of erstwhile NEFA originally written by a number of well-known administrators, military officers, missionaries and explorers like W. Robinson, A. Mackenzie, T.T.Cooper, E.T.Dalton, J.Errol Gray, Father Krick, J.F.Needhan, R.Wilcox, J.M.M.'cosh, J.B.neufville, C.R.Macgregor, W.Griffith and some others. All these writers had vast knowledge of the people and the land they visited. Some of them had become more famous as authors of some highly informative books on north east India. Elwin had done a remarkable job of collecting the articles containing excellent anthropological and historical materials and republishing them in the shape of a book for the benefit of the present and future generations of scholars. The book begins with an introduction where he tries to explain the European attitude towards the tribes of north east India and their general misconception about the tribal customs and practices. He also gives a brief account of the works done by some of the writers of the articles in respect of the areas they visited, and which he himself found so fascinating in his lifetime. It is a pity that during the larger part of the colonial period very little was known outside the north east about these people and the land they inhabited from time immemorial. And whatever little was known was not necessarily correct. An article published in 1865 in the *Pioneer* reported that "the only idea which most men had, with reference to the hills and forests (of Assam and the adjoining areas) was that they were the habitat of savage tribes, whose bloody raids and thieving forays threatened serious danger to the cause of tea".[3] The Naga tribes were known more for their head-hunting habits than for any other reason. John Butler, a military officer on civil duty and author of *A Sketch of Assam* (1847) and *Travels and Adventures in the province of Assam* (1855), despite his long stay in this region, described the Khamtis as 'a discontented, restless, intriguing tribe', the Singphos as 'a rude treacherous people' and the Abors (now Adis) 'as void of delicacy as they are of cleanliness', whereas E.A.Rowlatt, who explored the Mishmi hills in 1844, described the Mishmis as 'disgustingly dirty, with the exception of a few of the chiefs...'[4] Recent studies on these enterprising people have shown how inaccurate or exaggerated was the portrayal of the European writers. Fortunately, there were among European writers, not many, but a few, whose attitude towards these people was somewhat different, and who were impressed by their simple nature and their colourful lifestyle. Elwin was quite conscious of these lapses, deliberate or otherwise. Having known these people so well he was naturally pained and hurt when he found them projected as mere anthropological specimens or when they were looked down upon with contempt. Thus, while selecting the passages from old records for publication in the present volume Elwin was careful to avoid unnecessary details, omitting those parts which were marked by 'personal bias' and including those which have a greater bearing on them. Obviously, the passages were selected on the basis of their individual merit and not on the strength of the reputation the authors enjoyed. Out of total of fourteen chapters of the book, only four [5] deal with the people who are outside the territorial boundary of present Arunachal Pradesh, the rest then are devoted to the understanding of the various facts of the history and culture of the Arunchali tribes like the Daflas (Nishis), the Hill Miris, the Apa Tanis, the Abors (Adis), the Mishmis, the Khamtis, the Singphos and the Akas. The few illustrations appeanded in this volume are quite useful. The Bibliography is exhaustive; it gives the reader an insight into the volumes of books and articles written on these people during the colonial and post colonial periods. However, not much information is available in this book on the Monpas, the Tagins, the Sherdukpens, the Tangsas, the Noktes and the like.

On the whole Verrier Elwin's *India's North East Frontierin in the Nineteenth Century* is highly valuable account of the hill people of Arunachal Pradesh in the nineteenth century, when they lived in isolation and when they were not exposed to the so called 'civilized' world. The passages reproduced here are of 'unusual value' as they "give us a picture of the country as it was before it had suffered any external influence".[6] In the absence of other written records, other then the *buranjis,* these notes and articles, coming from the pen of the explorers, officers, military and civil, missionaries and the like, are of immense value to scholars, administrators and others who are interested to know what these tribal people were about a hundred years age or even earlier. However, all these accounts may not be hundred per cent correct and authentic, for there is, as admitted by Elwin himself, always a possibility of some being mere 'guess-work' and some others suffering from unavoidable lapses. The account writers were not necessarily trained and professional anthropologists or ethnographers in the modern sense of the term. The possibility of a communication gap between the writer and the reporter can not also be ruled out. But whatever little that turns out to be correct and true to a researcher after careful scrutiny, will prove to be useful for writing a comprehensive history of Arunachal Pradesh.

References

1. In an article entitled 'The Tribal Folk' Nehru wrote: "I have always.... Long before I became prime Minister... felt very strongly attracted to the tribal people of this country. This feeling was not the curiosity an idle observer has for strange customs, nor was it the attraction of the charitably disposed who wanted to do good to others..." Jawaharlal Nehru, 'The Tribal Folk' in *The Tribal People of India,* publication division, New Delhi, 1973, p. 2.
2. Verrier Elwin, *a Philosophy for NEFA,* Shillong, 1958, p.xiii, Foreword by Jawaharlal Nehru.
3. Quoted in Verrier Elwin, *India's North East Frontier in the Nineteenth Century,* Madras, 1959, pp. xv-xvi, Introduction.
4. *Ibid.*, p. xvi.
5. The Chapters are:
6. Chapter-I: The Frontier of Assam.

   Chapter-II: The Eastern Tribes in the Nineteenth Century

   Chapter-III: Tribal Warfare in the Nineteenth Century

   Chapter-IV: Travels in the Patkai Hills
7. Verrier Elwin, *India's North-East Frontier in the Nineteenth Century,* Madras, 1959, p. xv, Introduction.

22

Sources of History of Arunachal Pradesh: A Critical Study

S. Dutta

I

Introduction

Before going to deal with the paper it appears necessary to give certain important characteristics of the land and the people of the state. It would also be appropritate to point out cettain limitations while dealing with the subject.

By Arunachal and Arunachalee we mean here the landmass and its inhabitants evolved through historical process and names over time and space as a political unit of this vast Country. Aruanchal Pradesh, the erstwhile North-East Frontier Agency, the land of the rising Sun in the North Eastern tip of India, spreads over approximately an area of 84,000 sq. kms., which is the abode of a large number of tribes totalling a population of about 10,91,117 (as per 2001 census provisional) with their distinct culture, varied customs, own language and colourful costumes. Lying along the southern slopes of the Eastern Himalayas it is the largest state in the north eastern region of India in terms of area, having a strategic location with international borders with Tibet (China), Myanmar and Bhutan of about 1628 kms, of which 1030 kms. is with China, 441 kms., with Myanmar and 157 kms., with Bhutan.

Arunachal Pradesh has a very severe and rigorous topography. In the degree of hardship that depends on three main factors – the terrain, the climate and the degree of isolation (in terms of communication) from the rest of the world – Arunachal is very badly placed. In the words of waddell, "Driven into these wild glems by the advance of civilization up the plains and lower valleys, these people have become hemmed in among the mountains, where pressing on each other in their struggle for existence, they have developed into innumerable isolated tribes".[1] K.A.A.Raja, one of the pioneer Administrators of erstwhile NEFA and he first Lt. Governor of Arunachal Pradesh, has echoed a similar view:[2]

"Numerous communities in the earlier stages of material culture had moved away, over centuries, into these hills. They moved in batches and stages depending on pressure exerted. Each batch was self-contained and lost contact with the present stock and the related groups in the course of migration. Every fresh arrival pushed those that followed it, from place to place, till they all reached their present habitats. These movements accelerated and intensified the diversification".

Geography has also influenced the cultural development of the province to a great extent. The northern region had little contact with the lower region, particularly the Brahmaputra Valley and so it had been greatly influenced by the Indo-Tibetan culture. The Southern belt of foothills has had similar contact with plains of Assam with resultant cultural impact. But the middle zone has remained comparatively backward and both Tibetan and Assamese influences are visible in their way of life there.[3]

Most of the tribes of Arunachal Pradesh can boast of not only of a hoary past but also of a rich history and traditions. But because of lack of scientific data particularly of the ancient period, understanding and study of the past pause a Himalayan problem before a modern day researcher. Understanding and study of the past becomes easier if one can trace documents, relics, monuments and archaeological evidences. But most of the languages spoken by the tribes of Arunachal Pradesh, more than fifty in number most of which belong to the Tibeto-Burman group, do not have scripts and written literature excepting those of the Monpas and the Khamptis who have written literature and documents in Tibetan script and language and Tai script and language respectively. Thus, Arunachal Pradesh, an island of various tribes separated for so many factors, over the decades after independence, however, a common Arunachalee 'personality' has grown up, as the tribal people of Arunachal Pradesh have come into close contact with each other and the rest of the nation through various means of contact. The present democratic set up has contributed further to accelerate the process.

An evolution of names may be traced in case of the tribal groups of people in the north-east from the earliest blanket designations like *Nisada, Kirata* and *Asura* of the Vedic and Epic literature which made little distinction between the various peoples of the north eastern regions of India including Assam, Arunachal Pradesh and other tribal States of the present time to later appellations for different groups of people noticed in the Ahom Buranjis and British records.[4] The names of different tribes used in the present talk are those, which are being currently used by respective tribes in identifying them, since the names or appellations given to the tribes by the outsiders were mostly unknown to the tribal people themselves.[5] (However, in the excerpts quoted and wherever it was required to establish with distinction the contemporary historical context, the use of old names could not be avoided).

II

With these backgrounds in mind while dealing with the subject, I am aware of limitation of dealing with such a vast subject like History of Arunachal Pradesh (sources of the 'History of Arunachal Pradesh' from the ancient period to the modern time) in a single take. My attempt, therefore, will be of macro-nature leaving scope of micro warks on various aspects of the history of Arunachal Pradesh (studies of each source material in details). Like in most other cases, the sources of the history of Arunachal Pradesh also may be broadly divided into the following categories. Archaeological sources; Oral sources and literary sources.

Archaeological Sources

Inspite of having unfavourable climate and seismic disturbances, we are fortunate to have a good number of archaeological remains in Arunachal Pradesh, which help us in reconstructing the history of the State.

Stone Age tools and artifacts along with Neoliths and river terraces have been recorded by B.P. Boparkikar in his report of first ever scientific exploration in the Daphabhum area of the

Lohit district in 1969-70. S.N. Rao of Dibrugarh University detected some objects, which seem to be Palaeoliths in the Kamlang valley of the Lohit district in 1971. Y.A. Raikar of the Research Department of the Govt. Arunachal Pradesh, discovered chiefs of semi-precious stones from Vijaynagar of Tirap district in 1971, which he considered to be relics of Microlithic culture. These Reports appear to be significant in the background of discoveries of Stone Age relics from the adjoining region of Assam, Meghalaya and other parts of North East India.[6]

Neoliths have been found in plenty from all over Arunachal Pradesh chiefly as surface finds. All these indicate potentiality of the area awaiting further research for pre-historic remains. In this respect the discovery of a Megalithic site at Jamiri in West Kameng district is of much importance.[7] The fortification at Naksa parvat situated in the Seijosa circle in the foothills of the East Kameng district excavated during 1980-82 is considered to be of a somewhat later construction.[8]

Implements and utensils of the old period preserved in private households and monasteries indicate life-pattern and industry of their respective periods. Well-known specimens of Tibetan and Burmese types made of silver, brass, copper and other metals are seen in most of the religious centres. Apart from these, gongs and other items of heirloom preserved in the households of Non-Buddhist tribal folks occasionally having definite exchange value are also noteworthy in this context.[9]

Thus the results of various prehistoric explorations along with discovery of vertebrate fossils strongly suggest habitation of prehistoric man inside the territory of present day Arunachal Pradesh. Comparative study of materials and technology exhibit a close affinity of the neoliths of Arunachal Pradesh with objects of Assam, Burma, Indo-China, China and Malay Peninsula. The potteries from Parsi-Parlo in Lower Subansiri district from stratified deposits reveal its affinity with Chinese and South East Asian Pottery. We have no direct proof of an iron or copper age culture in Arunachal. The technology behind manufacture of certain Neolithic tools, however, is thought to be involved in use of metal implements and thus A.H.Dani believes that the neoliths themselves were perhaps products of Chalcolithic Age.

About the authors of the Paleolithic culture we can not say anything definitely. However, proximity, ecological identity and similarity of remains suggest that they belonged to the same ethnic tribes who were responsible for the contemporary cultures of North East India, Burma, South China and South East Asian Counties.[10] It seems that they would have been the Austric-speaking people who were supposed to have lived till their dispersal or miscegenation with later Mongoloid immigrants of North East India, who penetrated from China and South East Asia in the Neolithic period.[11]

Architectural vestiges of Arunachal are exemplified by Buddhist monasteries, *Stupas* and shrines, forts and hill-forets noticed at Bhalukpung, Nakshaparvat, Itanagar, Bhismaknagar, etc. and old Hindu shrines like Malinithan and *Tamreswari* Temple. These furnish valuable materials for study of various aspects of religious, social and political life and history of the territory. Architectural characteristics of these monuments indicate varying degree of impact and interaction of different cultural strains.[12]

Tawang, Zemithang, Kalaktong, Dirang, Rupa, Shergaon and other places of Tawang and West Kameng districts and Mechuka, Tuting, Gelling and other sites of the upper parts of West Siang and Dibang Valley are full of Buddhist *Gompas* (monasteries) and *Chortens* (*Stupa*) belonging to different sects of *Vajrayana* Buddhism constructed during different periods. Images preserved in monasteries and *Gompas* are traditionally ascribed to the eleventh-twelfth centuries AD or still earlier times. The *Theravada* monasteries and shrines of the Lohit and Tirap districts also contain numerous images of Buddha, other deities and monks in metals, wood or stone. Some of these are assignable to the 17th century, while others belong to later times. From an 18th century *Stupa* excavated at Vijayanagar of Tirap district have been found a number of Buddha figures made of stone and metals.[13]

Beautiful icons of Hindu divinities have been discovered from the temple of Malinithan in the foothills of the West Siang district bordering Assam which are variously datable to different periods between the tenth and fourtheenth centuries. The *Tamreswari* temple at the Lohit district and Naksaparvat ruins of the East Kameng district also furnish specimens of stone sculpture. These structures excavated mainly in the foothills near the Southern boundary adjoining Assam reflect a cultural penetration from the adjoining areas of Assam or the broader field of east India. It is to be noted here that numerous specimens have not yet been thoroughly investigated or studied, a lot can be known about migration of various ethnic groups, their admixture and cultural contact with the world beyond its present geographical limits.

The earliest datable inscription as found from the *Tamreswari* temple in the Lohit district. It is said to have recorded building of a boundary wall around the temple by one Muktadharmanarayana, supposed to be a Chutiya King, in 1364 Saka (1442 AD), which throws some light on the political, religious and cultural history of the period. Next may be mentioned of the short legends inscribed in a number of bricks found from the Bhismaknagar fort situated at a place not far from the *Tamreswari* temple. The Sadiya Snake Pillar Inscription found from Sadiya in Assam near the border of Arunachal Pradesh written in Tai script and language records some contract made between the Ahom King and the Mishmis. Numismatic evidence is very rare in the State and coins found are of the neighbouring rulers, which might have been brought in course of trade relationship.

Thus archaeological relics so far discovered in the State are not as prolific as in most other parts of the country. Still whatever little have come to light especially in recent years, deserves intensive examinations from various angles; and inter-disciplinary studies are likely to resolve many a knotty problems relating to the prehistoric period of Arunachal Pradesh. [15]

Oral Sources

Myths and legends represent quite an interesting and important source for the preparation of history of Arunachal Pradesh. Paucity of written literature, documents and other material-remains invest them with additional significance for having a direct access into tribal mind and tradition. Every village and community of the State has a rich heritage of such legends regarding its ancestors, origin, history of migration, etc, which exist mainly in the form of oral tradition. In the words of

Robinson, "History furnishes a very imperfect insight into the origin and descent of the tribes of the North East Frontier. We must, therefore, depend on the reflected light which is obtained by the comparison of languages, by the analysis of civil and religious institutions and mythological fables, or by trading clearly marked affinities in the manners and customs of different tribes".[16] It would, therefore, not be an exaggeration to state that the history of Arunachal Pradesh is mixed with legends. Folk-lore, folk songs and traditional accounts.

Oral traditions now-a-days are universally accepted as one of the complementary sources for recreating or reconstructing the past. In the words of Tomba Singh, "if history is the mother of the truth, folklore happens to be the mother of emancipation and reconstruction".[17] T. Mibang has echoed a similar view in the words, "Oral information becomes the only reliable source in areas where the documentary evidences are inadequate and especially for a society like Arunachal where and of whom history is yet to be written" [18] He further states, "*ponung* (folk dance accompanied with song of the Adi tribe) reflects the simple Sun, the Moon and the creation of the universe...... There may be certain fictitious plots in tale to amuse and entertain the listeners. But then here certainly the genesis of Adi cultural life is refered too. It remains an account of the past connecting the missing link in our history".[19] Here a special mention may be made of the *Abangs* of the Adis, an Indo-Mongoloid tribe of Arunachal Pradesh. Verrier Elwin has called tribal myths as *Puranas.* To quote him, "In the tribal *Puranas,* as we may call them, we find a strong sense of history, a pride in the descent of the race from a great ancestor, the record of a belief in the value of supreme self-sacrifice for the good of mankind".[20] Most of the tribes of the State are having such rich traditional sources. Infact Elwin's book *Myths of the North East Frontier of India* (1958) acquaints us with various myths of the tribals which are of great importance for the study of social history of the area.

Oral sources, however, have their limitations like subjectivity, personal biases and exaggeration. While using these sources, one should be careful to check and verify the facts in corroboration with other sources before arriving at a conclusion. Inspite of its limitations oral sources are valuable supplementary source for an imaginative reconstruction of the past, especially for filling up the gaps in our information. Although *Sources of the History of India* Vol. VI (N.R. Ray,1988) has compiled the archaeological and other literary sources relevant for use in the study of Arunachal Pradesh, these compilations did not mention the oral sources or data for historical research in Arunachal Pradesh. Though initiative in this respect have been taken by scholars like Sachin Roy, T. Nyori, T. Mibang and other, much more has yet to be done in this field to set right some distortions made by even some current scholars.

Literary Sources

Literary sources for convenience of our study may broadly be divided into those of (*a*) ancient and medieval periods, (*b*) colonial periods and (*c*) post-independence, post-Chinese aggression period.

(*a*) Literary Sources of Ancient and Medieval Periods

Starting from the earliest phase of Indian literary history, there are covert references to the non-Aryan autochthons like the *Nishadas, Kiratas,* etc and their settlements. Many of these accounts from the nature of their hints and description may well be construed as related to the areas ad people presently representing to region called Arunachal Pradesh and its inhabitants. Though the early and later Vedic literature, because of distance and lesser contact of the Aryans with this area, only vaguely mentioned about this region, in course of time because of eastward migration of the Aryans, greater knowledge about this area and people have been reflected in the *Mahabharata,* the *Ramayana*, the *Puranas* and the *Tantras*, especially in the *Vishnu Purana*, the *Kalika Purana* and the *Yogini Tantra.*[21]

Other works of both indigenous and foreign origin occasionally reveal awareness about this region. Early foreign account of the Indian Sub-continent like those contained in the *Periplus of the Enythraean Sea and Ptolemy's Geography* often are found to incorporate references to the land of the *Kiratas* and the trade that was carried with China.

In Hiuen Tsang's account (7th century AD) an idea is given of the hilly region east of Bhaskarvarman's Kingdom. It was full of folks living amidst forests infested with venomous snakes, herbs, etc. and extended upto the border of China. Muhammad Kasim, a Muslim historian, left an account of the Nyishis that in the days of Aurangzeb Nyishis (Dafalas) were entirely independent of Assam *raja* and plundered the country contiguous to their mountains whenever they found an opportunity. Shihabuddin Talish, who accompanied Mirjumla during his expedition to Assam (1662-63) left a detailed narrative on Assam.[22] In this he also incorporated available information about the tribal people residing in the region now comprising the hills of Assam and Arunachal Pradesh.

The Ahom *Buranjis* (Chronicles) which provide elaborate accounts of medieval Assam contain references to the people of Arunachal Pradesh. The relationship of the Arunachal Tribes with the Ahom monarchs have been recorded in details which are useful for construction of the political history of medieval Arunachal Pradesh. Besides political relationship, the *Buranjis* also throw light on the economic and cultural history of the people of Arunachal Pradesh.

Even some of the Vaisnava literature of medieval Assam refer about Arunachal and its people. The *Katha Gurucharita,* a biographical work of the medieval Vaisnava Saint of Assam, written in the later part of the 18th century, gives an exhaustive list of communities of Assam and the neighbouring areas which includes the names of many tribal communities of Aruanchal Pradesh. Similarly the book *Sri Sri Arinruddhadevar Charita aru Mayamara Gosain Sakalar Vamsavali* (1933) refers to the participation of Nyishi and Nyishi-*Bahatias* with the Mataks against the Ahom government in the Moamaria Rebellion.

(*b*) Literary Sources of the Colonial Period

After the establishment of British Superemacy in Assam in the 1st part of the 19th century, North Eastern Region gradually attracted the attention of a band of British adventurists and imperialists. The course of colonial intervention culminating into the establishment of British paramountcy over the hill-men of the region and their incorporation into the colonial cobwebs was determined by the colonial interests in the Brahmaputra valley and the commercial and strategico-political interests beyond the frontiers. By the beginning of the seventies of the 19th century, the economy of Assam had become promising and trade and industry had made a good start. Tea, petroleum, coal, rubber and timber became flourishing industries and items of business. As all the districts of Assam bordered on some hills inhabited by the tribes, further growth and consequent profit of the industries mentioned above greatly depended upon the Administration's capacity to maintain law and order in the foothill areas. The tribes on the other hand, driven or restricted into the hills by British commercial interest in the foothills, sometimes had to fall upon the plains to draw their supplies, which they did traditionally. So there was the need of regulation of hill-plain relationship for the Britishers and for this they needed intimate knowledge of the tribes and their land.

As a result, the British administrators, travellers and explorers – some of them were also trained anthropologists-left behind systematic accounts of the tribes they studied. Their studies, however, were the results of politico-economic needs of the Colonial State, which reflected the 19th century outlook of these ethnographers with an unchanging attitude for the oriental societies in general and the societies of this region in particular "with a view to projecting the British rule as the legitimate agency of progress".[23] The resultant monographs and studies followed a set standard pattern in which the tribes were depicted as "isolates", 'ignorants', 'uncivilized', 'culturally backward' 'belligerents', etc.[24]

Actually these days very few students of historiography would seem to believe that the colonial rule was 'governed by the motives of humanity' and it attempted 'to conciliate the hill-tribes'. Here lies the significance of the call given by B.K.Roy Burman in which he cautions the historians of India "to examine the events documented by sources close to colonial administration with conscious intellectual tuning".[25] Amalendu Guha echoes a similar view in which he wishes the historians writing on this region to be largely unconventional by delineating the characteristics of the colonial ethnography.[26] Actually the term 'isolation' was used to create a hill-plain dichotomy and negating the symbiosis that existed between the habitats of the hills and plains for centuries during the pre-colonial period. Similarly, by using the term 'Savage' the tribes were depicted as the fossilized segments of humanity around whom the colonial construct of "Wanton aggression and impulsive behaviour" could be foisted.

Even after admitting the facts mentioned above, we are also to admit it is infact the writings of the British historians, adventurists, anthropologists and sociologists, whose works can still be considered as the pioneering and scientific works on different aspects of Arunachal Pradesh. For the modern researchers one problem of considerable dimension is to check and countercheck such writings to make these presentable to the modern world. It appears proper here to mention some such important works, which throw light on different aspects of the State. These are:

Buhcanon Hamilton (Francis), *An Account of Assam* (1807-1814); R.B.Pemberton, *Report on the Eastern Frontier of British India* (1835); Montgomery Martin, *The History Antiquities, Topography and Statistics of Eastern India* (1836); John M'Cosh, *Topography of Assam* (1837); L.A.Waddell, *Tribes of the Brahmaputra Valley* (1837); Willaim Robinson, *A Descriptive Account of Assam* (1837); E.T.Dalton, *Descriptive Ethnology of Bengal* (1872) now printed with the title *Tribal History of Eastern India;* H.H.Rishly, *TheTribes and Castes of Bengal* (1872), W.W.Hunter, *A Statistical Account of Assam* (1872) J.F. Michell, *Report on the North East Frontier of India* (1883); Alexander Mackenzie, *The North East Frontier of India* (1884); E.A.Gait, *A History of Assam* (1905); L.W. Shakespeare, *History of Upper Assam, Upper Burma and the North East Frontier* (1914); R.S.Kennedy, *Ethnographical Report on the Akas, Knowas and the Mijis and the Membas of Tawang;* B.C.Ellen and E.A.Gait, *Gazetteers of Bengal and North East India;* Dorothy Woodman, *Himalayan Frontier;* C.U.Aitchison, *A Collection of Treaties, Engagements and Sanads,* G.A.Grierson, *Linguistic Survey of India;* R.Reid, *History of the Frontier Areas Bordering on Assam from 1883-1941; Reports on the Administration of North East India* (1921-22), etc. The list of sources is not an exhaustive one.

Apart from the above works, various unpublished works like Political Proceedings, Secret Proceedings, Judicial and Revenue Proceedings, Official correspondences, Census Reports, Military Reports concerning this area of the British period serve as primary sources for the study of territory of Arunachal Pradesh. These unpublished documents can be studied in the National Archive, New Delhi, India Office Library and Records, London; West Bengal Government Archives, Kolkata, of the Asiatic Society of Bengal and the National Library, Kolkata, Assam Secretarial Record office, Itanagar Archive, etc.

(*c*) Literary Sources of the Post-Colonial, Post-Chinese Agression Period

Even after independence the dominant trend of colonial historiography mentioned above about the tribes living in this frontier region or elsewhere in India took time for perceptible change. Even upto 1970s such an attitude was clearly manifested in the historiography of this region, whereas in the writings of the sociologists and anthropologist such perceptible changes occurred early. The historical writings took a broader time span to adjust with the changing situation. One more point to be noted here is that this was a period of Chino-Indian clashes of 1962 which had aroused a great interest in the history of the North East Frontier Agency and that elicited a spate of writings on the subject and the region.

The Post-colonial writing on the area requires some reference here. Verrier Elwin's *A Philosophy for NEFA* (1957), the foreword of which was written by no less a person than Jawaharlal Nehru, is still considered as a classic on Arunachal Pradesh. His other important works on the State are: *Myths of the North East Frontier of India* (1958); *Democracy in NEFA* (1965) and *The Art of the North East Frontier of India* (1959). H.K.Barpujari's *Problem of the Hill Tribes of North East Frontier* is of immense importance to understand the history of Arunachal Pradesh. S.K.Bhuyan's *Anglo-Assamese Relations* (1949, 2nd Edition, 1974) and Laxmi Devi's *Ahom Tribal Relations* (1968) have made considerable contributions in understanding the relationship of the different tribes of Arunachal Pradesh with the Ahom rulers and the people of Assam.

Other works on the State are: C. Von Furer Heimen-dorf, *Ethnographic Notes on the Tribes of the Subansiri Region* (1947); *Himalayan Barbery* (1955); *The Apa Tanis and their neighbours* (1962); G.Graham Bower, Hidden Land (1953); N.K.Rustomji, *Tribal Administration in the North East Frontier Agency* (1955);

B.K.Roy Burman, *Demographic and Socio-Economic Profiles of the Hill Areas of North East India* (1961); P.N.Luthra, *Constitutional and Administrative Growth of NEFA* (1961); B.C.Chakravarti, *British Relations with the Hill Tribes of Assam since 1858* (1964); J.N.Chudhury, *Arunachal Panorama* (1973); S.M.Dubey, *Modernization and Elites in Arunachal Pradesh* (1975); D.P.Chaudhury, *The North East Frontier of India 1865-1914* (1978), L.N.Chakravorty, *Glimpses of Early History of Arunachal Pradesh* (1997) and M.L. Bose's History of Arunachal Pradesh (1997); Y.A.Raikar and S. Chatterjee, *Archaeology in Arunachal Pradesh* (1981), Subid Chatterjee, *Comprehensive History of Arunachal Pradedsh* (1991); Sachin Roy, *Aspects of Padam-Minyong Culture;* S.Dutta, *Students Movement in Arunachal Pradesh*(1998). Here again the list is not exhaustive one.

The recent books from the Scholars from among the tribes of Arunachal Pradesh have thrown a lot of light on the history and culture of the region, which may be considered as insiders' scientific views on different aspects of the history and culture of Arunachal Pradesh. Noted among them are T.Nyori, *The History and Culture of the Adis* (New Delhi, 1993); T. Mibang, *The Social Changes among the Tribes of Arunachal Pradesh,* (New Delhi, 1995); N.N.Osik, *The Anglo-Adi relations,* (1995).

The Directorate of Research of the Government of Arunachal Pradesh has taken leading role in bringing out various books, booklets and pamphlets on different tribes of the State and their culture, religion, language, etc., which are the results of efforts of a group of dedicated Research Officers and Directors of the Department.

III

Conclusion

Since its inception in 1980 the North East India History Association (NEIHA) has been doing a yeoman job to being to light through its proceeding volumes the scholarly writings of the trend setters of historiography of North East India including Arunachal Pradesh. These writings have provided the young scholars with new themes, perspectives and methodology of interdisciplinary approach, and delineating the research designs so as to have even conventional "sources close to colonial administration with conscious intellectual tuning" to unravel new facts of the history of the region.

The research papers in NEIHA proceedings on the region show a significant shift from affirmation to negation of the dominant trend of colonial discourse outlined above. In this connection, we may quote from the presidential address of Prof .J.B.Ganguly, one of the prominent economists of the North East, who has postulated that the colonial interference and the resultant changes have much to do with the "inequality and poverty" presently manifesting in the area under discussion. [27] The research paper published in the NEIHA proceedings upto the 15th Session on the State of Arunachal Pradesh have been published in an edited volume[28] which can be considered as a mine of information and scientific data for scholars and researchers on the history and culture of Arunachal Pradesh, edited by S. Dutta.

One point to be noted here is that most of the modern scholars have studied the political and administrative aspects of the colonial period of this region on traditional lines chiefly to narrate the policy of the British government towards the tribes of Arunachal Pradesh. But the whole gamut of Socio-Economic or Cultural Aspects have yet to get adequate attention. "The migration and transformation of the tribes, their system of land tenure, their traditional system of law and justice, system of warfare, trend of modernization in their tradition bound society, economic transition, impact of two world wars, and search for identity in the recent scenario of Indian political changes require utmost research-oriented care".[29] Studies on the participation of the tribes in the Freedom Movement of the Country and reasons for less-intensification of the Movement in the area should also be studied scientifically

Finally, the acts, regulations, etc. of the independent Indian Union bearing on Arunachal Pradesh and Parliamentary Papers and decisions changing the status of the territory leading to its establishment of a full-fledged State may be perused for an upto date account of its political evolution and development of Arunachal Pradesh.

References

1. L.A. Waddell, *The Tribes of the Brahmaputra* Valley, Delhi 1986. 1st Published 1937, pp. 1f.
2. K.A.A. Raja, 'Arunachal: The Evolution of Personality', *Arunachal News,* June 1975, p. 5.
3. M.L. Bose, *History of Arunachal Pradesh,* New Delhi, 1997, p. 16.
4. Subid Chatterjee, *A Comprehensive History of Arunachal Pradesh,* Calcutta, 1991, pp. 20f.
5. *Census Report,* 1901, Vol. IV, Part. I, Chapter-XI, p. 120.
6. Chatterjee, *op. cit.,* p. 4.
7. Y.A. Raikar, 'Magaliths at Jamiri', *Arunachal News,* September 1997.
8. Y.A. Raikar and S.Chatterjee, *Archaeology in Arunachal Pradesh,* Shillong 1980p.46; D.K.Bora, 'Archaeological Ruins of Naksa Parvat' Resarun IX.1993, pp. 26f.
9. Chatterjee, p. 5.
10. E.C. Worman, 'The Neolithic Problem in the Prehistory of India', *Journal of Washingron Academy of Sciences,* Vol. 39, No. 6, pp. 181-201.
11. B. Tripathy, Archaeological Remains of Arunachal Pradesh (MS) (Unpublished).
12. Chatterjee, *op. cit.,* pp. 5f.
13. *Ibid.*
14. *Ibid.*, p. 7.
15. *Ibid.*, p. 30.
16. William Robinson, *A Descriptive Account of Assam,* p. 335.
17. T. Tomba Singh, 'Folk History and Historiography', North East India History Association (NEIHA) Proceeding Volume, 11th Imphal Session, 1990, p. 28.
18. T. Mibang, "Interpreting History through Ponung", S. Dutta (ed.) *History, Culture and Economy of Arunachal Pradesh,* New Delhi, 1998, p. 34.
19. *Ibid.*, p. 31.
20. Verrier Elwin, *W. Philosophy for NEFA,* 1988, p. 212.
21. Chatterjee, *op. cit.,* p. 11.

22. *Fathiyya-i-ibbriyya,* Portion Translated by J.N. Sarkar, *Journal of Bihar and Orissa Research Society.* Patna, 1915, pp. 182ff.
23. Amalendu Guha, Presidential Address, *NEIHA Proceedings,* 2nd Session, Dibrugarh, 1981.
24. Verrier Elwin, India's *North East Frontier in the Nineteenth Century,* Madras, 1959, Introduction; Sanghamitra Mishra, 'The Nature of Colonial Intervention in the Naga Hills, 1840-80'. *The Economic and Political Weekly,* Vol. XXXIII, 19th December, 1998.
25. B.K. Roy Burman, Prefatory Introduction to the new edition in Alexander Mackenzie, *History of the Relations of Government with the Hill Tribes of the North East Frontier of Bengal,* reprinted as the *North East Frontier of Bengal,* New Delhi, 1995.
26. Amalendu Guha, *op.cit.*
27. J.B. Ganguly, *Presidential Address,* 7th NEIHA Session, Pasighat, 1986.
28. S. Dutta (ed) *History, Culture and Economy of Arunachal Pradesh,* Delhi, 1998.
29. P.K. Nayak, Trends in the Historiography of Arunachal Pradesh, A brief discussion, S. Dutta (ed.) *op.cit.*, p. 23.

23

Aspects of Historical Sources of History in Arunachal Pradesh

Basudeb Malik

Arunachal Pradesh, also known as the dawnlit mountain where the sun rays reach first in our country, is a land covered with unknown history. It has, achieved its statehood on 20th February, 1987. Geographically the state is located between 26° 30′ and 29° 30′ N latitude and 91° 30′ and 97° 30′ E longitudes. The state is extremely beautiful studded with lush green forest, deep river valleys, picturesque plateau, snow capped peaks. The land mass of the state is mostly mountainous, overlapped by chains of Himalayan ranges. Only the foothill area of the state is plain.

This wonderful state remained unknown to most of the people due to its remoteness and inaccessibility. During the 19th century, the region started unveiling its darkness through the European explorers who started traveling in this regard. The first hand information about the area started coming through their reports. But the real activity of the state started in the post independence period. Different government agencies started working in the area and came close to the local inhabitants. Slowly but steadily, all-round information about the state started coming. The Research Department established in the early years of post-independence era undertook cultural, historical and philological research activity. Archaeological excavations, explorations and field survey started from 1950s. And through these archaeological activities various aspects of Arunachal history is known to us.

The sources of history are viz, (1) Archaeological objects (2) Literary works and (3) Myths legend, oral literature, etc.

The archaeological objects can be divided into two categories, pre-historic objects and proto-historic objects. It is possible to know about the prehistoric from the prehistoric objects like fossils, stone implements, prehistoric pottery, etc. These artifacts could be collected from the excavation, exploration and surveys conducted by the archaeologists, historians and explorers.

The European explorers and travelers who came in this part of the country from the middle of the 19th century could collect numerous prehistoric artifacts from different parts of Arunachal Pradesh. Among the prominent explorers mention may be made of John Lubbock who noticed a light green jade Celt collected from Tirap in 1870. Lt. E.H. Steel collected three more Celts from the same area. Another piece of stone tool was collected by Lt. Barron. Captain Gregory found one curvilinear butt axe from Mishmi hills in the end of the 19th century. In 1917 Healy collected a curvilinear facetted tool. J.P. Mills founded curvilinear facetted tool and three rounded butt axes from Nogra, north of Noa-Dihing river in Tirap in 1933. J.H. Grace collected three rounded butt from Sadiya Frontier Tract. Most of these artifacts have been preserved in the Pitt rivers Museum Oxford.

Quite a few discoveries of the prehistoric period has been done in the post-independence period by the Indian counterparts which provide information about the traces of Paleolithic culture in Arunachal Pradesh. Discovery of a vertebrate fossil by the Geological Survey in 1974-75 from the Upper Tertiary rocks of Ramghat in Lower Sunansir proves to be significant. The upper Tertiary horizon of Arunachal Pradesh seems to have inhabited by the Hominids and Paleolithic men.

B.P. Boperdikar of A.S.I. recorded Stone Age tools while exploring the Dephabhum area of the Lohit district in 1969-70. River section of the terraces were detected and artifacts like cleaver, ovate, chisels, cores, flakes, points, proto hand axe, unificial chopper, and Neolithic implements. S.N. Rao of Dibrugarh University traced out some objects from valley of Lohit district in 1971 which he claimed as Paleolithic object. Y.A. Raikar of Research Department, Govt. of Arunachal Pradesh found out some chips of semi-precious stones like chalcedony, jasper etc. from vijoynagar in Changlang in 1971 which he claimed as microlithic objects. A.A. Ashraf of the Directorate of Research unearthed Neolithic tools from Parsi-Parlo in the Lower Subansiri district in 1987. The present writer has also collected a Neolithic polished axe from Rayeng village in Lower Dibang Valley district in 2000.

The history of the later period *i.e.,* the 'Historical Period' can be ascertained from the architectural remains, sculptures, pottery, painting, terracotta, inscriptions and coins. The important secular architectural remains are Bhismaknagar fortress in the Lower Dibang Valley, Ita Fort in Itanagar, ruins of Chidu-Chimiri fort near Roing in the Lower Dibang Valley, Naksa Parvat ruins in East Kameng, Bhalukpong ruins in the West Kameng. Excavation and exploration conducted in these sites reveal lots of information which actually help to reconstruct the history of the area to a great deal. It is ascertained through archaeological research that these ancient structures belonged to 10th century AD. It could be also revealed that local dynasties viz. Kalitas, Chutiyas, Ahoms played important role in different foot hill areas in Arunachal Pradesh.

Among the religious structures some of the important ones are *Malinithan,* in foothills of West Siang district. *Tamreswari* temple and *Sivalinga* temple in the Lohit district, Injuno Ganesh temple at Injuno in the Lower Dibang Valley district - all these temples belong to the Brahminical faith.

Architectural remains of Buddhist faith can be seen in some parts of Aruanchal which help to ascertain in the rich Buddhist culture practised among the local people. The important areas of Buddhist monastery and *stupa* are Tawang, Zemithang, kalaktang, Dirang, Rupa, Mechuka, Tuting, Namsai, Vijoynagar, etc. The period of Buddhism started from 14th – 15th century.

Several sculptures of Hindu icons have been identified from Malinithan temple site. The important ones are Surya, Kartikeya, Vishnu, Saraswati, Nandi Bull, etc. There are also excellent sculptures of *Vidhyadhara, Gandharvas,* Sages, Door keepers, Animal Figures and motifs of vegetation. An important sculpture of Ganesh has been found at Injuno village near Roing. These sculptures provide enormous informations about the artistic skill and religious practice of Arunachal Pradesh in the past, specifically in the foothills area.

Large quantity of pottery could be yielded from excavations at Bhismaknagar, Chidu-Chimiri, Naksaparvat, Bhalukpong. Itafort, *Sivalinga* temple and several other sites in Arunachal. Pottery is considered as one of the most important sources to study the history of aparticular area or period.

Paintings of historical importance can be found in the Buddhist monastery and *stupa* in form of murals, miniature in manuscripts and painted scroll, etc.

Excavations at important sites in Arunachal have unearthed terracotta objects like figurines of gods and goddesses, animals, play objects, weapons, plaques with beautiful designs etc. These objects hear huge information in respect of constructing history.

So far the number of inscriptions found in Arunachal is very few. The earliest inscription has been found from *Tamreswari* temple in Lohit district. It is purported to record building of a boundary wall around the *Tamreswari* temple by Muktadharmanarayana in Saka 1364, *i.e.*, 1412 AD. The inscription is written in Sanskrit language and Assamese-Bengali script of the fifteenth century. This throws light on the political, religious and cultural history of the period.

Traces of inscriptions can be found on the bricks and tiles of Bhismaknagar fortress. Again it is written in Sanskrit with Bengali-Assamese script. The inscription is a repetititon of one sentence *'Sri Sri Laksmi Narayan Japa'.* These inscriptions throw important light on the religious and cultural history of the region.

Another inscription of Ahom period was discovered in the early part of the 20th century by O'Callghan, Political Officer. The inscription was found in two pieces in the bed of Deopani river near Roing. The content of the inscription is "I, the Dihingia Borgohain, do engrave on the stone pillar and copper plate these writing on the strength of which the Mishmis are to dwell on the hills near the Dihang river with their females, children, attendants and followers. They will occupy all the hills. They will give four baskets full of poison and other things as tribute and keep watch over the body of the fat *Gohain.* If any body happens to be in possession of and wishes to remain on both sides of the hills he is prohibited from encroachment. If any body should dwell by the side of the hills, he will surely become a slave of the Mishmis". The inscription is written in Tai script and language and dates back to the first part of the 16th century. It gives a clear idea of the socio-political situation of the region. It also throws light on demarcation of political boundary between the Idu-Mishmi and the Ahoms in this region.

Two more inscriptions could be seen engraved on the muzzle of cannons of Ahom king Gadadharsinha, from Chowkham in Lohit district are noticed. They are written in Sanskrit language and Assamese-Bengali script of the 17th century. These are dated Saka 1604 *i.e.,* 1682 AD. The content of the inscriptions was related to an important development in the struggle between the Mughals and the Ahoms for the control over Assam. It also reflected important side light on the history of Aruanchal Pradesh. The provenance of the inscription indicates relation and contact between the people of Arunachal and the people of Assam.

Several tablets in Buddhist monasteries, fort or *dzongs*, *stupas* or *chortens* and inscribed miniature *chortens*, stone plaque and pedestal of images are found in plenty in Tawang, West Kameng and Upper Siang districts. A memorial stone inscription has been found from the ruins of Naksaparvat in East Kameng.

All these inscriptions taken together furnish valuable information which help to verify, corroborate and supplement evidence available from other sources for reconstruction of history.

Numismatic evidence in Arunachal Pradesh is comparatively meagre. A few late Ahom issues of Sivasimha and Rudra Simha has been discovered. About three hundred silver coins of Muslim period have been discovered from coin hoard at Bhalukpong in East kameng district. The coins contain Arabic script mentioning the names like *Al Aminu Aazam* (chief treasurer) *Ms Jafurulla Shah, Abul Mujafar Uddin.* The date mentioned on the coin is 951 Macihe. The coins contain Arabic writing on both obverse and reverse sides. Detail study on the coins will definitely reveal lot of informations about the economic and political condition of Assam and Arunachal Pradesh during medieval period.

Literary evidence about Aruanchal in Indian literature is formidable. In the earliest Indian literature like the *Ramayana* and the *Mahabharata* there are references of the non-Aryan authochthons like the *Nisadas* and *Kiratas.* Description of these people and their location of habitation narrated in the epics could well be associated with the local population of Arunachal. The early Brahmanical literature viz., the *Taittiriya Brahmana* and the *Vajra Samhita* of the *Yajurveda* as well as *Atharva Veda* made frequent reference of the hill people and various medicinal plants grown in this region. In the early period very little was known to the Indo-Aryan people as there was hardly any possibility of interaction between them. However, in the later period the Aryan civilization gradually started spreading towards the northeast and the north Indians came in closer contact as well as clashed with the people of North-East region. Subsequently, mention of this region was found in the literature like *Mahabharata, Ramayana, Puranas, Tantras* and especially in the *Vishnu Puranas, Kalika Puranas* and the *Yogini Tantras*. Other works of Indian origin as well as works of foreign writers throw light on this regionl. They are the Manusmriti and the *Milindapanna*. Early foreign accounts on indian subcontinent like those contained in the *Periplus of the Erythrean* sea and Ptolemy's geography often are found to have mentioned about the land of the *Kiratas* producing malabathrus and offering routes through which trade was carried to China. Chang Kien also mentioned this trade in the second sentury B.C.These tracts may well be located in Aruancahl through which trade was regularly carried on. Hiuen Tsang has narrated about the hilly people inhabiting in the east of Bhaskarvarman's kingdom in his account which he described as barbarian folk living amid forest infested with venomous snakes, harbs, etc. and the area extended upto the border of China. Shihabuddin Talish accompanying Mirjumla during his expedition left a detailed narrative on Assam and also incorporated information about the tribal people residing in Arunachal. Ahom *Buranjis* provide an elaborate history of mediaeval Assam and Arunachal. Reports of occasional expeditions of British with the tribal Chiefs, furnish important information about the modern pariod of Arunachal history.

Finally, the regulations, treaties, acts of the government of indepenedent India related to Arunachal and Parliamentary papers and decisions changing the status of the territory ultimately leading to its establishment as a full fledged state may be understood with benefit for an up to date account of its political development.

Books and articles of foreign writers as well as their Indian counter parts dealing with various aspects of the life and culture of the people of Arunachal provide valuable information for writing the history. Census and statistical reports, periodicals journal, government magazines, research journals, viz., Resarun, Journals of Anthropological Survey of India, Journal and Magazines published by the Arunachal University, etc. deal with various socio-political and economic aspects of Aruanchal Pradesh covering from the earliest period to the modern day.

Buddhist manuscripts, *Thankas*, painted miniature etc. may be considered as a very rich treasure of art as well as important source of history and culture of Arunachal Pradesh and adjoining countries like Tibet and Burma. In most of the cases these manuscripts have been brought from the neighbouring counties like Tibet and Burma, except a few manuscripts which were created by the local inhabitants of this land. Majority of the manuscripts deal with religious aspects which reflect insight in the religious ideas and beliefs of the people as also the world of religious art. The books on secular subjects like history books of the *Gompas* or records kept in the monasteries and unpublished documents of treaties and *Sanad*, occasionally met with among the house holds of the Chiefs and dignitaries, provide valuable pointer to the contemporary economic, political and administrative system.

Myths, legends, folk tale, folk lore, etc. which can be called as 'Oral Literature' play a very important part in undesrstanding the history of an area. Most of the tribes in Arunachal Pradesh have no written language and as such the local people or this area are unable to record any event of their life in their own dialect or language. But interestingly all the tribal societies in Arunachal Pradesh possess a very elaborate oral literature which includes folk lore, folk tales, myths, legends etc. that treansmit from one generation to another since time immemorial. Particularly the priests of each of the tribal societies play very important role in narrating the stories of migration, origin, creation of universe, mythological story etc. All such narrations are usually made while performing rites and ritual practices in various occasions. Study of these lengthy utterance of the priests provide valuable information about the unknown and forgotten history of the tribes. Thus, it may not be exaggerated to say that without the help of the priests, the process of reconstruction of history of the tribal groups may not be possible especially whose culture is based on perishable material like bamboo, cane and wood and who has no script of their own.

Recently a project has been taken up the the Research Department, Govt. of Arunachal Pradesh to record and document the oral literature which is very much vibrant among the various tribal groups in Aruanchal Pradesh. Efforts have been taken up to record the chanting and the narrations of the *'Igus'* (the idu Mishmi priet) to collect the oral literature of the Idu-mishmi community. Among the other tribes, the educated modern societies have been trying to collect their respective folk lore, folk tales, myths, legends etc. The Adi Cultural Literary Society and the Idu-Cultural Literary Soceity have come forward in a big way in documenting and publishing literature reflecting various aspects of their societies.

Commendable works have been done by the foreign as well as Indian writers in regard to collection of folk lore, folk tales, myths, legends etc. of the tribes of Arunachal Pradesh. The famous writer Verrier Elwin's *'Myths of the North East Frontier of India'* and *'A new book of Tribal Fiction'* offer a rich collection of various folk literatrue popular among the tribal societies.

Proper study of these literatures and the narrations of the tribal priests should come handy in collecting information about the local history of the region.

References

1. S. Chatterjee, *A Comprehensive History of Arunachal Pradesh,* Calcutta, 1991.
2. G.C. Baruah (ed.), *Ahom Buranji*, Gauhati, 1930.
3. B.C. Allen, *Assam Gazetteers* Vol. IV, V, VII, VIII, Shillong, 1905.
4. A.H. Dani, '*Prehistory and Protohistory of Eastern India*, Calcutta, 1960.
5. V. Elwin, *Myths of NEFA*, Shillong, 1968.
6. D.K. Bora, *History and Archaeology of Itanagar*, Itanagar, 1996.
7. Y.A. Raikar & S.Chatterjee, *Archaeology in Arunachal Pradesh*, Shillong, 1980.
8. A.A. Ashraf, *Prehistoric Arunachal Pradesh*, Itanagar, 1991.
9. A.A. Ashraf *Prehistoric Archaeology of Lower Subansiri*, Itanagar, 1990.
10. D.K. Bora, *et. al.*, Medieaval Life of Naksaparbat, Itanagar, 1997.
11. L.N. Chakravarty, *Glimpses of Early History of Arunachal Pradesh, Shillong, 1973.*

24

Nyishi-Sulung Relationship: A Preliminary Enquiry into the Nature and Causes in Substantive Perspective

M.C. Behera

Introduction

Sulungs, a tribe recently being introduced as Puroiks by its members, is one of the least studied tribes of present Arunachal Pradesh. Commonly known as the slaves of Nyishis, a dominant and major tribe in the state, Sulungs have a beautific world of their own with a social and productive system as distinct from their 'masters'. The dual identity, slave tribe of Nyishis and a community having its own socio-cultural identity makes any study on them by social scientists in general interesting and challenging. It is challenging because with a long subordination it is difficult to get in to the data on Sulung way of life. On the other hand, it creates interest as one gets into it and understands their dual identity.

Interestingly, no serious research is available on Sulungs except a brief note by Haimendorf (1946) and two ethnographic accounts by Stonor (1972) and Deuri (1982). Dutta and Showren (2000) in a paper had focused on their problems after rehabilitation at Itanagar. Only a year ago, I have tried to understand Sulungs' social self (Behera : 2002) within the analytical frame of Foraging Mode of thought as propounded by Alan Barnard (2002) and their world view of man-nature relationship (Behera:2002b) in a comparative perspective with reference to Nyishi and Khampti tribesmen of Arunachal Pradesh. Yadav (1999) has prepared a note on Sulungs as a bonded labour group and Singh (19995) has referred to their relation with Nyishis during trade of the later with Tibet. But no study is available having made a critical analysis of the origin of such a relation as it exists. Stonor and Deuri, however, have attempted to trace its origin in to myths but without any serious analysis.

The present paper is an attempt to understand Nyishi-Sulung relationship as a typology within discussion frame of interaction between two distinctive systems.

Nuishi-Sulung Relationship: An Ethnographic Account

Sulungs (Stonor:1972; Deuri: 1982) are virtual serfs of Nyishi and Miji tribe of the state. They inhabit inaccessible terrains of East Kameng, Papumpare and Kurung Kumey districts. Their concentration is more in Chayeng Tajo, Bameng, Khenewa, Pipu-Dipu and Sewa circles in East Kameng district. Nyishi of Arunachal Pradesh (cf. Shukla: 1965) have spread over present Lower Subansiri, Kurung Kumey, Papumpare and East Kameng districts of the state. They inhabit almost central region of the state and to their northwest, there is the inhabitation of Sulungs. It is to be noted that Sulungs do not belong to Nyishi tribe as a whole. As a matter of fact Nyishi-Sulung relationship does not naturally fall within the domain of a tribe-to tribe relation, for, as has been mentioned, they are found to have entered into the same type of relationship with Mijis, another neighbouring tribe of Sulungs. Moreover, all the Sulungs are not slaves and even Stonor has mentioned of free Sulumgs and two cases where Sulungs have entered into the subordinate relationship with Nyishis. It is obvious that Sulungs living close to Nyishi habitation have entered into such type of relationship.

Sulung are considered to be "original inhabitants" (Elwin:1959:13) in their habitat (Yadav: 1999:20; Stonor:1972:2); at least believed to have been in the country when "the other races" migrated in (Haimendorf:1959:7). They constitute a "perfectly distinct tribal group" (Stonor:1072:1), their existence was only recorded in the 'Dafla Hills'. However, they came to lime light when they were 'rediscovered' by Haimendorf in 1944-45 (Haimendorf:1950:7) and there after were visited by Stonor (1972:1) between 1945-48 near Nyishi villages named Rio and Lidung Mundeng. Their distinct ethnic identity essentially stems from their distinct language group, pronounced prognathism and foraging economy (cf. Stonor: 1972).

The relationship between Sulungs and Nyishis is also described as a feudal arrangement (Stonor:1972:8). But Verrier Elwin writes," it is incorrect to say that there is no real slavery in NEFA and that the slaves should be called serfs" (Elwin:1959:230). He believes that Sulungs are "almost a slave tribe" (ibid: 229). In a recent writing Yadav (1999) uses the term 'bonded labour' for the Sulungs. In which way we describe the relationship between Sulungs and Nyishi, the fact remains that Sulung works in the field of his Nyishi master, fights for him (in old days) and works as his porter and shares the items obtained from foraging. It is to be noted that a Sulung slave is different from another category of slaves that unlike the Sulungs stay in their respective master's house. The second category of slave consists of *NERA* and *BETA.* "The *Nera* class are said to be Nyishis by birth. The other are purchased slaves of other tribes (Dun:1897:188). When a *Nera* or an Assamese slave is sold, the right of the master over the slave and his product is sold. The person shifts his residence along with his physical self. But in case of Sulungs, the rights to use Sulung labour directly or indirectly are sold. The total product of his labour is not sold. His resident as compared to the former class does not change, as he does not stay with the master. His residence in terms of his settlement, however, may change depending on the migration of the master's family to a far of place. In case of transfer/sale to another Nyishi clan, a Sulung is traded to another Sulung settlement, for the tribe "never shares a house with Daflas" (Stonor 1972:11). In spite of *Atok-akra* (Master slave) relationship, "the Sulung are to carry on with their own way of life undisturbed and unmolested". (Stonor:1072:8). It is difficult to say how old is such a relationship between Sulungs and Nyishis. Dalton mentions of Assam slaves. But both Robinson and Dalton have not mentioned of Sulung slaves in agriculture. Rather they have discussed about Nyishi division of labour and work participation in their traditional economic pursuits (cf. Robinson: 1851; Dalton: 1973). Haimendorf (ibid., 7) also has not mentioned of their slave status except that they "are familiar with the tongue of their neighbour". The only thing which can be deduced with certainty that they had interaction with the

Nyishis as he had studied them in Nyishi areas. Sulungs remain entirely self-respecting and give no impression of being downtrodden or a depressed class (ibid.10.). when Nyishi-Sulung or Miji-Sulung relationship is considered, a common factor of distinction stands out in both the cases. The productive system of both Nyishis and Mijis stands out superior to Sulung in that the economy of Sulungs is based largely on food gathering and hunting (Stonor: 1972:3), though presently they are both cultivators of grain crops and also food gatherers (ibid.13). Haimendorf writes that Sulungs subsisted "mainly by hunting and trapping and the collection of Jungle produce. They are believed to have had no cultivation until they came in contact with other tribes and learnt from them how to till the soil. Even now the areas they till are very small and they live in a semi nomadic style, leaving their villages for months at a time to range the forests and hills in search of game and wild jungle produce" (Haimendorf: 1950:7). Nyishis and Mijis, on the other hand, practise shifting cultivation and raise livestock.

Though Sulungs have entered in to the same type of relationship with Mijis, the discussion frame is designated Nyishi-Sulung relationship only to refer to the typology of relationsip between two groups with two distincts productive systems. Nyishi-Sulung relationship is preferred to Miji-Sulung relationship because of the fact that the first record of their existence was known with reference to Nyishi territory and then with Nyishi community. Only Deuri has mentioned of their relationship with both Nyishis and Mijis since time immemorial (Deuri: 1982: 7-8).

Conceptual Comprehension

Nyishi-Sulungs typology of relationship, *Atok-akra,* is an interaction between two groups of people with advanced and less advanced productive systems. The relationship is similar to that of the ones which exist between African hunter-gatherers and their neighbours (Woodburn:1988;31-64), Shans and Kachins (Leach:1954), and between Hindus and tribesmen (Bose:1996).

Woodburn discusses how stigmatized groups (hunter-gatherers in relation to farming neighbours) respond to teir vulnerability to domination and to persecution either "by dealing with outsiders only through ephemeral relations and thereby retaining control of themselves and their own labour or, alternatively, by entering into a relation of cliensthip with some outsider patron, to whom they will have to defer, but who may offer paternalist protection against other outsiders"(1988:54). The premise of his discussion is that "members of all hunter-gatherer societies (and indeed of all human societies) have been subjected to pressure of one sort or another from outsiders" (ibid.,34), and these outsiders, usually neighboring pastoral/or agricultural groups treat them as inferiors, as people apart, stigmatize them and discriminate against them (ibid., 37). Woodburn has used empirical data on the relationship between hunter-gatherers and their neighbours to study carefully how African hunter-gatherers social organization has been affected by pressure from outsider. Of course, the present paper does not attempt to study social organization of Sulungs in terms of their relations with Nyishis, but it attempts a theoretical understanding of 'oppositional solidarity' between two groups – one dominant and other subordinate. Nyishi-Sulung relationship is a typology that neither falls into 'ephemeral relation' type nor into a relation of 'clientship'. It is a permanent type relationship and contrary to ephemeral relations and associated "retaining control of themselves", Sulungs have been able to "keep their racial identity and at the same time a fair measure of self-respect and independence" (Stonor: 1972: 17). Sulung' dual identity, that they are subordinate to Nyishis and that they have their own social self, has its similarities and differences in Woodburn's contention that outsiders consider hunter-gatherers inferior. It agrees only with Woodburn in that Nyishis treat sulungs inferior, and consider them suitable for menial labour and so low that sexual contact is considered polluting.

Surprisingly Sulungs feel themselves inferior and during field study it was found that they used to display a sense of pride while introducing themselves in relation to their respective masters who enjoys one or other types of social status. A Sulung introduces himself as *his* (mentions master's name) Sulung. Self-accepted low status is reflected in the term *Ato*, meaning master, which they use to address Nyishi overlords. Sulungs not only have accepted subordinate status but feel as such inspite of the fact that they have forests to turn for subsistence, and actually they live on hunting and gathering. It contradicts Woodburn's notion that so long as hunter-gatherer "retain sufficient bush or forest in which to hunt and gather, when necessary, in which to conceal themselves, hunter-gatherers commonly do not themselves accept subordinate status, and indeed can be seen partially negating the discrimination practiced against them" (Woodburn: 1988: 49).

The correlation between real difficulty of hunter-gatherers and their subordination seems to hold less ground in explaining Nyishi-Sulung relationship. Sulungs are hunter-gatherers and so are not vulnerable to food shortage and famine. Contrarily, Nyishis depend on shifting cultivation and are not immune to crop failures due to one reason or the other. They also supplement their food shortage by foraging. As Sulungs are subordinate to their Nyishi and Miji neighbours, the question of protection by one against the other does not arise and there was no third neighbour against whom they needed protection by surrendering their independence partially.

Shan-Kachin model of relationship is "almost an ideal type' of the phenomenon of becoming another social being" (Firth: 1964: vii). Firth further comments that "the notion of 'becoming something else'... as Kachins become Shans, or *gumsa* people become *gumlao,* are specific ethnographic phenomena that may have only a restricted analogy" (ibid.). More or less a same type of relationship is found emerging among Shan group of tribes in Arunachal Pradesh. In Lohit district of Arunachal Pradesh, *Khamiyangs* and *Phakials* introduce themselves as *Khamptis,* another Shan group people with a higher social and economic status and widely known, though they have their own kinship and social relations. Leach (1954: 222) economically, are totally separated by barriers of kinship and religion".

What follows is that the notion of 'becoming another social being' has a contextual significance with a purpose and, therefore, is ephemeral. A Sulung's notion of becoming a Nyishi, however, has not been reported in earlier writings, nor it has been found during field study. At best, as is mentioned, Sulungs take pride in introducing themselves as 'Sulungs' of this to that master. However, the notion has another temporal implication in that Sulungs have created a myth by which they do not identify them with Nyishis, but with the Tani stock from which Nyishis have originated.

Sulungs, a distinct group linguistically and by a pronounced prognathism (Haimendorf: 1964: 7), did not have record of "any common descent, either recent or remote (Stonor: 1972: 3) in earlier writings. But Deuri (1972: 1) mentions of a Nyishi legend for the first time, which states that a Nyishi who was on a hunting expedition met an unknown girl named Konekongin in the jungle and from their union Sulungs, came into being. He also records Sulung's disapproval to such a possibility and contrary to Nyishi legend, he forwards a Sulung legend that traces their origin from *Khorongkhiya,* their mythical ancestor in the heaven. In a recent field study (May, 2002), I found that *Khorongkhiya* is identified as the son of *Abo Tani.* He is believed to have born out of the wedlock of *Tani* and *Nyidong Losine* and is believed to be the ancestor of Sulungs. *Mijis, Monpas, and Akas* are believed to be the offspring of *Tani and Aji Longsine Binyi,* who happens to be the owner of wealth. These tribal groups are not food gatherers like Sulungs and unlike Sulungs they posses *mithun,* which is a symbol and measure of wealth. This could be the reason to trace their origin from a wealthy parent. The informant, however, was not sure about the ancestral mother of Nyishis and that is why it is not mentioned here.

Contrary to the 'notion of becoming another social being' that operates between Shan and Kachin at the level of their interaction, Sulungs identity has bypassed Nyishi's contemporary position in relation to them but has asserted itself at a higher level. Arguably, it is the independent status of the Sulungs beyond their relations with Nyishis that has strongly acted upon to think for themselves of 'becoming another social self' at a higher level. The urge to maintain independent status as a trinbe, however, has not been so strong in other aspects of the culture. It is observed during field study that the dressing pattern, occasional intake of rice while working with Nyishis, influence of Nyishi language on the Sulungs, and above all, Nyishi system of paying bride price have found place in Sulung culture. Nevertheless, Sulungs have not become Nyishis.

Nyishi-Sulung relationship, however, resembles Hindu way of tribal absorption (Bose: 1996) in that Nyishis have allowed, if we believe so, their Sulungs to maintain their independent social identity. As Brahminical influence could be noticed in tribal communities in Orissa, Chotnagpur and Jharkhand areas because of their long interaction, so also Nyishi cultural influence could be found in many aspects of Sulungs' culture as mentioned earlier. Hindu way of tribal absorption, in other words Hindu-tribal relation is characterized, more or less by balanced exchange of goods and services, Hinduisation of tribal gods and goddesses, dependence on and acceptance of Hindu occupational pattern and so on. (ibid.). Historically, such a relation has a reference to crisis of the tribesmen either at economic level or at socio-cultural front or at security consideration (ibid). Bose holds that when population increased, slash and burn could not provide subsistence, people adopted the life of a people, their productive system (Bose: ibid; 50).

Discussion

As we turn our attention to Nyishi-Sulung relationship, we find that it is Nyishis who depend more on Sulung labour and products, but not the vice versa. Sulungs are expert blacksmiths and brass founders (Stonor: 1972:11-12, Deuri: 1982:2. Haimendorf: 1950:7). Their ladies are good weavers and mostly they weave for the masters (Stonor: 1972:12). It is to be noted that the design and clothes they weave for the masters have become the dress pattern of the Sulungs themselves. The economic pursuits of the Sulungs for subsistence needs do not require much of the iron works. They "acquired the crafts form the overlords" (ibid) because iron and brass-wares were used by the Nyishi extensively. Sulungs work in the jhum fields of the masters and work as porters for them. Sometimes, they hunt and collect honey for the masters and always share the catches from fishing and hunting. It is a type of negative reciprocity because Sulungs may or may not get any thing in exchange from the services. They work for the past obligation in terms of bride wealth paid by the master or some food items borrowed from the masters. Since the masters pay the bride wealth both husband and wife and their children are customarily obliged to work for the master. When the girl child of the Sulung parents gets married, the master gets the bride wealth from the girl's husband's master. When the boys grow up, masters purchase brides for them and in the process they become perpetual slaves. Added to this is occasional borrowing at the time of sicknesses or other emergencies. The bride wealth is paid in terms of *mithun* and borrowing consists of paddy, maize, pigs, and cows. These practices of borrowing and the payment of bride wealth by master have made them perpetual slaves. It is worth mentioning that Sulungs do not depend on Nyishi masters for their subsistence needs, rather Nyishi masters obtain items of subsistence needs from Sulungs' foraging activities. Not only Nyishi masters share catches from fishing and hunting, they also have a share from the sago, which is the staple food of the Sulungs. It is therefore, obvious that Sulungs' economic pursuits for their subsistence are independent of their relations with the masters.

Sulungs are "at heart food-gatherers and hunters who infinitely prefer a nomadic life in the forest" (Stonor: 1972:14; cf. Haimendorf: *op. cit.,*) even though "maize, millet are grown in fair quantities as subsidiary crops" (Stonor: ibid: 7). Food-gathering "consists almost entirely in collection of wild sago" (ibid: 15) along with occasional expeditions to collect a great variety of leaves, fungi, fruit, bamboo shoots, etc. (ibid.; 17). I was told during field study that collection of bamboo shoot is a regular feature in their annual calendar of food gathering, during July to September, because shoots are preserved for the whole year and used daily with staple food. It was also reported that all Sulungs do not cultivate rice, maize and millet regularly but most of them cultivate at least few sago palms from which they obtain their foodstuff. However, even to these days, bulk of the supply is obtained from the forest directly and as it was in 1940s, "for most of the wet summer months they live by food gathering and hunting" (ibid; 14). "Their poverty and their nomadic habits rule out the keeping of pigs or *mithun* and the domestic fowl is the only animals kept, with the exception of a few small dogs for hunting and watch dogs" (ibid; cf. Deuri: 1982). However, the fowls are used mainly for sacrifices in times of sickness.

Probably, Nyishi-Sulung relationship has undergone much transformation. Stoner enumerated mutual advantages out of this relationship. But what I find is nothing but a negative reciprocity (see Sahalnis: 1972), at the one extreme end is without any payment, where in Sulungs are always looser. Stonor rightly has pointed out that because of constant demand of their labour by their masters, Sulungs can not cultivate for their own (ibid; 14) though land is available for it and though they know the technology in course of their work in master's fields. They remain as food gatherers.

The question is why Nyishis did not absorb Sulungs in their community? Probably, Sulungs were not in subordination for a long time. As we see, there were efforts to bring Sulungs to Nyishi fold by creating a myth of their origin from a Nyishi father. Perhaps, it was not a success as administration had already recognized Sulungs as separate tribesmen and earlier writers have identified them differently both linguistically and by a pronounced prognathism. Before independence, Sulungs had not perhaps entered into *Atok-akra* bond for a long time.

Earlier writers have mentioned of the existence of slavery system among the Nyishis without reference to Sulungs. It cannot be said that the writes did not encounter them. As we understand these writers studied Nyshis where Sulungs are found subordinate to them. Moreover these writers have encountered *Beta* and *Nera* class of slaves and had report of the Nyishis in the hills from runaway Assamese slaves. With a degree of certainty we can say that Nyishi-Sulung relationship is probably a phenomenon during British rule.

Conclusion

Naturally, it warrants ones attention to enquire into the causes of such a relationship as the one that falls into the Nyishi-Sulung typology. Of course historical evidences available are fragmented and scanty. Ethnographic accounts are too inadequate at this stage for us, as we do not have any data on Miji-Sulung relationship, to be able to do more than speculate the possible reasons. From data available, we understand that Nyishis apparently have command over Sulungs labour than on Sulungs themselves. To get this labour, they have eveolved a mechanism at social level around marriage institution and, less frequently around rituals.

It this context, Nhyishi-Sulung relationship at social level is assumed to be the superstructures that support the infrastructure in the form of labour requirement in Nyishi productive system. The labour requirement may be viewed across subsistence requirement as it is embedded in the economy in substantive sense in that prestige, social status is associated with it. Sulungs used to fight for the masters, carry their loads and supply material products of their labour, whose possession enhances the status of the master. More of food supply in a Nyishi household not only ensures leisure to the master but also enables him to share it with clan members. In return, he acquires social status. The crux of the problem, in speculating Nyishi-Sulung relationsip, therefore, lies in understanding the labour requirement of Nyishi community. It is further assumed that both Nyishis and Sulungs were independent tribesmen before they entered into the interaction of the type as reflected in Nyishi Sulungs typology.

With identification of the 'demand' from Nyishis in the discussion frame, it is now imperative to speculate on 'supply' factor that effected the interaction to take a shape. Earlier studies provide sufficient evidences that substantiate to the point that Nyishi had a great demand for labour both in economic activities. That is why slavery was an institution during pre-British period and Nyishis used to raid Assamese villages to capture men, women and children. Even there are instances of Nyishis capturing people from tribal villages when they considered them to be the reason for loss of population in their villages. While writing in 1884 Mackenzie writies that "On the night of 12th February 1872, the village of Amtolla....was attacked by a body of two or three hundred hillmen. ...The hillmen had, it seems been much troubled, by an epidemic, which they believed to have been imported from the plains. They called upon the Duphlas of the plains to compensate them for the loss they had sustained in children and adults from the disease; and because the Duphlas of Amtolla declined to meet their wishes, they came down to recoup themselves by seizing them as slaves" (1994: 31). Allen (1905: 73) also writes that hill people have a strong desire "to keep up their population" and probably this could be a reason for their frequent raids into plains and other tribal villages and their habit of carrying off "Assamese subjects including women and children" (Bhuyan: 1949: 32).

When the British government fell on heavily on slavery system and took some other administrative measures (see Mackenzie: 1994: 32), Nyishis probably stopped their raids and thereby lost the source and mechanism of capturing slaves. It is evident from the writings of Mackenzie that, "from 1852, however, the Duphlas much to the relief of the local officials and somewhat to their surprise, settled quietly down" (ibid; 29). Probably, at this stage they found an alternative and a soft target in Sulungs. When the interaction of Sulungs and Nyishis got institutionalized the military mission came in contact with Sulungs during early part of the 20th century. Their existence was not probably noticed prior to that because of their nomadic foraging life in the jungle and shifting nature of settlement, which happens to be very small in size.

From the above speculation, it cannot be stated with certainty that Nyishis-Sulung relationship sprang up consequent upon the closure of the source of obtaining slaves from Assam. As Sulungs are different from the *Beta* and *Nera* categories, arguably there would have been a way other than raids and captures to enslave them. That the system is different, the two tribes have independent social organizations and the Sulung do not live in master's house are enough evidences to prove that the relationship evolved gradually. Obviously, this proposition assumes an earlier acquaintance and some short of interaction between the two tribes.

Material needs of Sulungs are of subsistence in nature and very few in numbers. Their subsistence needs have been patterned concomitant to environmental variability in various seasons. Consequently, they were not vulnerable to food shortages and that could not be a reason for their acquaintance with the Nyishis. According to Nyishi legend, Sulungs are up the *mithuns* given by Abo-Tani and borrowed them from Nyishis for payment of bride price. Since they could not repay the value of *mithuns*, they became perpetual debtors to the Nyishis. Stonor (1972) writes about few permanently free Sulungs and this evidently speaks that they do not owe any obligation to Nyishis, nor did their ancestors. However, Sulungs have a different story to tell. In course of their relation with Nyishis, Sulungs were enslaved by persuasion and offerings of salt, beads, clothing, local beer, etc. (Deuri, *op. cit.,*; 2), for they had to work in the fields of Nyishis in exchange of these items they obtained from the former. It is difficult to say if Sulungs brewed local beer prior to their relation with Nyishis or not. Of course, local beer can be brewed from sago but they do not know the yeast required to prepare it, which they obtain from Nyishis. Certainly, there is an economic content in the relationship between Nyishis and Sulungs. Mental enslavement to material goods made the Sulungs physically enslaved to the Nyishis who have had comparatively more resources (Danda: 2002: per.com). There are also instances to substantiate the point that a strong desire for sensual pleasure through material goods brings disaster. Bose (*op. cit.,*, 49-50) writes that when the King of Chotnagpur enslaved himself to sensual pleasure, forces of exploitation of the subjects were released in the form of free labour, increased tax and later in the from of traders' excess as the governance was left to them.

My informat of Pordung village in East Kameng district informed me that Nyishis were the first to contact Sulungs, when the famine broke out in their areas. During field study in Watte village of the same district, another informant informed me that his father, while a young boy, went to Sulung inhabited area to collect sago, which is still their staple food.

It can be argued with some degree of certainty that Nyishis were the first to depend on or to develop contact with the Sulungs to fight their vulnerability to food shortage during famine. This contact gradually developed into trade relations and Sulungs became middlemen between Tibetans and Nyishis and sometimes accompanied the latter (Deuri, *op. cit.,* 8; also see Singh, *op. cit.,*) to Tibet and other area. As time passed, goods from Nyshis productive system were exchanged with Sulungs. They became victim to local beer, which Nyishis prepare and consume, in large quantities. Probably, *mithun* was accidentally exchanged for something from Sulungs. Being an item of higher value, the exchange probably carried a promise of some future payment. It might have been the case that Sulungs borrowed *mithun* for rearing. Probably, they were not successful in rearing, or consumed it, and could not return the value of it either. In return, they might have entered into an agreement of labour exchange. During this period, probably Nyshis could not capture slaves from their raids and took advantage of Sulung labour, which was otherwise available to them in course of their interaction. As time passed, it became perpetuated through social systems and reflected in legends and customs.

References

1. Allen, B.C. (1905): *Assam District Gazetteers: Lakhimpur,* Shillong.
2. Barnard, A. (2002): "The Foraging Mode of Thought", in Henry Stewart, Alan Barnard & keiichi Omura (eds), *Self-and-Other Images of Hunter-Gatherers,* Senri Ethnological Studies-60, National Museum of Ethnology, Osaka.
3. Behera, M.C. (2002a): "A critique of foraging mode of thought and understanding Sulungs' social-self" presented at the Ninth International Conference on *Hunting and Gathering Societies,* 9th to 13th September, 2002, Heriot-Watt University, Edinburgh.
4. "Understanding forager worldview and changing ideology of man-nature relationship (A study with reference to Sulung, Nyishi and Khampti Tribes of Arunachal Pradesh in North-East India)", presented at the Ninth International Conference on *Hunting and Gathering Societies,* 9th to 13th September, 2002, Heriot-Watt University, Edinburgh.
5. Bhuyan, S.K. (1940): *Anglo-Assamese Relations,* 1771-1826, Gauhati.
6. Bose, N.K. (1940): *The Structure of Hindu Society,* Orient Longman, New Delhi, *Trans:Andre Beteille.*
7. Dalton, E.T., (1973): *Tribal History of Eastern India* (Revised), Cosmo Publications, Delhi. First published in 1872 at Calcutta (Kolkata) under the title *Descriptive Ethnology of Bengal.*
8. Danda, A.K., (2002): *Personal Communication.*
9. Deuri, R., (1982): *The Sulungs,* Research Department, Govt. of Arunahcal Pradesh, Shillong.
10. Dun, G.W. (1897): Preliminary Notes on Daphlas" in Verrier Elwin, (ed.), *India's North East Frontier in the Nineteenth Century,* 1959, OUP, Londom, pp. 185-88.

11. Dutta, S & Showren, T., (2000): "Internally Displaced Persons: A case study of the Sulungs (Puroiks) of Arunahcal Pradesh" paper presented at the Seminar on *Internally Displaced Persons in Arunachal Pradesh,* Itanagar, November 21, 2000, sponsored by ICSSR.
12. Elwin, V. (1959): *India's North East Frontier in the Nineteenth Century,* oup, London Firth, Raymond (1964): "Foreward to 1964 reprint of E.R.Leach: *Political Systems of Highland Burma, A Study of Kachin Social Structure,* G.Bell and Sons Ltd., London.
13. Haimendorf, C.V., 1946 (1950): *Ethnographic Notes on the Tribes of the Subansiri Region,* Assam Government Press, Shillong, 1950, p. 7. He uses the appellation 'Sulu' and 'Sulung' interchangeably.
14. Leach, E.R. 1954 (1964): *Political Systems of Highland Burma, A Study of Kachin Social Structure,* G. Bell and Sons Ltd., London.
15. Mackenzie, A. 1994 (1884): *The North East Frontier of India,* Mittal Publications, New Delhi.
16. Robinson, W. (1851): Notes on the Dophlas and the Peculiarities of their Language", *JASB,* Vol. XXX, pp. 126 ff., Produced in Elwin, V. (1959): *India's North East Frontier in the Nineteenth Century,* OUP, London.
17. Sahlins, M. (1972): "*Stone Age Economics*", Aldine, Chicago.
18. Shukla, B.K. (1965): "*The Daflas of Subansiri Region,* NEFA, Shillong.
19. Singh, S.K. ed. (1995): "*People of India: Arunachal Pradesh*", ASI, Kolkata.
20. Stonor, C.R. (1972): "The Sulung Tribe of Assam Himalayas", *Arunachal research Bulletin* DIPR, Government of Arunachal Pradesh, Shillong, pp. 1-18; The original paper was published in *Anthropos,* 1952, Vol. 47, pp. 947-62.
21. Woodburn, James (1988): "African hunter-gatherer social organization: is it best understood as a product of encapsulation?" in Tim Ingold, David Riches and James Woodburn, 1988, eds, *Hunters and Gatherers : History, Evolution and Social Change,* Berg, Oxford.
22. Yadav, Sajjan Singh, (1999): "Sulungs — The Traditional Bonded Labour Tribe of Aruanchal Pradesh", *Unpublished.* (He was instrumental in the rehabilitation of Sulungs during his tenure as Dy. Commissioner in East kameng district.